AN INTRODUCTION TO THE ENGLISH LEGAL SYSTEM

12

1

AN INTRODUCTION TO THE ENGLISH LEGAL SYSTEM

Second Edition

MARTIN PARTINGTON

OXFORD

UNIVERSITY PRESS

OXFORD

UNIVERSITY PRESS

Great Clarendon Street, Oxford OX2 6DP

Oxford University Press is a department of the University of Oxford.
It furthers the University's objective of excellence in research, scholarship,
and education by publishing worldwide in

Oxford New York

Auckland Bangkok Buenos Aires Cape Town Chennai
Dar es Salaam Delhi Hong Kong Istanbul Karachi Kolkata
Kuala Lumpur Madrid Melbourne Mexico City Mumbai Nairobi
São Paulo Shanghai Taipei Tokyo Toronto

Oxford is a registered trade mark of Oxford University Press
in the UK and in certain other countries

Published in the United States
by Oxford University Press Inc., New York

© Martin Partington 2003

The moral rights of the author have been asserted
Database right Oxford University Press (maker)

First published 2000

Reprinted 2003

British Library Cataloguing in Publication Data

Data available

ISBN 0–19–926057–5

Typeset in Adobe Minion and ITC Stone Sans
by RefineCatch Limited, Bungay, Suffolk
Printed in Great Britain by
TJ International Ltd., Padstow, Cornwall

Outline contents

Contents

INTRODUCTION

PART I LAW, SOCIETY AND AUTHORITY

CONCLUSION

List of boxes

List of diagrams

List of tables

Preface to the second edition

It is less than three years since I completed the first edition of this book. However such has been the pace of developments in the English legal system that my publishers have decided to commission this second edition.

The target readership for this book remains the same—those coming new to the study of law whether at A-level, degree level, or postgraduate conversion level who wish to get an overview of the context within which law is made and practised in England and Wales. Many new students will be asked to read a book about law before they arrive at university or college to start their studies. Many law courses no longer offer formal instruction on the legal system and its institutions; here students need a book that introduces them to these topics. I have sought to make the text as approachable as possible for all those who are, in essence, teaching themselves about these matters.

In addition, I have taken the opportunity to enhance certain features of the book designed to encourage readers to explore issues that interest them more fully, and to think critically about what they have read. These innovations include:

- Posing questions for consideration by the reader at the end of chapters;
- Placing suggestions for further reading at the end of chapters;
- Substantially increasing the number of references to relevant websites.

One of the features of the internet is its rapid development. Nearly all the links to websites which I included in the first edition are now defunct. I can assure readers that I have tested all the links published here. But it is inevitable that there will be changes to them. Up-dating material for students and lecturers will be found at the companion website **www.oup.co.uk/besttextbooks/law/partington2e/**. Information about broken links, or new sites which you find interesting and are not mentioned in the text may be fedback to me through the CWS.

Since completing the first edition, I have left—at least for the time being—the University of Bristol, having been appointed a Law Commissioner for England and Wales from January 2001. During that period, I have also served as an expert consultant to the Leggatt Review of Tribunals, and the Employment Tribunals Taskforce.[1] It must therefore be emphasized that I write here in a purely personal capacity. None of the official bodies with which I am or have been associated is to be taken as agreeing with what I have written here.

At Oxford University Press, my former editor Michaela Coulthard left, and has been replaced by Christina White. She has continued in the admirable OUP tradition of providing authors with helpful and supportive editors. Christina's contribution to

---

[1] Both mentioned in Chapter 6.

this edition has been of the greatest possible assistance. I am particularly indebted to my copy editor, Kate Elliott. I am also most grateful to the anonymous referees who, as part of OUP procedures, commented on the strengths and weaknesses of the first edition. While I may not have fully incorporated their comments, they all provoked thought and reflection. I remain responsible for all errors and omissions.

London

29 November 2002

Foreword and Acknowledgements
(Preface to the first edition)

The original proposal that I should write this book came from Professor Peter Cane when he, with Professor Jane Stapleton, were editors of the Clarendon Law Series, published by Oxford University Press. Though it has now been decided that the book should not appear in that series, I have nonetheless adhered to my initial instructions. These were that the book should: be genuinely introductory; be around 200 pages long; be relatively uncluttered by footnotes; be accessible to the more general reader; but at the same time offer an approach to thinking about the English legal system and its place in society not found elsewhere. With these strictures in mind, this book has been written particularly for those coming to the study of law for the first time. I also hope that others, keen to look behind the magical veil that all too often shrouds the legal system and its actors in mystery, will find the book of interest. It is, in short, intended for all those interested in the phenomenon of law and the important role it plays in the ordering of our society but without any detailed knowledge of it.

Over the last thirty or so years, I have been associated with a wide range of bodies and institutions, from whom I have learned much and who have helped to inform my ideas about the English legal system and the forces that shape it. They include, at different stages, and for different lengths of time: the Hillfields Advice Centre in Coventry; the Legal Action Group; the Training Committee of the Institute of Housing; the Management Committees of Citizens' Advice Bureaux in Coventry, Paddington and Uxbridge; the Education Committee of the Law Society; the Lord Chancellor's Advisory Committee on Legal Aid; the Independent Tribunal Service for Social Security Appeal Tribunals; the Judicial Studies Board (both the main Board and its Tribunals Committee); the Council on Tribunals; the Civil Justice Council (and its sub-committee on Alternative Dispute Resolution); the Committee of Heads of University Law Schools; the Socio-Legal Studies Association; and the Socio-Legal Research Users' Forum. I am grateful to the numerous friends and colleagues from all these bodies—too numerous to list here—for their generosity of spirit, enthusiasm, and sheer hard work in the development of the practices and institutions of law in England.

I also thank my colleagues at Bristol for their support, in particular Rebecca Bailey-Harris, David Cowan, Gwynn Davies, Clare Lewis, Donald Nicolson, Stratos Konstadinidis, and Andrew Sanders. I am grateful to successive generations of students at Bristol, and before then Brunel, Universities to whom I offered instruction in English Legal System and English Legal Methods for their critical responses to what I have had to say. I have been particularly fortunate that, as part of the writing process, I was able to deliver early versions of this text as introductory lectures to first year students at the University of Bristol; and to discuss them in an informal 'reading group'. They helped me determine important questions of structure and content. I am most grateful to all those who offered their comments. However, I remain wholly responsible for what follows.

My editor at Oxford University Press, Michaela Coulthard, has been a model of tolerance as I have failed to meet a variety of deadlines.

I am not sure that my children Adam and Hannah have ever been particularly conscious of what I do in my professional life. Nonetheless I am grateful to both for allowing me to share some of my initial thoughts about this book with them. They were particularly encouraging at times when encouragement was needed. As always I am especially indebted to Daphne for her insistence that I retain a sense of balance in my life.

I have sought to bring the text up to date to the date shown below.

Bristol
27 April 2000

INTRODUCTION

1

'Knowledge', themes and structure

Introductory

The purposes of this book are to consider a number of themes about how law and the legal system have developed over recent years, and how they may develop in future, to encourage the readers to think about law and the legal system and to question the extent to which that system is fit for its purpose.

The book is primarily about the *English* legal system (though for most practical purposes that also includes the legal system operative in Wales). There is a quite different system in Scotland and a rather different system in Northern Ireland, neither of which is considered in this book. There will be times when it is not sensible to refer just to 'England'—for example the phrases 'Great Britain' or 'United Kingdom' will be used where they seem more appropriate, particularly considering the place of this country in the wider world. However, the particular focus of the book is on the English legal system.

This does not of course mean that the exclusive focus of the book is on institutions located in England and Wales. The English legal system is also subject to external sources of law and legal institutions, in particular the law and institutions of the European Union and the European Convention on Human Rights and Fundamental Freedoms.

Many of those who study law in England come from other countries. Despite this focus, I nonetheless hope that readers from overseas can not only learn from the issues discussed here, but also relate the questions raised to the situation in their own home countries. Are the legal systems with which they may be more familiar fitted to their purpose? Are there lessons to be learned from the English experience?[1] What should the English be learning from experience elsewhere?

---

[1] A recent example of a book designed to explain part of the English legal system to a foreign audience is McConville, M., and Wilson, G. (eds.), *The Handbook of the Criminal Justice Process* (Oxford, Oxford University Press, 2002).

'Knowledge'

Images and pre-conceptions

Even readers of an introductory work on law will come to it with a good deal of 'knowledge'. This will have been shaped by personal experience or what they have otherwise read or heard in the media. Much of it will be wrong. It is impossible to identify all those images and pre-conceptions, but there are at least five which it may be suggested many readers of this book will have.[2]

The scope of the legal system

Many people define the scope of law and the legal system through what happens in criminal trial courts. After all, it is there that the major murder cases or other serious criminal cases (such as theft or fraud) are dealt with. This perception of the central place of the criminal justice system in the English legal system is quite understandable, taken from endless television dramas and press reports.

But such a view is far too narrow. First, as will be seen in Chapter 5, the vast majority of the key decisions in the criminal justice system are taken not in courts, but elsewhere, e.g. the police station or the parole board. Secondly, focusing on the criminal trial process results in a failure to appreciate the existence of other parts of the English legal system, the *civil justice, administrative justice* and *family justice* systems, considered in Chapters 6–8.

Providers of legal services

If asked who provides legal services, many would respond: the lawyers. Again this is too narrow a view. As will be seen in Chapter 9 (and part of Chapter 7) many others apart from professionally qualified lawyers provide legal services to the public.

In addition, perceptions of lawyers may be very unflattering. Some regard them as cynical parasites, willing to undertake any task for which a client is willing to pay—the 'hired gun' or 'prostitute' model of the lawyer. Others note the salaries lawyers are paid (indeed this may have been an element in the thinking of some of those readers now contemplating the study of law!). There may be views about the sort of person who becomes a lawyer. Some will describe them as pompous; conservative in temperament (or even Conservative in political outlook); pedantic; even untrustworthy. Some argue that lawyers use their legal education and training and professional status to enhance their earning capacity by creating a 'mystique' around the law which prevents the ordinary lay person from being able to make effective use of the law. There may be perceptions about the education, class background, gender or ethnicity

---

[2] For a more scientific survey of attitudes to the civil justice system see Genn, H., *Paths to Justice* (Oxford, Hart, 1999) Chapter 7.

of lawyers. While there may be *some* truth in some of these perceptions, a more detailed look provides a picture that is both more complex and more interesting.

The English legal system: resistance to change

Another perception people may have of law and the legal system is that they are very backward looking. The Victorian architecture of law's landmark buildings, such as the Old Bailey or the Royal Court of Justice in London, harks back to a bygone age, as do the robes and old-fashioned styles of dress that lawyers adopt, particularly when appearing in court. This may lead to a more general impression of conservatism and resistance to change. It is natural that many who practise law will resist change. It is disturbing and unsettling.

Again, these perceptions, though perhaps correct in part, do not reflect the total position. For many change is what prevents life becoming boring. The last thirty or so years have witnessed a large number of changes in law and legal process, many of which have been very dramatic. Indeed the number of changes which have had to be considered in this second edition demonstrate that the pace of change is, if anything, increasing.

Another of the themes to be explored in this book relates to the forces for change— the *dynamism*—within the law and the legal system. In Chapter 4 we consider the contribution of Government to the pressure for change. And throughout the work, we note numerous examples of how practice and procedure have changed in recent years. Implicit in this discussion is a question whether those who work in the legal system should be more willing to embrace change and proclaim it as an important part of our legal culture than they have perhaps been willing to do in the past.

Inefficiency, expense and delay

A further perception is that legal proceedings are too long-drawn-out and that the whole system suffers from inordinate delay and expense. This is, perhaps, a perception that is closer to the truth than some of the others suggested above. It is certainly a perception that has driven much current debate about reform of the civil justice system, discussed in more detail in Chapter 8. It underlies many of the other changes made to the justice system. However, before concluding that the whole of the system is dogged by inefficiency, delay and expense, we once again need to consider the evidence carefully to see how far popular pre-conceptions reflect the whole truth about the English legal system. We also need to ask whether pressure for greater speed and efficiency can, in some circumstances, act against the interests of justice.

Miscarriages of justice

A final issue which dominates media treatment of law relates to miscarriages of justice. This may suggest that there are serious, even structural, defects with the legal system that result in these miscarriages. There is no doubt that from time to time things do go seriously wrong. Cases are improperly investigated, or inadequately presented in court, or inexpertly handled by the trial judge, or insufficiently considered on appeal. It is right that the media draw attention to them.

But miscarriages of justice also demonstrate another side to the English legal system. Whatever the difficulties, there are those within the system willing to challenge decisions that have not been arrived at by 'due process of law'. Many of those arguing that miscarriages of justice have occurred are themselves lawyers. Miscarriages of justice may lead some to perceive the legal system as a system in crisis. Paradoxically, though, they may also be a source of reassurance, that the system and those who work within it are sufficiently independent and robust to challenge those who have made mistakes.

The primary purpose of this book is to provide a general overview of the framework within which the law of England (and Wales) is made and practised, which will illuminate and where necessary alter such initial images and pre-conceptions. Where there is truth in those images and pre-conceptions, particularly negative ones, I hope the reader will be able to learn from the fact that not everything is perfect and reflect on what may need to be changed. Where images of law and the legal system are unfair, I hope the reader will at least be better informed.

Themes

Although an introductory book, it seeks to address themes inadequately considered in other books with the same or similar titles.

- First, many current accounts of the English legal system are rather 'practitioner-driven'; they focus primarily on those parts of the system in which professionally qualified lawyers practise their law. Here a more holistic approach is taken, designed to introduce the reader to a wider range of activities and functions often ignored elsewhere.

- Secondly, other introductory accounts are somewhat descriptive and 'static' in nature, providing a snapshot of the system at the moment of writing. As already suggested, the English legal system is considerably more complex, more dynamic and more responsive to change than is often realized. A recurring theme will be on change and the forces that have shaped and are shaping the English legal system. At the same time, questions will be raised about the extent to which particular changes are desirable or should be resisted.

- Thirdly, the English legal system is often portrayed as something distinct from the British system of government. Indeed one of the important claims made for law and its practice is that it is 'independent' of Government. Yet the government of the country is based in law; the institutions of law derive their power and authority from the system of government. Understanding the constitutional function of the English legal system and the relationship of the legal system to other branches of government will therefore be another theme underpinning the discussion in this work.

- Finally, the assertion is often made that 'we have the best system of justice in the world'. It may be a good system, indeed a very good system. But this conclusion should be arrived at on the basis of evidence, not mere assertion. This book is intended to provide a basis for thinking critically about the institutions and practices of the law and contemplating change where inadequacy or inefficiency is demonstrated to exist.

Structure

Having considered the knowledge which those coming new to the study of law may have about the legal system, and the extent to which images and pre-conceptions held by such newcomers may, or may not, be well-founded; and having set out the themes that underlie the book, the structure of the book is as follows:

Part 1 consists of two chapters that discuss the social functions of law and the legitimacy of law. Chapter 2 considers the roles which law plays in the regulation of modern society. Chapter 3 considers how law is made, who makes it, where they get the authority for making it, whether the processes currently used for making law should be changed and, if so, how.

Part 2 considers the institutional framework within which law is developed and practised. The discussion opens, in Chapter 4, with an account of the role of Government in shaping the institutions and practice of law. Chapters 5 to 8 look in turn at the four legal systems which, for the purpose of this account, comprise the English legal system:[3] the *Criminal Justice* system, the *Administrative Justice* system; the *Family Justice* system; and the *Civil and Commercial Justice* system. In each chapter there is consideration not only of formal legal institutions such as courts, but also informal or other processes that do not catch the public eye (or indeed which are not known about or properly understood by professional lawyers) but which form an essential part of the framework of the English legal system seen in the round.

Part 3 looks at the personnel of the law, and the tasks they perform in delivering legal services. Chapter 9 considers the role not only of those professionally qualified to practise law, but others who play a part in the workings of the legal system, including adjudicators and jurists. Chapter 10 reflects on how the provision of legal services is paid for.

Finally, a short concluding chapter asks whether the English legal system is in fact fit for the purposes it is required to perform. Is the English legal system 'the best in the

---

[3] Most other accounts draw a distinction between two systems only—criminal, and civil. But I argue that the four-pronged approach adopted here offers the newcomer a clearer way of understanding the whole picture.

world' in need of little or no change? Or is the system simply not delivering what is required of it, and thus in need of fundamental change? If changes are needed, what are they? What are the forces likely to render change difficult, if not impossible?

Questions for discussion

1. To what extent do you share the images and pre-conceptions set out in this chapter?

2. What other images of law do you have?

3. How have you acquired your knowledge about law?

   A useful exercise, to see the extent to which law permeates our lives, often without realizing it, is to read any daily newspaper carefully from cover to cover. Ask yourself: which items deal with some aspect of the practice of law, the making of law, the resolution of disputes? Consider not just home news pages or specialist law pages, but the whole paper, including the international pages, the business pages, and the sports pages. You will be surprised how many stories have a legal dimension to them.

4. Have you any personal experience of going to law? If so, what did you learn about the legal system as a result?

Further reading

BAILEY, S.H., and GUNN, M.J., *The Modern English Legal System* (4th edn., London, Sweet & Maxwell, 2001)

BANKOWSKI, Z., and MUNGHAM, G., *Images of Law* (London, Routledge and Kegan Paul, 1976)

COWNIE, F., and BRADNEY, A., *English Legal System in Context* (2nd edn., London, Butterworths, 2000)

GENN, H., *Paths to Justice* (Oxford, Hart, 1999)

JUSTICE, *Miscarriages of Justice: A Report by Justice* (Chairman of Committee, Sir George Waller) (London, Justice, 1989)

PODGORECKI, A., *et al.*, *Knowledge and Opinion about Law* (London, Martin Robertson, 1973)

WARD, R., *Walker and Walker's English Legal System* (8th edn., London, Butterworths, 1998)

WHITE, R.C.A., *The English Legal System in Action. The Administration of Justice* (Oxford, Oxford University Press, 1999)

ZANDER, M., *Cases and Materials on the English Legal System* (8th edn., London, Butterworths, 1999)

——*A Matter of Justice: The Legal System in Ferment* (London, Tauris, 1988)

Websites

www.bailii.org/ *(Electronic library of legal materials)*

http://library.ukc.ac.uk/library/lawlinks/default.htm *(Legal information on the internet)*

www.venables.co.uk/ *(Privately run gateway to information about law and solicitors)*

www.beagle.org.uk/hra/newindex.htm *(Human rights legal material)*

www.sosig.ac.uk/law/ *(Social sciences information gateway, material on law)*

www.coe.int/portalT.asp *(Council of Europe portal)*

http://europa.eu.int/eur-lex/en/index.html *(European Union legal portal)*

www.lcd.gov.uk/ *(Lord Chancellor's Department home page)*

PART I

LAW, SOCIETY AND AUTHORITY

This Part considers, first, what functions law plays in the way in which society is ordered (Chapter 2). Secondly, it asks what are the sources of authority from which those who make law base their claim to have the power to make law (Chapter 3).

2

Law and society: The purposes and functions of law

Introduction

One purpose of this book is to enable the reader to understand the *framework* within which rules of law are made and utilized, not to analyse specific rules of law, for example, 'what is the legal definition of murder' or 'when is a contract legally binding'. Nonetheless, it will be hard to make any sense of that framework without at least some indication of what the rules of law are to which the framework of the English legal system applies and, in particular, what the *social purpose* or *social function* of those rules of law is. In considering this, a distinction is drawn between what may be described as the macro and the micro functions of law. The macro functions of law are those which relate to the general role law plays in the running and ordering of society. The micro functions—which derive from those macro functions—relate to more specific uses to which law is put. The distinction should become clearer as the discussion proceeds.

The macro functions of law: law and orders

If the question were posed: 'what is the role of law in society?' a common response would be 'to maintain order'. Much public debate and political rhetoric makes the link between 'law' and 'order'. However, such a response disguises considerable ambiguity about the concept of order. There is a variety of orders in relation to which the law may be playing a role. These include:

- public order,
- political order,
- social order,
- economic order,
- international order, and
- moral order.

In addition, the interactions of law with each of these orders are extremely complex. To start, two general points may be made. First, the extent to which law is able to shape these different orders is not unconstrained, but is itself shaped by the political and other forces which are at work in the society in which law functions. Thus the role law plays in one society differs from that which it plays in another. Secondly, and related to the first point, law is not a 'neutral' force which contributes to the organization of society, but which is otherwise and in some peculiar way detached from that society. The functions of law in any given society cannot be understood without an understanding of the political, social and economic ideologies that underpin that society. These provide the context within which law functions.

Law and public order

Many would argue that a—possibly the—primary function of law is to assist in the preservation of public order. Maintaining public order is not exclusively a task for law; many other factors such as pressure from family or friends or work colleagues play an important part. Nonetheless the fact that law sets the boundaries of acceptable behaviour and prescribes sanctions for breaches of those boundaries (which is in essence the function of criminal law) makes a significant contribution to preserving public order.

The preservation of public order, however, immediately raises another but not necessarily consistent function for law: the *protection of civil liberties and human rights*. The ability of people to argue freely about their beliefs is an important aspect of life in a democratic society. Limits may need to be set to the freedom of individuals to advance unpopular views, for example those that are obscene or defamatory or which incite racial hatred. Nevertheless, within those limits, freedoms of speech and thought must be protected by law.

British constitutional arrangements have not, in the past, gone as far as, for example, the Bill of Rights formally enshrined in the constitution of the United States of America. Even so there are long-standing principles of English law which seek to allow people to indicate dissent, for example, by demonstrating peacefully, or engaging in other public activities such as political marches. The coming into force, in October 2000, of the Human Rights Act 1998 has resulted in increased interest in the development of human rights as a fundamental part of English law. Protection of human rights and civil liberties can therefore be identified as another function of the law, but one not always consistent with the aim of preserving public order. There will be occasions when the preservation of public order may result in the imposition of restrictions on civil liberties. Conversely, the protection of civil liberty will on occasion result in some limitations on the ability of the authorities to control public order.

In highly repressive societies, the function of law in preserving public order may result in the destruction of civil liberties and other fundamental freedoms. In more tolerant societies where dissent is permitted, there will always be sharp debate about the extent to which law's function is to preserve public order, as opposed to protecting

other rights and freedoms. *Liberty*[1] and other pressure groups may not always persuade governments to change their minds on proposals relating to the development of
law. But their ability to challenge and criticise is fundamental to ensuring that
governments do not step too far over the boundary of what is politically acceptable.
The law's function in relation to the maintenance of public order is, thus, highly
contingent upon the nature of the society in which law operates.

Law and political order

Another primary function of law is to underpin the political order of the country—
the constitutional function of law. In this respect, the United Kingdom is something
of an oddity. It is one of a very few countries that does not have a written constitution.
There are indeed many important practices within the British Constitution that arise
from the operation of practice and 'convention', rather than from identifiable rules of
law. (*See below, Box 3.1*). Some of the most important aspects about the way the
system of government is organized in England fall outside the scope of law altogether.
Their basis is found more in political theory than in legal rules. In view of this, it
might be thought that support for constitutional arrangements should not be
regarded as one of the macro functions of law.

However, despite this lack of a written constitution, it is appropriate to include this
topic under the macro head. It emphasizes the point that, although there is no written
constitution in the United Kingdom, there is still a great deal of fundamental law
which regulates the way in which our political system operates. Indeed as a result of
many of the changes being introduced to our constitutional arrangements by the
present Labour Government, it is arguable that, whatever may have been the correct
analysis in the past, we are currently witnessing the birth of a legally based constitutional settlement. There are so many aspects of our constitutional arrangements
that are either now enshrined in law or shortly will be. To give some examples.

- British membership of the European Union, recognized in such fundamental
  statutes as the European Communities Act 1972 and as amended to take account
  of changes to the European Treaties has, among other things, set limits to the
  legislative power—the sovereignty—of the British Parliament.

- The Scotland Act 1998 and the Wales Act 1998 both provide for devolution of
  powers from the government in London to, respectively, the Scottish Parliament
  and the Welsh Assembly. This provides a new legal framework for the regulation
  of the relationship between central and regional governments.

- The enactment of the Human Rights Act 1998 has affected the practice of
  government. Legislation must be compliant with the provisions of the Act,
  and the provisions of the European Convention on Human Rights which are
  incorporated in that Act.[2]

---

[1] Formerly known as the National Council for Civil Liberties.
[2] For an account of developments under the Human Rights Act see www.lcd.gov.uk/hract/hramenu.htm.

- Reform of the House of Lords—still in progress as this book is being written[3]— will only be achieved by the enactment of legislation which will form another part of the new British Constitutional arrangements.

- Laws relating to official secrecy on the one hand and freedom of information[4] on the other determine the extent to which governments can operate openly or in secret. This is another example of the use of fundamental law to support constitutional arrangements.

- Many other examples can be given: the detailed law relating to the running of elections;[5] or the law regulating the relationship between central and local government.[6]

In the light of this rapidly growing body of law, the argument is now heard that the British should take the last step and adopt a written constitution, which would codify into a single legislative measure all these constitutional provisions.[7] It is ironic that one of the legacies left by the British in the vast majority of its former colonies was a written constitution, including a Bill of Rights, when no such document exists in the UK itself.

Law and social order

Law also contributes to the preservation of the country's 'social order'. Defining the nature of social order is extremely complex and an issue on which there are wide differences of opinion. However, it is clear that in the UK, as in many other countries in the Western democratic tradition, there are substantial differences between individuals that may depend on differences of ability, or differences of income or wealth, or differences of birth or class. These differences are reflected in many rules of law, in particular those that define concepts of property and contract. The present social order and the law that supports that social order have the effect of protecting the rights of those with property and the economic power to enter and enforce contractual arrangements. Much criminal law also seeks to protect rights of property. On this analysis, the relationship between law and social order may be seen as conservative, in the sense that it seeks to conserve current social arrangements.

However, as with the role of law in relation to public order, there are other ways of

---

[3] See www.lcd.gov.uk/constitution/holref/holrefindex.htm.

[4] The Freedom of Information Act 2000 will not come into effect until 2005; until then government departments are required to operate under the terms of a non-statutory *Code of Practice on Access to Government Information*. See www.lcd.gov.uk/foi/foidpunit.htm.

[5] Proposals for the much greater use of information technology to enable citizens to participate in the political process may also require legislative action in the future. See *In the service of democracy* at www.edemocracy.gov.uk.

[6] For recent examples of legislation in these areas see the Political Parties, Elections and Referendums Act 2000 and the Local Government Act 2000.

[7] The Constitution Unit at University College London is taking a lead in this debate. See www.ucl.ac.uk/constitution-unit/.

thinking about the relationships between law and social order. Many would assert that a fundamental purpose of law today is to promote a more dynamic social order, designed to ensure that society is not locked into structures which sustain inequality, but is based on principles of equality and the prevention of social exclusion.

The bases for attacking inequality are the subject of fierce debate. Some argue that 'equality' can be achieved only if there is a complete levelling of the differences between people—so that, for example, everyone in employment receives more or less equal pay, that there is equality in the amounts of wealth capable of being held by individuals, and so on. Others take the view that equality in this sense is neither the right nor a sensible way to promote a new social order. They argue that the focus should be on *equality of opportunity*, for example in the provision of education or health care or work opportunities.

Many rules of law now exist which have as their specific objective the promotion of equality of opportunity. Both within the UK and more broadly in the European Union, there is law designed to combat the impacts of discrimination based on grounds of gender, ethnicity and race, disability or age. This is driven not by simplistic notions of 'political correctness' but by the very practical belief that the collective good of nations will be enhanced by ensuring that all citizens are in a position to play a full part in the economic and social life of those nations. To give a simple example, if women are excluded from the workforce, 50 per cent of the available talent is thereby excluded.

In addition to specific measures of anti-discrimination legislation, a great deal of political debate and public policy-making is directed to devising social, welfare and educational policies which seek to assist in the creation of a new social order. Law gives legitimacy to those policies. There is nothing new about this. Since the development of the concept of the Welfare State in the middle of the nineteenth century, the argument has been heard that it is right that governments should seek, to varying degrees, to promote equality. The law has clearly had and will continue to have a part to play in these developments.

The mere fact that policies are developed and enshrined in legal Acts of Parliament does not mean that a new social order is thereby automatically created. The evidence is that in modern Britain there remain very marked inequalities—whether based on class, education, employment, health or other life opportunities. While there may be aspirations towards equality, the social reality is that equality—however defined—has not yet been fully realized.

The claim that law has a role in the promotion of equality is one that is frequently made, and can thus be included as one of the 'macro' functions of law. However the part played by law in maintaining the existing social order may be said to be in conflict with that function. This leads some to argue that law has another, more political, function of supporting the status quo against any other ways of promoting social order. As with the tension between public order and human rights, there are tensions between the role of law in the preservation of the existing social order and its role in the promotion of a new social order.

Similarly, claims are made that a function of law is to promote social justice. The extent to which law and the legal system, by themselves, can deliver social justice is limited. Social justice is more a political concept than a legal one. Law may be able to support steps taken to achieve social justice and thus promote a new social order; but it would be unrealistic to claim that law can achieve this in isolation from other non-legal factors which underpin modern society.

Even if the ability of law directly to foster social justice or equality is limited, there is nevertheless an important claim for law: that it does have a role to play in protecting the weak against the powerful. This has become a very important function for law in the twentieth century as notions of the Welfare State have developed, not just in England but across the developed world.[8]

Law and economic order

The relationship between law and economic order raises similar matters to those considered in the relationship between law and social order. The dominant economic philosophy in the United Kingdom, indeed throughout the Western World, is market capitalism.[9] Here, a very important function of law has been and is the recognition of rights in private property, whether in land or other forms of security. It is in law that definitions of the ownership rights in property are to be found. The law provides procedures for the transfer of property from one person to another. The law enables different property rights to co-exist in the same piece of property. And the law provides mechanisms for the enforcement of those rights. There is little doubt that the notions of property developed in the law have, historically, assisted in the development of this economic framework and continue to sustain it.

Similar arguments can be made in relation to the law of contract. The recognition of the principle of the enforceable bargain (contract), breaches of which can be pursued and enforced through the courts, has been an essential tool in the development of the modern market capitalist economy. As with the function of law in the maintenance of the social order, law can also be seen as instrumental in the creation and underpinning of the economic order.

Nevertheless, there are other ways in which law is now used to regulate the economic order. It has long been recognized that there are activities which market economies are very bad at undertaking, or which do not make sense in crude market terms. Operating factories or machinery with proper regard for health and safety is one example. Certainly a great deal of modern law-making activity has been focused on the creation of regulatory frameworks within which business activity is required to

---

[8] Indeed there is a more historical claim that there have been situations in the past in which the law sought to intervene to offer at least some protection to the weak: see Thompson, E.P., *Whigs and Hunters* (London, Penguin, 1990).

[9] Differences between different models of capitalism—e.g. the North American model, the European model or the Japanese model—are not considered here. But it should not be assumed that the principles of capitalism are applied in exactly the same way in all countries.

be undertaken, which are justified on the basis that they fill the gaps left by market failure.

Similarly, it has long been recognized that untrammelled capitalist activity contains its own contradictions. There is an inexorable tendency for capitalists to wish to accumulate market position, and if possible dominate that position by the exercise of monopoly power. However, the shift from competition to monopoly poses a fundamental threat to the operation of the market. Thus legal mechanisms have been put in place to promote competition and to limit the development of monopolistic positions.

There is also an inevitable tendency for those with greater bargaining power to seek through contract to impose their wishes on parties with weaker bargaining positions. A great deal of modern law is designed to 'level the playing field'. There is a vast body of consumer law which has the effect of softening the binding nature of contractual relationships by giving added rights to consumers in situations where the bargaining power between the supplier of goods or services and the consumer of those goods or services is regarded as unequal. Thus, there are legal requirements that those who sell insurance policies or other expensive financial products should allow the purchaser a 'cooling-off' period within which she may change her mind. Housing law regulates the relationship between landlords and tenants. Employment law seeks to regulate the relationship between employer and employee. More generally there are measures which enable the consumer to challenge terms in contracts thought to be 'unfair'.

Here again, as with law and public order or law and social order, in relation to the economic order the law may be said to perform functions that to some degree are in conflict. Law has helped to legitimate the tools essential to the commercial context within which market capitalism is able to flourish. At the same time law is used to limit the excesses of market behaviour that can arise from the unregulated operation of market capitalism.

Law and international order

Another function for law is the provision of support for international order. This is a complex and controversial subject not considered in detail here. There are those who argue that there is really no such thing as international law; rather that maintenance of the international order is sustained by international relations and diplomatic pressure. But in many respects, international bodies and politicians like to point to legal authority for what they are trying to achieve. For example:

- Recent incursions by the United Nations into particular world trouble spots have been justified in part by reference to the legal framework of the United Nations Charter and its executive bodies, in particular the role of the Security Council.[10]

---

[10] Much of the present controversy about the war against Iraq arose from arguments that any resumption of hostility against Iraq should be properly justified in international law.

- Attempts to deal with 'crimes against humanity'—a particular curse of the modern age—are being made through a special War Crimes Tribunal which has been established by the UN and which sits in the Hague.

- In other areas, such as the regulation of world trade or the protection of the environment, the regulation of the use of the sea, or even space, there is an increasing tendency not only to enter treaties—which historically was common practice—but also to create special institutions and mechanisms for enforcement like courts or tribunals, which are independent of particular national governments.

- The conduct of war has long been subject to international legal constraints, for example the Geneva Convention on the treatment of prisoners of war. Similarly other constraints on behaviour in war and other situations of conflict, such as the prevention of torture, have been prescribed in instruments of international law.

- One of the most pressing of current social issues, the protection of those seeking asylum in one country because of a well-founded fear of persecution in another, is essentially shaped by principles of International Law.

These are important and controversial issues. Even though the focus of this work is on the rather more parochial subject of the 'English legal system', we cannot ignore the global context in which countries now operate. It has been argued that, following the collapse of communism, a 'new world order' has emerged. Legal instruments and institutions play a significant part in its development; this wider dimension of the role of law should not be forgotten.

Law and moral order

Another broad function of law is the provision of support for the moral ordering of society. This is extremely controversial. Some theorists argue that there should be little, if any, distinction between law and morality; that the law should clearly and deliberately mirror those issues of morality which people think 'ought' to inform the way we should behave. Others seek to draw a clear distinction between law and morality. They argue that the mere fact that many people *believe* that certain forms of behaviour or activity are morally wrong (for example engaging in homosexual activity) should not mean that they should be defined as unlawful.

There are clear dangers and considerable difficulties in seeking to equate law and morality, not least because of the problems of determining what the common morality is on any given issue. Nevertheless many rules of law are founded on a moral view of society. Perhaps the clearest example is the moral imperative not to kill people, reflected in rules of criminal law which outlaw such activity.

In general it may be suggested that rules of criminal law which reflect some common morality, however defined, may be more acceptable and effective in regulating behaviour than those rules which do not. For example, there may well be behaviours which many would regard as undesirable—dressing shabbily or drinking cheap alcohol in the streets—but which should not of themselves be defined as criminal. Conversely, there may be rules of criminal law, for example not exceeding speed limits, which many would not regard as particularly morally repugnant, but which should nevertheless be defined as criminal.[11]

In a different context, much of the law which seeks to regulate relationships between individuals is also based in concepts of morality, for example the law relating to marriage. To an extent, therefore, it can be said that another function of law is to provide at least some support for the moral order, a function now reinforced by the protection of family life under the European Convention on Human Rights (Art. 8).

Related to the relationship between law and moral order is the relationship between *law and religious order*. Despite the apparent decline in religious belief in England, there are still many who argue that religion—both formal and informal—remains an important facet of society at large. However, and in contrast with discussion about the relationship between law and morality, it is not now often argued that law should be directly supportive of religion. Indeed many would argue, whether in general principle or because of their own religious (or anti-religious) beliefs, that law should *not* be used to support the religious order. Questions of spirituality and religious belief should fall within that private sphere of activity in which the law should not intervene.

Nevertheless, the historical role played by religion in the development of modern England cannot be wholly ignored. At its most basic, our calendar and major festivals are firmly based in the Christian tradition, not that of other religious groupings. There are a number of legal privileges that attach exclusively to the Church of England; there are others that apply to religious groups more generally. There remains a specific law against blasphemy which effectively applies only to the Christian religion. Thus it is arguable, though not often seen in this light, that present-day law still plays a residual part in the support of religious order, in particular the Christian religious order.

This is controversial, not least because of the rise in a number of countries of various forms of religious fundamentalism. These are often accompanied by degrees of intolerance towards others that many regard as quite unacceptable in a modern pluralistic society. Indeed it may be the case that, in order to protect social pluralism, the law should be used more to protect the ability of those of different religious beliefs to hold and practise their religion, another issue embraced in the European Convention on Human Rights (Art. 9).

---

[11] Current campaigns to change people's perceptions about the non-desirability of driving above the speed limit are being directed as much to the moral issues as the legal issues involved.

Other macro functions

In addition to the ways in which law may interact with the maintenance of and challenges to different types of order, law also has a number of other macro functions.

The resolution of social problems

The response of politicians and their officials to many of the issues perceived as social problems is to create more laws seeking to regulate the behaviour complained against. This is regarded as the appropriate or expected political response. Only rarely do politicians concede that there may be enough law, and that what is needed is better understanding of or enforcement of existing law. Even more rarely are politicians willing to accept that a possible solution to a problem might be to repeal existing rules of law or to develop the law in such a way as to 'decriminalize' the activity in question.[12] Their mindset assumes that a function of law is 'to solve social problems'. Indeed whole careers are devoted to the promotion of legislation allegedly designed to address particular social issues—even if, as often happens, there is already perfectly satisfactory law already available, or where changing the law is not really a solution to the problem. (Perhaps civil servants and politicians who are responsible for *preventing* legislation from reaching the statute book should be rewarded more generously than those who seek to drive legislation forward.)

In addition, one obvious consequence of creating legal provisions to 'solve social problems' is that people—ever mindful of their own self-interest—respond to new legal frameworks in ways not predicted by the law-makers. A hidden but often inevitable consequence of using law to solve social problems is, therefore, that the very process of creating new law results not in the solution of an existing social problem but rather in the creation of new social problems. The process of dealing with one issue leads to the creation of another issue, which in its turn has to be solved at a later date.

The regulation of human relationships

Another important function of law is the regulation of the nature and extent of human relationships. The definition of and the formalities relating to the creation of marriage are determined by legal rules, often supplementing different religious rules.

---

[12] Historically this has often happened. For example many of the criminal offences that two or three hundred years ago might have led to draconian punishments such as transportation or even the death penalty now seem very trivial, and are either not criminal at all or dealt with much less severely. Today many argue that a less criminal approach to the use of 'soft drugs' might not only lead to more equitable treatment of drug users, as compared with those who use alcohol or nicotine, but also lead to reductions in other forms of criminality resulting from the need for drug users to obtain the money to buy their drugs. On the other hand, there are powerful political arguments that any relaxation in the Government's approach to drug use would send 'the wrong signal' to the community at large.

Law provides a framework for the distribution of assets on the breakdown of marriage. The law is also currently being developed in relation to the regulation and underpinning of other long-term relationships—both heterosexual and homosexual—where persons have not gone though the formalities of marriage. Law sets boundaries to the scope of sexual relationships, prescribing for example the minimum age of sexual consent, and making certain sexual relationships within the 'prohibited degrees of consanguinity' (incest and other close relationships) unlawful. The law also sets down a framework for the treatment of children and other family members.

The educative or ideological function of law

A further function of law, almost irrespective of its impact in particular cases, is an educative one; it contributes to shaping part of the 'ideology' of a nation. To give a simple if significant example, there is no doubt that attitudes to drinking and driving have changed dramatically over the last twenty years. In part this is the result of powerful advertising, demonstrating the devastating impact that drink-drive accidents can have on victims and their families. But the change in attitude has also been the result of changes in the law contributing to a climate of opinion in which drinking and driving is just no longer regarded as socially acceptable behaviour.

Another example is law, already mentioned above, dealing with various forms of discrimination. When such laws are brought into effect, those who argue for their introduction often accept that the law will not, on its own, alter the attitudes of mind that lead to the patterns of discriminatory behaviour which result in the creation of those laws. However, those who have sponsored such laws see them as not only creating certain legal rights which may be enforceable by individuals, but also sending a more general educative signal to members of society at large that discriminatory behaviour is not acceptable.

More generally, countries that embrace the principle of the 'rule of law' are, in effect, asserting that powers of officials of the state must be limited and that the individual citizen should have both the right and the opportunity to challenge decisions where they are thought to be wrong or in some respect unfair.

The decision by the British Government to introduce the Human Rights Act, incorporating the European Convention on Human Rights directly into English law, is another example of legislation that not only will create legal rights which individuals may seek to pursue through the courts, but which also sends an important educative signal about the limits within which people, particularly those who work within government, must behave. In this sense, therefore, another function of law relates to the education of the public.

Micro functions of law

Turning from the 'macro' to the 'micro' level involves consideration of rather more specific functions for law, many of which derive from the 'macro' functions identified above. A number of examples are offered; this does not purport to be a comprehensive list. The reader is invited to think of other functions not identified here. In addition, the reader may be able to think of other examples to illustrate the particular functions which have been identified.

Defining the limits of acceptable behaviour

The area of law with which most people have at least some familiarity is the *criminal law*. A major objective of this branch of the law is to prescribe the limits of behaviour which is socially acceptable. The criminal law seeks to prohibit many kinds of activity about which there would be widespread agreement, such as murder and violent crime. It also outlaws a wide range of other activities about which there may be more debate, such as the use of particular types of drugs. The following points may be made in this context:

- Not all behaviour which may be regarded by many as undesirable is thereby characterized in legal terms as criminal. Thus there is no law preventing a person over the age of 18 from drinking alcohol. However, where the consequences of that conduct may impinge on others the law often steps in. There is a strict law which makes it unlawful for persons who have been drinking alcohol to drive their cars.

- There are more ways in which human conduct is regulated than simply the use of law. Codes of morality, religious principles, the pressures of friends are all other factors which constrain the ways in which people behave.

- Different countries set the boundaries of their criminal law in different places: what is criminal in one country is not necessarily criminal in another.[13] Although there is a great deal of commonality between different bodies of criminal law, in important respects the boundaries of criminal law are *culturally determined*, set by the demands of the specific society. There are particularly important distinctions in societies with different religious traditions or moral backgrounds: laws operating in Islamic countries are often quite different from those in countries founded on the Judaeo-Christian tradition.

- The boundaries of the criminal law are *dynamic*. Activity which has been

---

[13] This can have an important practical consequence in that if a person commits a criminal act in one country and flees to another country where that act is not criminal, this is often the basis for successfully resisting extradition proceedings—official proceedings to bring the alleged miscreant back for trial to the country where the original act took place.

regarded as criminal at one point in time will not necessarily be regarded as criminal at another point in time. The prohibition of alcohol in the USA during the 1920s is a good example.

The attempt by law to regulate human behaviour is not exclusively through use of the criminal law. Areas of *civil law* also seek to do this. For example, if parties to a contract break that contract, rules of law allow the party affected to claim compensation or other remedies from those in breach of contract. The law of negligence prescribes situations in which a person who has negligently injured another has to compensate that other for the injury. In short, law seeks to define the scope of the obligations that exist between individuals. Although the objectives of rules of civil law are not to punish an offender, in the sense used in the context of the criminal law, it is nevertheless the case that rules of civil law indicate that a contract cannot be breached with impunity, nor can one person act negligently in relation to another. In this sense, the rules of civil law also send the message that certain types of behaviour are not acceptable or are undesirable.

Defining the consequences of certain forms of behaviour

Law does not of course simply define those forms of behaviour which are unacceptable. It also prescribes consequences. In the case of criminal law, these are the punishments that attach to a finding of guilt. Similarly in the area of civil law, law prescribes the remedies that the person affected by a breach of contract or a negligent act may obtain from the perpetrator.

In some situations the same facts may generate a variety of legal consequences. For example, a road accident may be caused by a person driving a car carelessly or recklessly. This may result in the police seeking to get that person prosecuted through the criminal courts; if found guilty this may result in the imposition of a fine or even imprisonment. If the accident causes damage to another, that other person may seek compensation by bringing an action for damages in negligence. The driver may argue that the accident occurred because her car was improperly serviced, and may therefore bring an action for breach of contract against her garage. Three different legal consequences have thus arisen from the same incident.

Defining processes for the transaction of business and other activities

A rather different function of law is to define procedures by which certain transactions must be carried out. Some of these are quite simple, such as those relating to the making of simple contracts. In other cases, particularly where there is concern to prevent fraud, considerable formality may be required. Many of these relate to transactions dealing with the transfer of entitlement to property rights. For example, the process of buying and selling houses is subject to a number of formal legal requirements, known collectively as the rules of conveyancing. There are detailed rules relating to the creation of leases. There are special rules for the creation of wills. Similarly, there are detailed requirements for the creation of trusts or settlements of property.

One of the problems with prescribing formal requirements is that, whatever the law states, people in practice attempt to carry out these transactions in ignorance of the rules. The law then has to develop supplementary principles to prevent injustice occurring, notwithstanding the existence of procedural irregularity. Many of the principles of the law of equity have developed in response to this problem.

Creating regulatory frameworks

A great deal of law seeks to regulate those who provide services to the public. For example, substantial bodies of law regulate the activities of solicitors, doctors, architects, nurses or estate agents. There is a vast regulatory framework designed to control the activities of those who provide financial services to the public to prevent fraud and other breaches of trust. A consequence of the privatization of the bulk of the former nationalized industries has been to create a vast body of law designed to regulate the activities of companies now in the private sector (such as telecommunications, utilities and transport) including the promotion of competition and the regulation of prices. And specific areas of economic activity are subject to the most detailed legal regulation designed to promote standards and give the consumer value for money. The regulation of the housing market through housing law is a prime example.

A different form of regulatory law, but one that has been in existence for many years, is planning law regulating the use to which land can be put in this country. Law which seeks to regulate industry in order to protect the environment is another example. In this context, the law operates at an international as well as a national level.

Regulatory law also serves another purpose. It defines the categories of persons able to make representations to government about a particular policy or decision. For example, again in the context of planning law, the relevant law determines who may challenge decisions of the planning authorities and who may appear to make their case at any public inquiry resulting from a planning decision.

Giving authority to agents of the state to take actions against citizens

Another function of law is to give power to state officials to take action against members of the public. There are numerous examples: the powers of the police to stop, search, question, arrest and caution members of the public are one; the power of doctors to detain in mental hospitals those diagnosed as suffering from acute mental illness is another; the power of social workers to remove children from families where they are thought to be at risk and to place them in the care of the local authorities a third. Similarly, agents of both central and local government are given power to take money away from members of the public through the taxation system.

A rather different example is the power given to government and other agencies of the state to acquire land compulsorily in the public interest.

Preventing the abuse of power by officials

Set against the last head, much law is designed to prevent abuses of power by public servants. For example, the police are required to operate within a framework of powers prescribed by the Police and Criminal Evidence Act 1984, designed to set boundaries to their powers of arrest, search and questioning.

The heart of the principles of administrative law, considered further in Chapter 6, relates to the importance of officials acting within the framework of the law which prescribes their power; not allowing officials to make use of discretionary powers in an abusive way; and giving people the opportunity to take advantage of certain procedural safeguards—for example a right to a hearing—before adverse decisions about them are taken. These are further examples of rules of law setting boundaries to the power of state officials.

Giving power/authority to officials to assist the public

In contrast to the preceding category, the law also sets down a vast range of requirements whereby agencies of the state must provide services or other goods to the public. At the most general level, all public expenditure has to be legitimated by special Acts of Parliament known as the Appropriation Acts. These give general authority for the expenditure of public money on the range of social and other policy programmes run by government.

More specific bodies of law deal with the details. Social security law is one example, setting out as it does the entitlements to social security benefits which have been created by government. Many other examples could be given: entitlement to free education is one, free treatment within the National Health Service another. All these activities, of the social security, education and health authorities, are underpinned by detailed legal frameworks.

Prescribing procedures for the use of law

In addition to prescribing procedures for conducting different types of transaction, there is another important body of law—procedural law—which seeks to control the ways in which courts and other adjudicative bodies are to operate. This body of law may set limits to the evidence that can be brought in different types of cases. It also prescribes the way in which different types of proceedings, whether in the courts or other forums, are to be conducted.

Conclusion: law and society

It is not claimed here that these examples of the 'macro' and 'micro' functions of law in society are exhaustive. Readers should ask themselves whether there are other functions for law and whether they should be regarded as 'macro' or 'micro' in character. There is indeed a huge literature on the relationship of law and society of which the foregoing is only a very limited summary. However a number of points can be noted.

(1) All the functions of law, whether defined as 'macro' or 'micro', are *contingent* upon the stage in the development of that society. While many of these functions of law will be common to very many societies, others will certainly not be.

(2) The laws that exist and the ways in which they are used are dependent on the ideology and politics of the particular country. For example, current notions of social justice and equality in the UK have developed in the light of particular socio-political and economic theories. They will change again in the future. The list of functions proposed here should not therefore be regarded as set in concrete; it will reflect other broader changes in the social and political ideas and ideals of that society.

(3) The functions of law are by no means always consistent with each other: preservation of social order may on occasion be in sharp conflict with the function of protecting civil liberties; the role of law in advancing equality, or social justice may be in conflict with its role in supporting current social and economic orders.

(4) It should be remembered that there are still activities which are not currently the subject of legal regulation. Governments frequently claim that they are seeking to limit the encroachment of law. Interestingly, however, when a new technology arrives which actually enables activities to occur outside conventional regulatory frameworks—the internet is a good current example—politicians and others quickly become agitated.

(5) There are many mechanisms, apart from law, which are used to regulate and alter the ways in which people behave. Much of the practice of economics is based on the assumption that, if financial incentives are right, behaviour will change. An interesting example is the proposal that problems of global pollution and global warming must be tackled not just by laws saying what should or should not be done, but also by getting financial incentives right—higher taxes paid by those who pollute, for example.

(6) More fundamentally, there are significant issues about the way in which we order our society which are either not touched on at all by law or only in relatively insignificant ways. For example, one of the major social issues of our time relates to the extent to which groups in the community are excluded from the mainstream of social life, whether through lack of monetary resources or other material resources such as housing. To be sure, there are legislative provisions relating to the provision of

social security benefits or to the provision of accommodation to the homeless. But the entitlements contained in these bodies of law are not absolute but are highly contingent on legal tests being met. Those claiming benefits or access to housing have a substantial list of conditions that they must satisfy before they will be helped. The fact that the rhetoric of law employs concepts such as 'liberty' or 'justice' does not mean that the body of substantive law is actually able to deliver 'social justice' to all the citizens of the UK.

With these examples of the use (and non-use) of law in mind, together with others that may well come to the attention of the reader, the rest of this book will consider the ability of the English legal system to enable the functions of law to be performed.

Questions for discussion

1. Are there other functions that you think law plays in the ordering of society? Would you classify these functions as 'macro' or 'micro'?

2. Is it necessary for a society to reach a particular level of development before law can play a useful role?

3. What are the consequences for a country or society of not accepting the importance of the rule of law?

4. How can the balance between the preservation of liberty and the maintenance of social order be best preserved?

5. Can law protect the economically weak?

6. What should be the relationship between law and morality? When should things we disapprove of be made unlawful?

7. To what extent can principles of law be employed in the ordering of international affairs?

8. How successful is law in shaping people's behaviour?

Further reading

ABEL-SMITH, B., and STEVENS, R., *In Search of Justice: Society and the Legal System* (London, Allen Lane, 1968)

ANDERMAN, S., *et al.* (eds.), *Law and the Weaker Party: an Anglo-Swedish Comparative* (Abingdon, Professional, 1981)

BARKHUYSEN, T., VAN EMMERIK, M.L., and

VAN KEMPEN, P.H.P.H.M.C. (eds.), *The Execution of Strasbourg and Geneva Human Rights Decisions in the National Legal Order* (The Hague/London, Martinus Nijhoff, c1999)

BRAKE, M., and HALE, C., *Public Order and Private Lives: the Politics of Law and Order* (London, Routledge, 1992)

COTTERRELL, R., *The Sociology of Law: an Introduction* (2nd edn., London, Butterworth, 1992)

DELUPIS, I., *The International Legal Order* (Aldershot, Dartmouth, c1994)

DICKSON, B. (ed.), *Human Rights and the European Convention: the Effects of the Convention on the United Kingdom and Ireland* (London, Sweet & Maxwell, 1997)

DRZEMCZEWSKI, A.Z., *European Human Rights Convention in Domestic Law: a Comparative Study* (Oxford, Clarendon Press, 1997)

DYZENHAUS, D. (ed.), *Recrafting the Rule of Law: the Limits of Legal Order* (Oxford, Hart, 1999)

FREEMAN, M.D.A., *The Legal Structure* (London, Longman, 1974)

HONORÉ, T., *The Quest for Security: Employees, Tenants, Wives* (London, Stevens & Sons, 1982)

JACOBS, F.G., WHITE, R.C.A., and Ovey, C., *The European Convention on Human Rights*. (3rd edn., Oxford, Oxford University Press, 2002)

McDOUGAL, M.S., LASSWELL, H.D., and LUNG-CHU CHEN, *Human Rights and World Public Order: the Basic Policies of an International Law of Human Dignity* (New Haven, Conn., Yale University Press, 1980)

RAINE, J., and WALKER, C., *The Impact on the Courts and the Administration of Justice of the Human Rights Act 1998*, LCD Research Series (London, LCD, 2002)

REINER, R., and CROSS, M. (eds.), *Beyond Law and Order: Criminal Justice Policy and Politics into the 1990s* (Basingstoke, Macmillan, 1991)

ROBERTS, S., *Order and Dispute: an Introduction to Legal Anthropology* (Harmondsworth, Penguin, 1979)

SCHACHTER, O., and JOYNER, C.C. (eds.), *United Nations Legal Order* (Cambridge, Grotius, 1995)

SHAPIRO, I. (ed.), *The Rule of Law* (New York, New York University Press, 1994)

DE SMITH, S.A., *The New Commonwealth and its Constitutions* (London, Stevens, 1964)

TOWNSEND, P., *Poverty in the United Kingdom: a Survey of Household Resources and Standards of Living* (Harmondsworth, Penguin, 1979)

VAN WYK, D., *et al.*, *Rights and Constitutionalism: the New South African Legal Order* (Kenwyn, Juta, 1994)

Websites

www.lcd.gov.uk/hract/hramenu.htm *(Lord Chancellor's Department Human Rights Unit)*

www.beagle.org.uk/hra/newindex.htm *(Site dedicated to human rights material)*

www.echr.coe.int/ *(European Court of Human Rights)*

www.liberty-human-rights.org.uk/ *(Liberty, formerly National Council for Civil Liberties)*

www.un.org/english/ *(United Nations home page)*

www.un.org/law/ *(United Nations International Law)*

www.icj-cij.org/ *(International Court of Justice)*

www.un.org/icty/ *(International Criminal Tribunal for the Former Yugoslavia)* www.wto.org/ *(World Trade Organization)*

www.uncitral.org/ *(United Nations International Trade)*

www.un.org/Depts/los/index.htm *(United Nations Law of the Sea)*

www.un.org/law/icc/index.html *(United Nations proposal for an International Criminal Court)*

www.citfou.org.uk/ *(Citizenship Foundation, promoting citizenship through education about law and democracy)*

www.citizen.org.uk *(Institute for Citizenship, materials for teachers)*

http://teachingcitizenship.org.uk *(Association for Citizenship Teaching)*

3

Law-making: Authority and process

Introduction

In the last chapter, we considered a number of functions that law plays in the ordering of society. In this chapter we examine the principal law-making institutions and how they operate. First though we ask: what gives these institutions their authority? What gives the law-makers their legitimacy?

Power, legitimacy and authority in the law-making process

One of the functions of law identified in Chapter 2 was support for the political order. Law provides much, if not all, of the legal framework within which power is exercised. But simply stating that constitutional principles provide governments or other executive agencies with the power to make law begs a further, more fundamental question: whence do these constitutional legal principles derive their authority?

The answer is far from easy. Different societies base their claims for the legitimacy of their law-makers on different theoretical foundations. In broad terms, however, law-makers may be said to derive their authority from two principal sources:

(a) the basic constitutional framework or constitutional settlement which operates within that country;

(b) the underlying political ideology of that country.

The reasons people in general are more or less willing to accept these bases for the exercise of power are complex. One is that, once they have established a claim to exercise power, states invariably create the machinery—police, security services and the like—whose function is to enforce the law. Another is that most people do want to run the country themselves and are happy to let politicians and bureaucrats get on with the job.

But it should always be remembered that even the most fundamental of constitutional arrangements will fail if significant groups within a particular society find that constitutional basis unworkable. The fact that in some countries in the world there have been civil wars, that in others there have been *coups d'état*, demonstrates the point. The destruction of the Berlin Wall and the collapse of apartheid in South Africa may be cited as two particularly dramatic instances. But many countries, even those which now have the most stable and secure of constitutional arrangements, trace their current situation to resistance to or even rebellion against earlier unacceptable constitutional arrangements. The United Kingdom and the USA both stand as examples. Constitutional arrangements ultimately depend on the consent of the governed.

In the United Kingdom, and in many other developed countries, that consent is more taken for granted than actively sought (save on particular issues which are the subject of referenda). Free and regular elections are usually seen as the primary institution from which continuing consent is implied.

Constitutions and constitutionalism

One basis for the authority given to the law-makers can therefore be found in a country's constitution and its related principles of constitutionalism. What are these?

In most countries there exists a *written constitution* or other form of 'basic law' which defines the powers of the law-making institutions of the country. In the United Kingdom, the constitutional arrangements are unusual in that there is no formal written constitution. Many of the most important constitutional principles are to be found not in any written document but embraced in unwritten practice, known as *constitutional conventions.* (*See Box 3.1.*)

These unwritten principles are now accompanied by an increasing number of fundamental statutory provisions.[1] Devolution, reform of the House of Lords, the Human Rights Act 1998, the Freedom of Information Act 2000 all involve the use of legislative measures which have transformed the constitutional landscape. In addition British membership of the European Union and other international bodies such as the Council of Europe and the United Nations has had significant constitutional implications. These all help to set the framework within which power in the United Kingdom is exercised.

British *constitutionalism*—the principles which underpin the constitution—rests on three essential features: the *sovereignty of Parliament*, the *rule of law* and the *separation of powers.*[2]

- The *sovereignty of Parliament* asserts that the ultimate legal authority for law-making in the United Kingdom is Parliament.

- The *rule of law* insists that power should not be exercised by persons acting by or

---

[1]   See the examples given in Chapter 2 at pp. 13–14.
[2]   The definitions of these concepts have, over the years, been the subject of fierce intellectual and political debate—see further reading.

Box 3.1 Constitutional conventions

A detailed account of the nature and extent of constitutional conventions is beyond the scope of this work; there is a substantial literature on what they are and the extent to which they have changed over the years and are still effective. But some examples of constitutional conventions may be noted:

Constitutional monarchy. Although the theoretical Head of State remains the monarch, the principle of constitutional monarchy means that the Queen takes no active part in the running of the country. Though the Parliamentary year starts with the 'Queen's Speech' and though bills are given 'royal assent', the Queen does not intervene in the politics of the law-making programme. The Queen is still kept informed about what is happening in Parliament and, through audiences with the prime minister of the day, is briefed about significant developments. It would be surprising if, on occasion, she did not offer her views on particular issues. But the monarch is no longer the source of political decision-taking or law-making.

Prerogative powers. Nevertheless, there are still certain functions of government which are based not in legislative authority, but on the historic exercise of power by the monarch. These are known as 'Prerogative Powers'. The most dramatic example of this is the power to go to war, which is exercised by ministers not under the authority of any Act of Parliament, but by exercise of prerogative powers. The Home Secretary's 'Prerogative of Mercy' to reduce a sentence imposed by the courts in a criminal trial may be seen as another example.

Cabinet government and collective responsibility. The very existence of a Cabinet—the central committee of ministers chaired by the prime minister and responsible for determining the government's programme—is another aspect of the British Constitution founded in convention, rather than legislation. The related doctrine of collective responsibility, whereby ministers who do not agree with the policy of the government as determined in Cabinet are supposed to resign from the government, is also based in constitutional convention, rather than constitutional law.

Individual ministerial responsibility. Another constitutional doctrine is that ministers should take ultimate responsibility for what goes on in their departments. This certainly means that they must answer questions in Parliament or select committees about the work of their departments. On occasion, this may also lead ministers to resign, where something has gone very seriously wrong, though in practice these days this is a rare occurrence.

on behalf of the state, without their being able to point to some form of legal *authority* for their actions.

- The *separation of powers* suggests that, to prevent any particular arm of government from becoming too powerful, there should be a separation between the legislative (law-making), executive and judicial functions of government.

Thereby each branch of government is subject to *checks and balances*. This in turn leads to the proposition that the judges in particular, and lawyers in general, must have the power to act independently of government.

These principles relate to the central issues of power: who may exercise it, how it can be controlled and how those who exercise power can be called to account.

Political ideology

Stating these principles still leaves unanswered the question: what is the theoretical basis on which power to make law may be asserted by political institutions? To answer this it is necessary to consider the underlying political ideology of the country.

In the United Kingdom, and indeed many other countries, the currently dominant political ideology is *representative democracy*, expressed principally through the holding of regular elections. Democratic theory suggests that society is unable to function as effectively as it might if everyone retained their unique power to control their own life or the lives of others. Instead, by electing Members of Parliament to *represent* the views of electors, individuals pass to those elected to Parliament some of that control or *sovereignty* which gives them the authority to govern on behalf of the people.

Those in power are also subject to the principle of *accountability*. For example politicians are regularly called to account for themselves or their political parties when general elections are held. From the electoral process those elected to political office derive their authority to make laws on behalf of the citizens of the country, knowing that if their actions are not approved of by the electorate they will be defeated at the next general election. They are also subject to accountability through the range of *checks and balances* that exist, both within the Parliamentary system (such as Parliamentary debates or questions to ministers) and outside. These comprise a wide variety of bodies and activities, including the essential part played by the press and other mass media in exposing things that go wrong within government.

Principles in practice

The application of these principles is not as clear in practice as theory might imply.

- First, in the British system, the fact is that the Parliamentary process is strictly controlled by the political party which forms the government of the day. There are very few issues on which MPs will vote independently of what the party wants. There is the occasional backbench revolt; and the occasional 'free vote' on a matter of conscience where the party 'whip' is not applied. But these are the exception, not the rule.

- Secondly, all legislation in the United Kingdom passes through not only the elected House of Commons, but also the non-elected House of Lords. Although the House of Lords rarely exercises the power it theoretically has to delay bills becoming law, on many occasions the House of Lords amends, often very substantially, legislation coming to it from the House of Commons. The threat of delay may also result in substantial amendment or even the dropping of legislative proposals. While there is in the Commons a clear link between the democratic process of election and the outcomes of the legislative process, in the Lords this is not so, and even after reform will not be the case.[3]

- Thirdly, knowing the extent to which the electoral process does in fact represent the 'will of the people' is also very difficult. In the United Kingdom, the voting system of 'first past the post' has meant that nearly all recently elected governments have attained power on the basis of a minority of the popular vote. This leads many, particularly those in the smaller parties who struggle to get elected under the present system, to argue that a 'fairer' voting system would incorporate proportional representation, whereby seats in Parliament would be distributed in proportion to votes cast. The primary argument against this apparently attractive proposition is that this tends to lead to coalition governments, in which the small minority parties thereby acquire a disproportionately powerful position. Experiments with proportional representation have recently occurred in the United Kingdom in the elections of members to the European Parliament.

- A further issue which could be said to weaken the democratic process is that the percentage of the population voting in elections has been declining in recent years. This has led to a variety of suggestions to make it easier for people to vote in elections, for example setting up electronic voting systems in supermarkets or increasing the ease with which people may vote by post. There have even been calls to make voting compulsory, as happens in a number of other countries: Australia is a prime example.

- Fifthly, there are important sources of law other than Parliament. Under the British system of separation of powers, judges in the higher courts have power to make new rules of law. They do this through the development of rules of 'common law'—long-standing principles of law developed over the years, in some cases centuries, by the judges. Many examples of judicial law-making can be given:

  - the fundamental principles of the law of contract on which much economic activity is based;

  - the principles of the law of negligence, which relate among other matters to dealing with the aftermath of accidents and other forms of misfortune;

  - the development of procedures for dealing with disputes between the citizen and the state, especially the principles of *judicial review*, which is the basis on which judicial control of the administrative arm of government is achieved.

Yet judges are not elected; they do not get their authority from any democratic theory. The legitimacy for their activity has to be found in other constitutional

---

[3] Precise details of the membership of the reformed House of Lords were not decided at the time of writing, but it is already clear that the reformed House of Lords will not be a wholly elected body.

principles, in particular the separation of powers. The judges are recognized to be both a part of the machinery of government and, paradoxically, at the same time independent of it.

Membership of the European Union

One respect in which the law-making process in the United Kingdom has been significantly altered in recent years has arisen from the United Kingdom's membership of the European Union. The fundamental constitutional documents of the Union, starting with the Treaty of Rome and developed by, for example, the Treaties of Maastricht and Amsterdam, provide not only that member states must abide by those principles of European law that are made by the institutions established by the Treaty of Rome, but also that failure to do this will result in sanctions being imposed by the institutions of the European Union. As a result of these principles, the British Government is *required* to incorporate certain rules of European law into British law, whether or not it likes them. Furthermore, the House of Lords has decided[4] that if the provisions of a British Act of Parliament are in conflict with European law, then the British Act is to be regarded as of no effect. Until this point was reached, the British courts had never claimed the power to overrule an Act of Parliament, which was always regarded as the sovereign law-making authority.

One criticism of the institutional arrangements of the European Union is said to be 'democratic deficit'. It is argued that too many of the institutions established to run the European Union operate without the authority/legitimacy bestowed by some process of democratic accountability. For example, the exclusive right to initiate legislation is held by the European Commission, whose twenty Commissioners are not directly elected by the people of the European Union. In practice, the powers of the Commissioners are constrained by the Council of Ministers, comprising elected ministers from each of the member states, and whose approval of legislative proposals was always required.[5] But the argument was often made that the European Parliament—the only body with directly elected members—had no part to play in the law-making process, certainly compared with the part played by the British Parliament.

These criticisms have been acknowledged, at least to a degree. Since the Maastricht Treaty was concluded in 1992, and more particularly since the 1997 Treaty of Amsterdam came into effect (on 1 July 1999), the European Parliament has acquired significantly more legislative power. It still cannot initiate legislative measures. But it now has significant power to control the content of measures. Around 75 per cent of all European law-making must now be approved by a majority of the European

---

[4] *Factortame v. Secretary of State for Transport (No. 2)* [1991] 1 AC 603; the jurisprudence of the European Court of Justice had long been clear on the point: *Costa v. ENEL* Case 6/64 [1964] ECR 585.

[5] Initially, the Council of Ministers had to be unanimous; a single vote against a proposal would result in its not being adopted. In many circumstances the principle of unanimity has been replaced by the principle of qualified majority, which at least enables measures to be introduced despite the opposition of some ministers.

Parliament as well as the Council of Ministers. The poor participation by the British electorate in European elections may be the result of the widespread lack of knowledge about the role of the Parliament and how it has changed.

European Convention on Human Rights and the Human Rights Act 1998

The incorporation of the European Convention on Human Rights[5a] into British Law, through the Human Rights Act 1998 raises similar issues. All bills presented to Parliament now contain a statement that, in the view of the relevant sponsor, the bill complies with the Articles of the European Convention. Nevertheless, it is not inconceivable that particular rules of statute law will be held by the English courts (as they have from time to time been so held by the European Court of Human Rights in Strasbourg) to be contrary to the Convention. The Human Rights Act specifically prohibits the English courts from declaring principles of legislation invalid,[6] thus preserving the notion of the sovereignty of Parliament. However the Act does give the courts power to issue a 'declaration of incompatibility' which, in effect, is a direction to the government of the day that a particular statutory provision must be amended in order to comply with the provisions of the European Convention.

The law-making institutions

With these points in mind, we take a closer look at the functions of a number of the law-making institutions that exist in the United Kingdom:

- The British Parliament and central government;
- European institutions;
- The courts;
- Other sources of law-making.

The British Parliament and central government

The principal law-making body in the United Kingdom is the British Parliament. Its legislative programme is at the heart of the law-making process. By no means all legislative measures are the subject of detailed Parliamentary scrutiny (*see Box 3.2*),

---

[5a] The European Convention on Human Rights is the work of the Council of Europe, *not* the European Union: see below p. 50.

[6] S. 4.

but the vast bulk of legislative measures derive their authority from the Parliamentary process. The nature of that process has undergone significant though inadequately publicized change in recent years—an example of the often understated dynamism that characterizes many developments in the English legal system.[7] The discussion here focuses on the process of enacting an Act of Parliament. Apart from the inherent importance of the subject there is a good practical reason why lawyers need to know about this. There are now circumstances—albeit limited—in which what was said about a bill as it passed though Parliament may be used by a court when dealing with a question of statutory interpretation.[8]

Box 3.2 Statute law: the classification of legislative measures

The vast bulk of the new law that is brought into effect in England is statute law, that is law which has been passed through Parliament following analysis and debate in both the House of Commons and the House of Lords. Statute law comes in a variety of forms:

- primary legislation

- secondary legislation

- tertiary legislation, and

- (not strictly statute law) 'quasi-legislation' or 'soft law'.

Primary legislation comprises the eighty or so *Acts of Parliament* that are passed through Parliament each year. The process consumes a great deal of Parliamentary time; indeed lack of time is a significant constraint on the law-making process. Many legislative proposals—particularly if they are not high on the government's political agenda—are brought forward only when 'time is available'. This can be used as an excuse for a government delaying bringing a new measure forward; but the non-availability of Parliamentary time is also a real constraint on the opportunities for introducing and then amending legislation.[9] Most Acts of Parliament are 'Public General Acts', applying throughout the land; some are 'Local or Personal Acts' applying only in particular localities or to specific people. (*See Box 3.3.*)

---

[7] One of the most recent innovations—introduced in November 1999—is that of *backbench debates*. Because of the amount of time the legislative process takes in the House of Commons, backbenchers have only limit opportunity to raise matters of more general concern. Three days each week are now available for backbench debates on matters not related to the legislative programme. These take place not in the chamber of the House of Commons, but in Westminster Hall, which for these purposes has been arranged in a horse-shoe formation—thought to be less confrontational than the familiar 'head-on' arrangements in the House of Commons.

[8] *Pepper v. Hart* [1993] AC 593 (HL); on statutory interpretation see below p. 58.

[9] There are occasions when measures can be introduced and passed with extreme rapidity; the enactment of the Northern Ireland (Emergency Provisions) Act 1998 in the aftermath of the Omagh bombing in August 1998 is an example.

Primary legislation is supplemented by a vast body of *secondary legislation*—regulations and orders made under the authority of an Act of Parliament. There are typically in excess of 3,000 such items, known generically as *statutory instruments*, made each year. These run to many thousands of pages of text. They are not subject to detailed Parliamentary scrutiny, though in many cases statutory instruments cannot be made by the Government without a process of consultation with a specialist Advisory Committee. (*See Box 3.5.*)

In addition to primary and secondary legislation, there is also a vast array of *tertiary legislation*—legislative instruments which are made under the authority of an Act of Parliament, but which are subject to no Parliamentary scrutiny at all. For example, in Housing Law, numerous powers are given to ministers to issue 'directions' or other instruments, which are drafted in the form of legislation and which effectively have the force of law, but which are simply issued by the government department in question. Similar examples are found in many other areas of government.

There is, finally, a fourth category of instrument, sometimes referred to as *quasi-legislation* or *soft law*, which comprise statements of good practice or guidance. These may be made under the authority of an Act of Parliament and may in some cases be subject to Parliamentary approval. But, as with tertiary legislation, they are subject to no detailed Parliamentary discussion. Examples include codes of practice such as the Highway Code or the Codes of Practice relating to police behaviour made under the Police and Criminal Evidence Act 1984. (See Chapter 5.) Many other examples could be given.

One practical problem with tertiary and 'quasi'-legislation is that it is not published in the normal way by the Stationary Office—the official outlet for government publications. For example ministerial directions will usually be made available to those who need to know about them; the ordinary member of the public who may wish to know about the existence of these documents may find them hard to track down.

An important issue of principle flows from this. There is a simplistic assumption that because legislation is published by a single authoritative source, 'everyone is deemed to know the law'. Such a claim is simply not sustainable in the case of such instruments.

Primary legislation

Acts of Parliament all start as bills. In addition, nearly all bills are now accompanied by an Explanatory Note, a detailed note drafted by the bill's sponsoring department, which sets out the background to the bill and explains what it is trying to achieve in policy terms.[10] They are all published on the internet.

---

[10] This is one of the most important, though again inadequately publicized, procedural innovations of recent years. These notes set bills in both their policy and legal context.

Four distinct types of bill may be identified:

(1) 'Political' bills, the result, usually, of the political programme of the party in government. Here the initial idea for a bill will be found in the political manifesto of the party in power. (Indeed, Acts of Parliament have been referred to as the 'corpses' of political debate: the remains left over from the sound and fury of political struggle.) The majority of bills presented to Parliament are designed to further the political objectives of the government in power. These are often referred to collectively as government bills and are sponsored by individual ministers.

(2) 'Law Reform' bills which arise from time to time as the result of recommendations made by law reform agencies, such as the Law Commission. These tend to be less politically controversial.[11]

(3) 'Consolidation' bills, which bring together into a single place a wide range of legislative provisions scattered through many Acts of Parliament and thus difficult to find.[12] These measures do not themselves introduce new law but tidy up and re-present what is already on the statute book. There is a special procedure to enable such measures to reach the Statute Book without going through the full Parliamentary process discussed below.

(4) 'Private Members' bills' are a special type of bill introduced by backbench MPs.

(For further consideration of these different types of Act of Parliament, *see Box 3.3*.)

Box 3.3 Acts of Parliament: Public General Acts and Local and Personal Acts

Most Acts of Parliament are known as *Public General Acts*, which means they apply throughout the United Kingdom. Because of their different legal systems, Acts which apply only in Scotland may now be made by the Scottish Parliament; and there are special rules relating to legislation which is effective in Northern Ireland. Each Public General Act contains a section which defines in which parts of the United Kingdom the Act will apply. All such Acts are of *general* application in all those parts of the countries to which they are stated to apply.

By contrast, *Local and Personal Acts* are of limited scope only. They may apply only to a local area (say a town) or to a specific institution (say a body such as a university, or a particular individual). The procedure by which Local and Personal Acts become law is quite different from the procedure by which Public General Acts become law. The detail is not considered here, but in essence such Acts are passed through a procedure involving committees of the House, not the full House of Commons.

---

[11] For further information on the work of the Law Commission see Chapter 4, p. 79.

[12] Failure to consolidate adds to the complexity of carrying out legal research; printed versions of Acts of Parliament may be quite misleading, having been substantially amended. New computer technology creates the opportunity to keep texts of statutes up to date. In some countries, e.g. Canada, the statute book is automatically consolidated every ten years.

Private Acts must be sharply distinguished from *Private Members' Acts*, which are Public General Acts, but sponsored—as their name implies—not by government ministers, but by ordinary backbench Members of Parliament. (*See Box 3.4.*)

Box 3.4 Private Members' bills

Private Members' bills are introduced by MPs who are not members of the government. They are subject to special rules relating to their content. Most important of these is that they cannot contain any provision that would result in the expenditure of public money. These bills are also subject to special procedural rules, which mean that only a very few such measures reach the statute book in any given year.

The backbenchers who bring these bills forward are selected following a ballot—a process which takes place early in each Parliamentary session. Private Members' bills are debated only on Fridays—a day when the pressure of government business is usually less. Twenty Private Members are able to introduce their measures following the ballot, but those near the top of the list have a greater chance of seeing their bills introduced into law. For a bill to have any chance of success it must either be supported by the government, or at least not actively resisted by the government.

The Housing (Homeless Persons) Bill 1976 is a good example: as originally drafted it would have given a range of legal rights to the homeless which the government regarded as wholly unacceptable. In that case, the government offered the bill's sponsor an alernative, which was the bill he then took forward. With this government support the bill did eventually pass into law.

Private Members' bills can be used to introduce measures on which there are fierce divisions of opinion, but where those divisions are not the subject of party political debate. An excellent example of this is the Abortion Act 1967, which was a very important, but obviously controversial, measure introduced by Mr David Steel, in relation to which none of the main political parties wished to tie their political reputations. The willingness of a private member to take such an issue forward can mean that the political parties, in particular the government party, can distance themselves to some extent from such an issue.

Over the last fifteen years, or so, the average 'success' rate for Private Members' bills has been about eight out of twenty reaching the Statute Book each year. In addition to the ballot process, there are three other means by which backbenchers may attempt to introduce legislation: 'presentation bills', Ten Minute Rule bills and bills from individual members of the House of Lords. The numbers of such bills passing into law are tiny and are not considered further here.

Preparatory stages

Before getting to Parliament, many bills start the process of becoming law by being part of the political manifesto produced by the party that won the last general election. Political parties seek to achieve power in government in order to turn their ideas into legislative form. Issues that involve a good deal of specialist know-how may also be the subject of consultation with persons or other agencies outside government. There are various ways in which this is carried out. Commonly, ideas for new policies and related changes in the law will be floated in a *Green Paper*;[13] this will often set out a number of proposals for change and ask for comments on them. The government may attempt to steer response by indicating its preliminary view on what should happen.

Following this initial consultative process, a further and firmer statement of the government's policy objectives may be set out in a *White Paper*[14] that summarizes the consultation and sets out the government's view on what it plans to do. At this stage there will be no detailed draft bill to consider, just the underlying policy.

The Queen's speech

Each session of Parliament[15] starts with the Queen's speech. Written by the government of the day, it sets out the legislative priorities for the coming Parliamentary session. Getting a slot in the Queen's speech is a key objective for ministers seeking to introduce a bill into Parliament. Without it, their legislative ambitions will be thwarted.[16] The details of the Queen's speech are determined each year by one of the committees of the Cabinet.

Procedural changes

Until recently, Parliamentary practice required all bills to be presented first to Parliament. Failure to do this was regarded as an insult to Parliament. The process of enacting bills has recently undergone three important changes.

Consultation. The wisdom of the principle that bills must not see the light of day until they are brought to Parliament has been increasingly challenged. As the result of very important procedural changes,[17] some bills are now published in draft and circulated for comment and criticism by those most likely to be affected, prior to their formal introduction into Parliament.[18] In the last session of Parliament, six bills were

---

[13] So called because years ago they were published with green covers. For some years, however, image-conscious governments have used designers and printers to produce Green Papers with covers containing all the colours of the rainbow!

[14] They too are no longer distinguished by the colour of their covers.

[15] The date is usually in November. Following a general election, the opening of the session will start shortly after the results are declared and the new government formed. The November date applies in those years when there is no general election.

[16] The only exception to this is emergency legislation needed to deal with an urgent and unexpected issue.

[17] See Select Committee on the Modernization of the House of Commons, *The Legislative Process* (July 1997) (HC 190, 1997–1998).

[18] The Employment Rights (Dispute Resolution) Act 1998 is an example.

so treated, up from three the session before. The Select Committee on Modernization has recommended that this procedure be followed as much as possible.[19]

Hearings. In addition there are now cases where a draft bill is subject to special hearings by a committee of MPs—a practice common in the USA and other countries but not until recently used here.[20] Thus, in the case of the Financial Services and Markets Bill 1999 a consultation paper was issued in July 1998, with a draft Bill attached to it. This was the subject of consultation with those likely to be affected by it. In addition it was the subject of hearings before two Parliamentary committees: one the Treasury Committee of the House of Commons,[21] the other a joint committee of the House of Commons and House of Lords, both of which issued reports on the draft bill. All these consultations led to further changes to the bill being made before it was formally introduced into the House of Commons in June 1999.

Carry forward. A further significant procedural experiment has been introduced whereby a bill can be considered over two Parliamentary sessions. If the passage of a bill through Parliament is not completed before Parliament is prorogued in late October/early November, it can be taken forward into the following Parliamentary session. So far only the Financial Services and Markets Bill 1999 has been subject to this procedure. The Select Committee on Modernization of the House of Commons has recently recommended wider use of this practice, which is common in most other political systems with Westminster-style Parliamentary procedures.[22]

The advantage of these developments is clear. Those affected are given the opportunity to comment on the adequacy of the legislation from a practical point of view before it reaches its final form. The ability to carry bills from one Parliamentary session to another means that there can be greater flexibility over the dates on which bills can be introduced into Parliament. The practice of 'front-loading'—the presentation of new bills in the first half of each Parliamentary session—will, to an extent at least, be mitigated. (Present practice effectively prevents any new measure being introduced later than May in any year.) It also represents a sensible attempt to prevent the detail of complex legislation being rushed through Parliament, at the end of a Parliamentary session, often with undesirable drafting consequences.

Parliamentary stages

The formal procedure for passing an Act starts with the presentation of a bill in one of the Houses of Parliament. Most measures designed to advance the political objectives of the Government are presented first in the House of Commons; less controversial

---

[19] Modernization of the House of Commons Select Committee, 2nd Report, *A Reform Programme*, HC 1168 September 2002; www.publications.parliament.uk/pa/cm/cmmodern.htm.

[20] An early example was the pre-legislative scrutiny by the Social Security Select Committee of the Government's draft bill on pension sharing on divorce, published in June 1998.

[21] Their report, *Financial Services Regulation*, was published in February 1999, with a response from Government in March 1999.

[22] It is hard to say how often this procedure will be used. It was not used in relation to measures such as the Social Security Bill 1999, which proved to be extremely politically contentious.

measures (including consolidation bills) may start in the House of Lords. The analysis here assumes the bill starts in the House of Commons.

The bill's objectives will have been determined by the political imperatives of the Government or other person presenting the bill. Those principles are transformed into legislative form by teams of specially qualified and trained lawyers known as Parliamentary Counsel.

The Parliamentary process starts with a *first reading*, a formal stage when the House orders the bill to be printed.[23] No progress can be made on a bill until it has been printed.

The first opportunity for debate arises at the *second reading*. Here the minister responsible sets out the main policy objectives; the opposition parties set out their objections. This is followed by comments from other Members of Parliament—the backbenchers. At the end of the debate, there is a summing up by a government minister. It is rare for a government bill to be defeated at this stage.[24] If a bill implies either the raising of taxation or the expenditure of public money, Parliament also has to pass (respectively) a Ways and Means Resolution or a Money Resolution.

The bill then moves to the *committee stage*.[25] Detailed scrutiny of the text is carried out by a small group of MPs, usually about eighteen in number, known as a Standing Committee. They consider the clauses[26] of the bill, as drafted, consider amendments proposed to those clauses, and determine whether or not such amendments should or should not be accepted. This is a highly 'political' stage in the legislative process. Not only do the Opposition members put down such amendments that they have thought of, but members of the Standing Committee are also subject to intense lobbying from groups outside Parliament, with a view to their putting down amendments which reflect the interests of those lobbying groups. (These groups will also, of course, exert pressure in other ways—press releases, airing their views on TV and the radio, and so on.)

Given that the government party always has a majority on the committee, and those MPs from the government side are instructed to vote as the Whip tells them, it is usually the case that the government side either gets its way, or makes only those concessions which it is prepared to accept. Despite the degree of control that government has, bills are actually frequently amended and often emerge from the overall process significantly changed from the form in which they were first advanced. On

[23] All bills are printed on a light blue-coloured paper, to distinguish them from the subsequent Act, which is printed on white paper.

[24] This was a fate suffered by the Shops Bill 1986, designed to deregulate Sunday trading.

[25] The committees of the House of Commons which look at bills are known collectively as 'standing committees'. Rarely, on a very controversial measure, the committee stage may be taken 'on the floor of the House', in other words before the House of Commons as a whole. In the House of Lords, the committee stage is always taken before the whole House. Standing committees should be carefully distinguished from 'select committees' which have the task of examining the activities of government carried out in the various government departments.

[26] Each of the separate provisions in a bill is called a 'clause'; after the bill has passed through Parliament and become an Act, the clauses are transformed into 'sections'.

occasion, where a bill is being rushed though Parliament, or on a very significant constitutional change, the committee stage may take place in the whole House, but this is a rare occurrence.

Next comes the *report stage*, in which things that have happened to the bill in committee are reported to the main House. This may provide the government with the chance to undo things that the committee may have done to the bill which the government does not like. It is often the point at which amendments which the government wishes to introduce into the bill (perhaps following debate in committee) are introduced.

The final stage is the *third reading*, a more formal stage in which the bill in its then form is brought together but no more amendments are made. The bill then goes to the House of Lords, where it begins a similar process.

Usually the progress of a bill is the subject of an informal timetable agreed between the Government and the opposition whips. Where a bill is extremely politically controversial, and the Opposition parties are taking every opportunity to slow progress of the bill through committee, the Government may decide that a strict timetable for the discussion of the measure is to be imposed. A timetable order, commonly known as a *guillotine motion*, is passed which prescribes the date by which each stage of the bill's progress must be completed. If it is not, the bill nevertheless proceeds to the next stage of the Parliamentary process, without any further debate or analysis of the draft provisions. Decisions to impose the guillotine are not taken lightly, but are not uncommon. In most recent years there have been a small number of examples; the record was in 1988–9 when ten such motions were passed.

Another important procedural innovation in recent years has been the creation of the *programme motion*. Here Government and Opposition agree a timetable, which can be amended, that sets out publicly the dates by which each stage of the bill will be complete. This provides more transparency than arrangements reached 'through the usual channels'.

The House of Lords

Procedure in the House of Lords is broadly similar to that in the Commons. The major differences are:

(i) the committee stage is taken 'on the floor of the House', i.e. there are no specially designated committees of peers whose task it is to report back to the House as a whole;

(ii) there is no guillotine, and thus debate on amendments in not restricted;

(iii) amendments can be made at the Third Reading stage.

These potentially can be, and on occasion are, a source of delay. But although the Lords are in theory able to wreck or seriously delay legislation, they are aware that, given their current status as a non-elected legislative body, the ultimate decision on legislation must lie with the elected House of Commons. While they do not in practice destroy bills, there have been a number of occasions in recent years where they have secured significant amendments or even caused a bill to be withdrawn.[27]

Once the Lords' stages are complete, there has to be a process for the Commons and the Lords to agree a single version of the text. Particularly at the end of the Parliamentary year (late October/early November) this can lead to dramatic horse-trading between Lords and Commons, especially where measures are very controversial. In the last resort, the House of Lords does have power under the Parliament Act 1911 to delay a Commons bill for up to one year (though not a money bill). If there is an ultimate impasse, then the view of the elected legislature, the House of Commons, will prevail. Reform of the House of Lords will bring detailed changes to these procedures.

Royal assent and commencement

The final stage is the granting of the *royal assent*. This has not been withheld since 1707, but, reflecting the fact that the United Kingdom is a constitutional monarchy, is still a formal step that has to be completed.

The mere fact that an Act has completed the legislative process does not mean it at once becomes effective. Commonly, new administrative arrangements have to be put in place before an Act can become operational. In such cases, the legislation will be effective only when a *Commencement Order*—a special type of statutory instrument (see below)—is made. (The Easter Act 1928 has still not been brought into force.) It is clearly essential that those who may seek to take advantage of new rules of law discover whether or not statutory provisions are in force.

Reports of debates

The debates on all the Parliamentary stages are the subject of verbatim reporting in the Official Reports of the Houses of Parliament (known collectively as *Hansard*). Thus it is possible to research what was said and by whom at each stage of the Parliamentary process. These reports also detail how MPs voted. These reports are now also available on the internet.

Secondary legislation

Because of the length of time which has to be taken to ensure the passage of legislation through Parliament, modern practice is for Acts of Parliament to contain the essential principles of legislation only. The detail is filled in by *secondary legislation* made under the authority of the Act, but which is not subject to the full Parliamentary scrutiny that a bill undergoes. Secondary legislation is technically known as *statutory instruments*, which come in two forms, *regulations* (the most common) and *orders*.

---

[27] A recent example was the Criminal Justice (Mode of Trial) Bill 1999; this had been introduced in the House of Lords, but was withdrawn following an adverse vote there. The Government decided to introduce a new bill, revised in content but with the same title, in the House of Commons; this was the subject of a wrecking amendment in the House of Lords. See further Chapter 5.

Underpinning the creation of secondary legislation is a number of controls designed to ensure that governments only introduce measures which they have authority to introduce:

(1) regulations are subject to formal vetting by the Statutory Instruments Committee of the House of Commons;

(2) many categories of statutory instruments also have to be shown in draft to particular bodies or organizations detailed in the 'parent' Act. Many governmental advisory committees are given the specific task of commenting on and vetting proposed regulations. (See *Box 3.5.*) Some parent Acts require the Government not just to consult with a specific nominated body, but with 'such bodies as appear to have an interest in the legislation'. This is code for requiring the Government to discuss with a range of interested groups the content of proposed delegated legislation;

(3) there is the potential for some Parliamentary input, though this rarely happens. All regulations are subject either to a *negative resolution procedure* or to a *positive resolution procedure.* (Two particular types of SI, Commencement Orders (which bring Acts of Parliament, or parts of Acts of Parliament into effect) and Orders in Council, are not subject to any Parliamentary procedure.) The *negative resolution procedure* is the more common. It means that, once laid before Parliament, a new regulation will become effective on the date stated in the regulation, *unless* Parliament passes a resolution stating that the regulations should be annulled. Given that regulations are introduced by government and that (usually) the Government has a majority in the House of Commons, it will be realized that this will happen very infrequently indeed. By contrast, the *positive resolution procedure* means that a regulation laid before Parliament cannot become effective unless Parliament adopts a resolution which states *positively* that the regulation should become effective. It cannot be said that this process actually gives the House of Commons much control over the detail, since debate is permitted only on the underlying issues, not the specific details. But positive resolution debates do give some opportunity for opposition parties to make broad political points about the regulation in question;[28]

(4) in an extreme case, the validity of a statutory instrument may be challenged in the courts and, if found to be *ultra vires* (outside the legal framework provided by the parent Act), will be declared by the courts to be a nullity.[29]

---

[28] An example is found in the annual up-rating of social security benefits. The relevant regulations are subject to the positive resolution procedure. Debate on whether the new amounts should be 50p more or less is not permitted; but general debate about social security provision and social welfare policy is allowed.

[29] Although a relatively rare occurrence, there have been two recent examples: *R v. Secretary of State for Trade and Industry, ex parte Thomson Holidays, The Times,* 12 January 2000 and *R v. Secretary of State for the Environment, Transport and the Regions and Another, ex parte Spath Holme Ltd* [2000] 1 All ER 884.

Box 3.5 Consultation on regulations: social security and administrative justice

An interesting example of the use of a specialist committee to review delegated legislation is the work of the Social Security Advisory Committee which looks at draft regulations relating to social security policy. It not only considers the proposals itself, but also consults on those proposals with a wide range of bodies and pressure groups outside government. It reflects on these comments before making its own report to the Government. The Government then decides whether or not to accept the advice of its Committee.

When it brings forward the final version of the regulations, the Government is required to publish a special report which not only reproduces the report from the Advisory Committee, but also details why the Government has (or more often has not) followed the advice of the Committee.

This represents a particular form of accountability which to some extent replaces normal Parliamentary debate; arguably it is more relevant since most of the commentators will have a specialist interest in and knowledge of the area. This is a model which, it has been forcefully argued, should apply in other regulation-making contexts.[30]

Another example is the work of the Council on Tribunals which scrutinizes draft statutory instruments relating to the practice and procedures of tribunals and inquiries.

Amending legislation

The process of amending legislation is usually done by the enactment of a new Act which alters an Act already on the statute book. Thus amending legislation has to take its turn in finding a slot in the legislative programme. On occasion, ministers have sought to make their lives easier by providing that provisions in an Act of Parliament can be amended by statutory instrument, thereby avoiding Parliament. These provisions, sometimes called 'Henry VIII clauses',[31] are not regarded with favour.

In recent years, it has come to be accepted that where changes in legislation which impose unnecessary burdens can be removed they should be without waiting for a full Parliamentary legislative slot. The first Act to move in this direction was passed in 1994. The Deregulation and Contracting-Out Act 1994 provided that, subject to detailed safeguards, ministers could lay orders before Parliament which had the effect of amending legislation. The power was used forty-eight times to remove burdens from business and individuals which might not otherwise have received Parliamentary time.

This trend has been continued with the enactment of the Regulatory Reform Act 2001, which gives ministers wider powers to lay orders before Parliament to amend

[30] Harden, I., and Lewis, N., *The Noble Lie: The British Constitution and the Rule of Law* (London, Hutchinson, 1986).

[31] Reflecting the propensity of that monarch to ride roughshod over Parliament.

legislation, so long as any such amendment removes burdens. It is anticipated that this measure will enable a number of more substantial statute law reforms, including, for example, some reforms proposed by the Law Commission, to be achieved. (*See Box 3.6*).

Box 3.6 The Regulatory Reform Act 2001

Scope of the Act

Orders under the Act, which are called regulatory reform orders, are capable of:

- making and re-enacting statutory provisions—the order can amend or repeal statutory provisions, it can replace provisions with a restatement of the law, or it can modify or replace them with new provisions;

- imposing additional burdens where necessary, provided that they are proportionate, that the order strikes a fair balance between the public interest and the interests of persons affected by any such burdens, that the order also removes or reduces other burdens and that the extent to which other burdens are removed or reduced or there are other beneficial effects makes it desirable to make the order;

- removing inconsistencies and anomalies in legislation, provided the order also removes or reduces other burdens;

- dealing with burdensome situations caused by a lack of statutory provision to do something;

- applying to legislation passed after the Act if it is at least two years old when the order is made and has not been amended in substance during the last two years;

- relieving burdens from anyone, including ministers and government departments but not where only they would benefit; and

- allowing administrative and minor detail to be further amended by subordinate provisions orders, subject to either negative or affirmative resolution procedure.

The Act also requires that any burdens imposed by an order must be proportionate to the benefits expected. Two further stringent tests (fair balance and desirability) apply if an order would increase or impose a burden. Requirements for extensive public consultation and thorough scrutiny by two Parliamentary Committees remain. Ministers bringing forward regulatory reform orders are required to present explanatory information to Parliament. The importance of full and thorough consultation was stressed during debate in both Houses.

Parliamentary procedure

The special Parliamentary procedure which orders will undergo (sometimes called the 'super-affirmative' procedure) affords a greater degree of Parliamentary scrutiny than that which ordinary affirmative resolution orders receive. First, the minister lays a regulatory reform proposal before Parliament 'in the form of' a draft order together with a full explanatory document. Following the sixty-day period of Parliamentary consideration, during which time the proposal is referred automatically and simultaneously to the committees appointed by Parliament for the purpose, the committees make their first reports to their respective Houses. If the reports are favourable, the next stage is for the minister formally to lay a draft order in each House, along with an explanation of any changes made compared to the earlier proposal. If the minister accepts any changes that are proposed to the draft order by the committees or others between this stage and the final vote on the order, he must formally withdraw the draft order he has laid and replace it with another which incorporates the changes. The ability to make changes (minor or otherwise) to the draft order is a key feature of the order-making power, which is not available to statutory instruments dealt with in the usual way.

The final procedural stages for Parliamentary scrutiny of draft regulatory reform orders are set out in Standing Orders. The Commons committee produces a report on the draft order within fifteen days. The Lords committee has no set time period but usually reports within the same time period. Each House then considers the relevant committee report on the draft order (this is the main feature that makes this form of Parliamentary consideration 'super-affirmative').

Comment on the legislative process

Given the domination of the Parliamentary timetable by the government machine, it is sometimes asked whether the amount of time spent debating proposals in relation to which the outcome is totally or largely predictable is worthwhile. Elected Members of Parliament do not, in general, have any detailed control over the content of Acts of Parliament; indeed, there is no guarantee that all provisions of bills are subject to considered debate. The vast bulk of legislation—secondary legislation—reaches the statute book with no consideration by Members of Parliament at all.

Nevertheless it should be remembered that much of the detail of the Parliamentary process was developed in an age where the party machine and the discipline over the Parliamentary party provided by the Whips was not as it is today. But the enormous power of the modern party machine in government to dominate the legislative process is perhaps the best reason for retaining the detailed process that currently exists. This arises from the very political theories, noted above, which underpin the British Constitution and its system of government. Although ministers may be able to achieve their desired goals in the end, the process ensures that they will have been subject to challenge by elected Members of Parliament. Without these procedures it would be far harder for ministers seeking to defend a particular measure to claim legitimacy for their legislative acts.

European law-making institutions

There has been much debate about the impact that the involvement of the United Kingdom 'in Europe' has had on British law and the English legal system. Two quite separate institutional frameworks are often muddled. They are:

- the Council of Europe; and
- the European Union.

The Council of Europe

The Council of Europe was established after the end of the Second World War. Its task was to prevent the human rights outrages of the Second World War period. More recently it has engaged in a process of assisting those countries of the former Eastern Bloc to create the institutional arrangements that will permit democratic principles to develop. Its most significant act in terms of its impact on English law was the creation in 1950 of the European Convention on Human Rights. This is a charter of fundamental rights and freedoms agreed by all the member states of the Council of Europe. As is common with all treaties, the Convention did not come into effect until it had been ratified by a number of governments. This happened in 1953. The Convention has been amended a number of times. The current version, amended by Protocol 11, came into effect in November 1998.

Normally treaties seek to regulate relationships between nation states. They may provide that one country may take action against another where there is an alleged breach of an international treaty obligation. The European Convention on Human Rights is quite distinct. In it, provision is made for *individuals* to take proceedings where it is alleged that a government is in breach of its obligations under the treaty. Individuals cannot start proceedings unless the government in question has permitted this to take place. In the case of the United Kingdom, the right of an individual to take proceedings against the British government for alleged breaches of the Convention was agreed in 1966.

The impact of the Council of Europe on the law-making process in the United Kingdom has been indirect. Where cases are taken before the European Court of Human Rights in Strasbourg which result in a decision that a rule of British law or some practice of the British government is contrary to the provisions of the Convention, this will lead to the British government changing the law to bring it into line with the Convention, as interpreted by the Court.[32] The Interception of Communications Act 1985, which regulates phone-tapping, was the result of an adverse decision by the Court of Human Rights.

With the terms of the European Convention being directly introduced into British

---

[32] There have been over thirty adverse decisions of the Court affecting the United Kingdom.

law following enactment of the Human Rights Act 1998, most of the Articles of the European Convention have become directly enforceable in the English courts. It is specifically stated in the Human Rights Act that, in interpreting its provisions, English judges must take account of the jurisprudence developed by the European Court of Human Rights in Strasbourg.

The Act has two principal effects on the law-making process in the United Kingdom. First, in presenting bills to Parliament, ministers must declare that in their opinion the proposed legislation complies with the Convention provisions. Secondly, as noted,[33] British courts now have power to declare a legislative provision incompatible with the provisions of the Convention. Although not declaring an Act of Parliament, or a provision in an Act, unlawful, this will bring overwhelming pressure on ministers to introduce changes so that the incompatibility is removed. In this important sense, the legislative freedom of ministers is reduced.

There is much debate about the impact that the Human Rights Act will have on British law. The British government introduced a number of measures to deal with law it thought was not Convention-compliant; the Regulation of Investigatory Powers Act 2000 was an example. Policy-makers within government are very conscious of the need to ensure that new policies will be Convention-compliant. To that extent the Act has had significant impact. However, although many practising lawyers have been advancing arguments about whether some aspect of British law does or does not offend against the principles of the European Convention, the extent to which these arguments have so far been upheld in the courts has been quite limited. Whether this restrained approach by the British judges will be sustained cannot be predicted. Thus what the long-term impact will be is harder to gauge. It should also be remembered that, despite the ability of the judges in the United Kingdom to apply the provisions of the Convention, they do not have the last word; applications to the European Court of Human Rights in Strasbourg will continue to be made.

The European Union

Although being a signatory to the European Convention on Human Rights has had an indirect impact on United Kingdom law-making, the accession of the United Kingdom to the European Economic Community in 1973 has had a direct impact on the English legal system. Ever since it became a member of the European Union, there has been an obligation on the United Kingdom to incorporate rules of law prescribed by the institutions of the European Union: the European Commission, the European Council of Ministers[34] and the European Parliament.

---

[33] Above p. 36.

[34] Although in the formal descriptions of the EU there is only one Council of Ministers, there is in fact a substantial number of Councils of Ministers reflecting the different portfolios of those ministers, for example, agriculture, foreign policy, economic matters, trade matters, and the like. The supreme Council of Ministers is that which comprises the leaders of the governments of the Union, brought together to determine the most fundamental issues affecting the EU.

The essential purpose of the European Union is to create a huge free market for the provision of goods and services throughout the area of the EU. In order to achieve this, European law seeks to provide a framework within which trade between the countries of the EU can fairly take place. Thus, for example, the EU provides a framework for the promotion of competition and the regulation of anti-competitive practices.[35] It aims to liberalize industries, such as telecommunications or the airline industries, to allow greater freedom of consumer choice. It seeks to prescribe EU-wide standards for the manufacture of goods, in order to protect consumers and to try to ensure that industry overheads are broadly in line. Examples include European standards on the manufacturing of cars or the quality of food labelling.

In addition to trade policy, the EU also seeks to promote human rights and tries to support measures for social cohesion. Thus certain common standards of social security provision for workers are set down, as well as entitlements for citizens of one country in the EU to work in other countries of the Union. There are specific rules relating to measures of employment protection, including safety at work and the prohibition of discriminatory employment practices, particularly those based on gender and race or ethnic origin.

The existence of law-making powers in the institutions of the EU means that in those areas covered by the EU Treaties British law-making institutions no longer have exclusive power. In the language of common political debate, the 'sovereignty of Parliament' has been diminished. This fact of modern political life causes much heated argument.

In recent years there has developed within the EU an emphasis on a different principle—that of 'subsidiarity'—designed to ensure that the European institutions exercise their law-making powers only in relation to those matters which are truly essential to the working of the aims and objectives of the Common Market. Other, subsidiary, matters are to be left to the national law-making bodies in each of the member states. It is beyond the scope of this work to assess the extent to which adoption of the principle of subsidiarity has in fact reduced the amount of law-making activity undertaken in the institutions of the EU. But the tension between law-making bodies within the United Kingdom and those outside should be noted at this stage.

The law-making processes of the EU are extremely complex. They are not at all like the Parliamentary processes familiar in the United Kingdom. Under the European Treaties, the European Commission has the exclusive right to initiate proposals for legislation. Whether or not those proposals become law, and if so in what terms, depends on the outcome of a complex process of negotiation and consensus-building between the Commission, the Council of Ministers and the European Parliament. The details of these procedures will change again once the Treaty of Nice (2001)—which provides for the expansion of the EU—becomes fully effective. The nature of the exercise is more like the legislative system in the USA, where the President proposes legislation and the Congress decides whether or not it passes into law.

---

[35] The content of the Competition Act 1998 was greatly influenced by the demands of EU law and policy.

A number of technical points need to be made about the different types of law that emerge from the EU institutions.

First, all the institutions of the EU draw their ultimate authority from the treaties that underpin the establishment of the EU.[36] These may be regarded as the *primary legislation* of the EU. While many of these fundamental provisions of Community law are designed to deal with obligations between states, some have been held by the European Court of Justice to have 'direct effect' in the determination of individual rights and duties. For treaty provisions to have this effect, the content of the provision must be clear; the provision must be self-executing, in the sense that it imposes a specific duty; and the provision must not contain any conditions of qualifications.[37] There are many European Court of Justice decisions which have held particular Treaty Articles to be of direct effect; for example Article 81,[38] which outlaws anti-competitive agreements, or Article 141, establishing the principle of equal pay between men and women.

Secondly, where a treaty provision is found to be of direct effect it may be both vertically and horizontally effective. 'Vertical' effectiveness arises when an individual uses a treaty provision to challenge an act of the government or some other public body; 'horizontal' effectiveness arises where one individual or other body wishes to use EU law to challenge the behaviour of another individual body of similar status.

Thirdly, more detailed legislative measures which seek to implement the detailed policies of the EU can collectively be described as the *secondary legislation* of the EU. This emerges in three different guises: regulations, directives and decisions.

Under Article 249 of the Treaty establishing the European Community, *regulations* are—like the treaty provisions considered above—of 'direct effect', that is to say they automatically become part of the internal law of each of the member states of the EU. An example is Regulation 1408/71, which deals with aspects of social security law and the need to insure workers under a scheme of national insurance. As with treaty provisions, regulations may have both vertical and horizontal effectiveness.

Directives are more general in tone. They set down standards towards which member states are required to aim, but some discretion as to the detail of how that is to be done is left to the member states. The recent debate about the implementation of the Working-Time Directive, which seeks to regulate the number of hours worked each week, provides a good example. The principle of direct effect may arise if there is a complaint that a government has failed so to incorporate the provision into national law. In the United Kingdom, directives are usually brought into effect in statutory instruments.

Decisions are rulings on particular matters addressed to either governments of member states, corporations or individuals. For example, an argument about whether a particular take-over bid was or was not anti-competitive could be the subject of a decision. Decisions are binding on those to whom they are addressed (Article 249).

---

[36] In particular, the Treaty of Rome, the Single European Act, the Treaty of Maastricht (the Treaty on European Union), the Treaty of Amsterdam and the Treaty of Nice.

[37] O'Neill A., and Coppel, J., *EC Law for UK Lawyers* (London, Butterworths, 1994).

[38] Following the adoption of the Treaty of Amsterdam in 1997, the Treaties have been officially consolidated and the Articles renumbered.

In addition to these forms of secondary legislation, the EU may also make *recommendations* and *opinions*, but these do not have any direct effect.

The courts

There are three principal ways in which the courts contribute to the development of English law:[39]

- *The development of common law*. England is a 'common law' country. This means that many of the principal doctrines of law were first established, not by Parliament, but through cases determined in the higher courts.

- *Statutory interpretation*. The courts play a crucial role in the interpretation of the statutes that Parliament has enacted.

- *Procedural law*. The courts also make important contributions to the development of procedures which the courts follow.

The development of common law

It may seem odd today, but the power of the judiciary to make law was, for many years, denied by it to exist. Judges were said merely to 'discover' the basic principles of the common law. No one seriously believes that now. It is recognized that judges do make law. There is however often unease about the theoretical basis for this power. Certainly it cannot derive from any theory of democracy or electoral representativeness. Rather, the power of the judiciary depends on the doctrine of the *separation of powers*, that to prevent dictatorial powers from being asserted there must be checks and balances in the Constitution. The independence of the judiciary is at the heart of this separation, for it is the judges who have the primary task of ensuring adherence by ministers and other agents of the state to the principles of the *rule of law*. No specific legislative provisions give the judiciary that power. Rather it is the assertion of this power by leading judges over the years, and the place that they occupy in the structure of the government, that has resulted in the development of this fundamental judicial function.

The law-making powers of the judiciary are themselves supported by two other fundamental principles: the hierarchical structure of the courts and the doctrine of precedent.

The hierarchical structure

The idea of courts being arranged within a hierarchical framework is quite straightforward. The courts are organized on the basis of seniority (*see Diagram 3.1*); the

---

[39] It should be stressed that not all courts have the authority to make law; only the higher courts—the House of Lords, the Court of Appeal and the High Court—have it. For further discussion of the courts see Chapter 9.

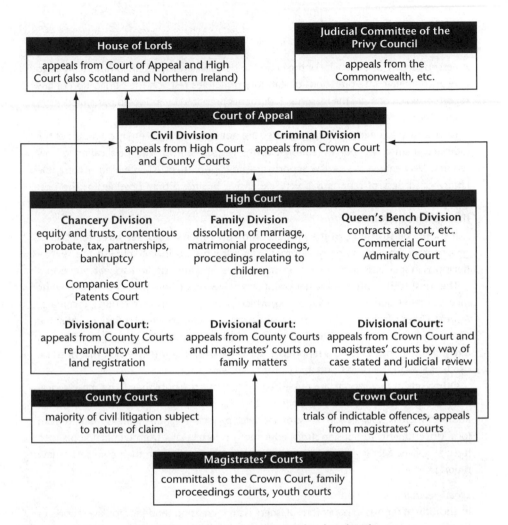

Diagram 3.1 An outline of the court structure in England and Wales

higher the level of seniority, the greater the authority of the court. Thus the decisions of the House of Lords[40] are the most authoritative; those of the Court of Appeal are next; those of the High Court third. Decisions of courts at lower levels are not regarded as precedents, though very occasionally the judgment of a county court judge on a novel point of law may get reported. (On the importance of law reporting *see Box 3.7*.)

---

[40] Although the name is the same, the House of Lords sitting as a court is quite distinct from the House of Lords acting in its legislative capacity. The judges in the House of Lords can take part in debates in the House of Lords, but they sit on the cross benches—outside the control of any political party—and by convention usually only intervene in debates on law reform or the administration of justice.

Box 3.7 Law reporting

An essential part of the ability of the courts to develop principles of common law or to give authoritative interpretations of statutory principles rests on the publication of law reports—which contain the reasoned judgments prepared by judges in particular cases, from which general principles may then be drawn.

Decisions as to which cases get reported are not, in general, taken by members of the judiciary themselves, but by editorial teams responsible for the publication of law reports. Very many sets of law reports are now published. Maintaining a complete library of all sets of reports is a very expensive business, only possible for the best endowed university libraries, the libraries of the Law Society and the Inns of Court, and the most prosperous law firms.

It should be stressed that the production of law reports is not seen as a function of government (though some government departments do in fact publish the text of decisions in specialist areas, such as taxation cases, and immigration appeal reports).

The most authoritative of the generalist sets of law reports are those published by the Incorporated Council of Law Reporting, which publishes a range of reports, including: Appeal Cases (decisions of the House of Lords), the Queen's Bench Reports, and the Chancery Division Reports. The Council also publishes the Weekly Law reports. There is a requirement that if a case is reported in these reports, that is the version that must be used, at least in the High Court and Court of Appeal.

Other sets of law reports are published by commercial publishers. The most widely available generalist set is the *All England Law Reports*, published by Butterworths. In addition there is now a wide range of specialist reports available in areas ranging from local government, to housing, from education to family law, from criminal appeals to judicial review. Many sub-specialisms in legal practice now have their own sets of law reports.

Legal electronic databases

In addition to reports in paper format, there is an increasing tendency for law reports to be published in electronic format. For many years a vast electronic database, *Lexis*, has been available, providing full-text versions of decisions from a range of the most senior courts. The use of these reported cases as precedents has, however, been limited by the refusal of the judiciary to take into account judgments that appear only in the Lexis format. If they have not been reported elsewhere, in printed form, they have not been usable.

The internet

A more recent development has been the appearance of a range of decisions on the internet. The House of Lords has all judgments since 14 November 1996 on line; the Court Service website carries reports selected by the judges from the Court of Appeal and Administrative Court. There are other on-line sources available too (see the list of websites at the end of this chapter). For those who have access to the internet, the costs of obtaining the report of a particular case are limited to the costs of going on line and printing the text. The provision of the reports themselves is at present free. In order to facilitate the use of these sources, a system of 'neutral citation' of judgments has been introduced. (*See Box 3.9.*)

There have been occasions on which this hierarchical structure has been challenged, most notably by the late Lord Denning when, as Master of the Rolls, he was the senior judge in the Court of Appeal. He argued that, since most appeals ended in his court and did not proceed to the House of Lords, his court should have similar law-making power to that of the House of Lords. His arguments did not prevail, though they do provoke a broader question: do we need all the levels of court, in particular all the levels of appeal, that currently exist?

The doctrine of precedent

This is also a simple idea, though not always easy to apply in practice. The essence of precedent is that a principle of law, established in one case, must be applied in a similar situation in a later case. Indeed, such a rule of law will continue to be applied either until another court decides that, for some reason, the case was incorrectly decided, or for some other reason cannot be allowed to stand, or until a court higher in the hierarchy overturns the decision; or until Parliament decides to change the law by passing a new Act of Parliament which has the effect of overruling or altering the rule that has been laid down by the court.

There have long been arguments for and against the use of precedent. Against, it is argued that precedent introduces unnecessary rigidity into the law, thereby preventing legal doctrine from developing as society develops. In its favour, the use of precedent is said to bring certainty to the law by enabling people to know how issues in the future will be resolved. The principle of law in one case which forms the precedent is known by the Latin phrase, the *ratio decidendi*. Any part of a judgment that does not form part of the *ratio* is not part of the precedent, and thus not relevant in later cases. These are referred to as *obiter dicta*.

There are many reasons this apparently straightforward principle can be exceptionally hard to apply in practice.

(1) The facts on which the ratio of one case is based never replicate themselves exactly in a later case. Thus lawyers wishing to argue that a particular precedent does not apply to the later case will seek to *distinguish* the two fact situations, thereby, they hope, rendering the earlier decision irrelevant.

(2) Given the large number of reported decisions, there may be situations where a decision reached in one case was reached in ignorance of other relevant decisions. The argument will thus be made that the precedent in question was made incorrectly or, again to use the Latin, *per incuriam*.

(3) Again resulting from the very large number of cases that are now reported, there may simply be two inconsistent decisions in the law reports, so that a straightforward application of a particular decision to a new situation is just not possible.

(4) Since 1966, the House of Lords has taken to itself the authority, in very exceptional circumstances, to change its mind and alter a precedent. It may therefore, on occasion and notwithstanding the existence of clear precedents,

decide that earlier cases were wrongly decided and that the law should now be changed.

There are also more technical reasons why the doctrine of precedent is not always simple to apply in practice. It can be very hard to decide what the precedent is. When the House of Lords found[41] that a manufacturer of ginger beer was negligent after it allowed a decomposed snail to enter the ginger-beer bottle, was this a case about not allowing snails into ginger beer bottles? Or about not allowing foreign bodies in general into manufacturing processes? Or was it about the care which any person—including a professional person giving advice to a client—should demonstrate in preparing that advice? In short, what was the 'level of generality' at which the particular instance of snails in ginger-beer bottles was to be treated in future cases?

Even if the principle of law which can be derived from the cases is clear—such as the principle of negligence, that one person owes a 'duty of care' to his 'neighbour'—who will be categorized for these purposes as a neighbour? And what will be the standard of behaviour that will result in a conclusion that the 'duty of care' has been broken? If teachers take a party of teenage pupils to the seaside, and one of the pupils is washed out to sea by a freak wave, were the teachers in breach of a duty of care in those circumstances to the pupil who drowned? Or did that fault lie with the pupil who ignored advice and went clambering onto the rocks from which he was swept?

Much of the litigation that arises out of the principles of the law of negligence is not seeking to redefine the principles of the law, but rather exploring the extent to which those principles will be applied in new situations of risk. This is not the place for a detailed analysis of the law of negligence. The point to be stressed here is that, even though at one level the law may be quite clear, the situations to which the law may be applied in future can be far from clear.

Statutory interpretation

Statutory interpretation is another way in which the courts that have authority within their hierarchical structure are able to develop the law. The work of the courts when interpreting statutes may not be as dramatic as when they develop principles of common law, as they clearly have to work within a framework that has been prescribed by Parliament through the legislative process. Nevertheless the interpretative process can lead to the clarification of words in statutes, and thus in the implementation of those statutory rules. (For a particular example *see Box 3.8.*)

The development of the power of the court to interpret statutes has increased now the Human Rights Act 1998 has been brought into force. This has given power to the British courts, not just to interpret legislative provisions, but also to test the substance of legislative provisions against the standards laid down in the Human Rights Act, which derive from the Articles of the European Convention on Human Rights. In cases where the courts find that they must declare a statute or provision within a

---

[41] In *Donoghue v. Stevenson* [1942] AC 562.

Box 3.8 Statutory interpretation: the case of Mr Fitzpatrick[42]

There is a right, in housing law, for a tenant to pass on his right to occupy premises on death to a 'member of his family'. The question has arisen in a number of cases over the last fifty years: who is a member of the family? Initially, in the 1940s, it was held that the phrase was limited to blood relatives only; thus the former mistress of a deceased tenant could not take over the tenancy, despite having lived together with her partner for many years. Later, in the 1960s, it was held that, with changes in the nature of relationships and society's attitudes, the mistress of a deceased male tenant could in such a circumstance be regarded as a member of the family and thus take over the tenancy.

Most recently, in 1999, the House of Lords decided that the long-standing homosexual partner of a deceased tenant could similarly take over the tenancy. The judges found that, in terms of love and affection and thus the attributes of family, a distinction could no longer sensibly be drawn between a couple of the same sex living together and a couple of different sexes. Reference was made to the provisions of the European Convention on Human Rights protecting family and family life.

This case illustrates that, even within a single statutory framework, there can be scope for the development of the law to reflect changes in social practices and attitudes.

statute to be incompatible with the Convention—thus in effect requiring ministers to change the law—the courts will have acquired a significant new power to develop English law.

One question that may be asked is: why—if Parliament has passed legislation—should there be any need for the courts to intervene at all? There are two basic reasons why this needs to happen: the unpredictability of fact situations and the ambiguity of language.

The unpredictability of fact situations

However detailed the provisions of statutes or statutory instruments may be, they can only set down rules at a certain level of generality. There will always be those whose particular situation is not captured *precisely* by the legislative provisions. In such cases the facts will need to be determined by the courts—in itself not always a straightforward task—and once this has been done, a judgment reached as to whether or not the relevant legislative provision covers that situation. Particularly where legislative provisions seek to impose some burden or penalty on the citizen, there is a general judicial policy that this should not happen unless those provisions quite clearly 'bite' on the individual circumstances concerned. To give an example: the 'tax avoidance industry' is dedicated to the careful and detailed analysis of the provisions of tax legislation to see whether there are arrangements which can be reached whereby those

---

[42] *Fitzpatrick v. Sterling Housing Association* [1999] 3 WLR 1113.

who might otherwise have to pay tax may—quite legitimately—be able to avoid paying it.[43]

Many of the apparently pedantic points that are taken in some criminal trials are, similarly, the result of the principle that a person should not be able to be convicted of a crime unless the factual situation that has been established in the court is quite clearly caught by the relevant statutory provisions.

The ambiguity of language

The other justification for the role of the courts is that the meaning of language is not itself precise. There may be ambiguities arising from the way particular rules have been drafted. There may be differences in the meaning of words chosen. Some statutory provisions are deliberately drafted using words such as 'reasonable' or 'fair' which do not have a precise meaning and which therefore give scope to officials and others for the exercise of discretion or judgement. There may be changes in the meaning of a word—(*see Box 3.8*)—resulting from broader developments in society.

There is, in the literature on statutory interpretation, a set of principles—rather inaccurately described as 'rules'—designed to be of assistance. These include:

- the literal rule;
- the golden rule;
- the mischief rule; and
- the 'unified common approach'.

The *literal rule* is what it implies. The words of a statute should be given their literal meaning. This does not avoid the problem of linguistic ambiguity.

The *golden rule* suggests that the courts should use the literal rule unless this would lead to manifest absurdity.

The *mischief rule* asks the judge to consider what was the legislative purpose of the Act—what was the 'mischief' the Act was trying to deal with. Any question of interpretation should be resolved in such a way as not to thwart that purpose. The problem with this view is: how does it relate to the concept of the independence of the judiciary? If the mischief rule is rigidly adhered to, does this not result in the judges losing their independence and doing the government's job for it? On the other hand, if the legislative intention is wilfully ignored by the judge, how does that square with the constitutional principle that the primary law-making authority should rest with the democratically elected Parliament, not the unelected judiciary?

It will be quickly appreciated that these principles are not consistent with each other; they offer great scope for reaching different conclusions. The reality is that

---

[43] The distinction between tax avoidance, which if successful is lawful, and tax evasion, which is clearly unlawful, should be noted. In recent years, governments have become increasingly adept in their attempts to thwart the tax avoiders. Tax incentives—schemes which attract tax advantages and are part of the government's fiscal policy, e.g. tax relief on pension premiums—are quite different.

Box 3.9 Neutral citation of judgments

Since 11 January 2001 every judgment of the Court of Appeal and of the Administrative Court, and since 14 January 2002 every judgment of the High Court, has been prepared and issued as approved with single spacing, paragraph numbering (in the margins) and no page numbers. In courts with more than one judge the paragraph numbering continues sequentially through each judgment and does not start again at the beginning of each judgment. A unique reference number is given to each judgment.

Each Court of Appeal judgment starts with the year, followed by EW (for England and Wales), then CA (for Court of Appeal), followed by Civ (for Civil) or Crim (for Criminal) and finally the sequential number. For example *Smith v. Jones* [2001] EWCA Civ 10.

In the High Court, abbreviated as HC, the number comes before the divisional abbreviation and, unlike Court of Appeal judgments, the latter is bracketed: Ch(ancery)), (Pat(ent)), (Q(ueen's) B(ench)), (Admin(istrative)), (Comm(ercial)), (Admlty (Admiralty)), (TCC (Technology and Construction Court)) or (Fam(ily)) as appropriate. For example, [2002] EWHC 123 (Fam) or [2002] EWHC 124 (QB) or [2002] EWHC 125 (Ch).

Paragraph numbers are referred to in square brackets. Thus paragraph 59 in *Green v. White* [2002] EWHC 124 (QB) would be cited: *Green v. White* [2002] EWHC 124 at [59]; paragraphs 30–35 in *Smith v. Jones* would be *Smith v. Jones* [2001] EWCA Civ 10 at [30]–[35]. Page numbers are not given.

This 'neutral citation' is the official number attributed to the judgment and must always be used at least once when the judgment is cited in a later judgment. It is designed to facilitate the use of websites so that the confusion that is caused by differences in pagination that occur when information is down-loaded to different computers with different printers is avoided.

different judges favour different approaches; indeed individual judges are themselves not consistent.

The *unified common approach* is a label that seeks to provide a broader, less specific label to the process. It implies that judges should start by considering the literal meaning of the words; but if they are really not clear or would lead to absurd results then the judge should consider what the purpose of the Act was and interpret the Act so as to advance that purpose.

The inference should not be drawn from this discussion that the bases on which the judiciary interprets legislation are so varied that there is no principle at all. Reading the reported judgments in decided cases reveals that those judges in the higher courts whose decisions get reported go to great lengths to try to ensure that their decisions are founded in rationality and principle. But that there are different approaches cannot be denied, and the inevitable consequence is that different judges may, as a result, reach different decisions in individual cases.

Procedural law

A third way in which the judges may be said to make law is by the development of new procedures. A number of examples may be briefly mentioned:

* The day-to-day practice of litigation is regulated by rules of procedure which are drafted by the judiciary—Rules Committees—acting under legislative authority. Many rules of court are supplemented by Practice Directions, also made by the judiciary. (See Chapter 8.)

* The rules of evidence—what evidence is or is not admissible in a court of law— has to an important degree been developed by the judiciary, though supplemented by very important statutory provisions, for example the Police and Criminal Evidence Act 1984 or the Civil Evidence Act 1991. (See Chapter 5.)

* A number of powers of the court are asserted on the basis of what it claims as its 'inherent jurisdiction'—the High Court's powers of wardship over children may be given as an example. (See Chapter 7.)

* Perhaps the most important judicial development of the last generation has been the shaping of the rules and practice relating to judicial review, which goes to the heart of the powers of the judiciary to render government departments and other public bodies legally accountable for their actions. (See Chapter 6.)

The European Courts

The European Union has, as one of its constituent bodies, the European Court of Justice, which sits in Luxembourg. The Council of Europe has the European Court of Human Rights, which sits in Strasbourg. Both courts have played a significant role in the development of the jurisprudence of, respectively, the European Union and the European Convention on Human Rights.

It is hard to summarize the 'European' approach of the judges in these courts, though it is the case that the legal instruments of both the European Union and the Council of Europe, with which the European Courts have to deal, are drafted more in the relatively broad-brush European continental tradition than in the more linguistically precise tradition familiar in the United Kingdom. As a consequence the approach of judges in the European Courts has been to decide cases very much bearing the purposes of the relevant Treaty provisions in mind. British legal minds often regard this as a rather distinct approach. Perhaps more accurately it may be said to represent something of a hybrid between the common law and statutory interpretation. Decisions of the European Courts lead to the development of legal principle on a case-by-case basis, not dissimilar to the common law tradition. At the same time, these developments are set within a framework of treaties and other instruments which have emanated from the institutions of the European Union and the Council of Europe and which require interpretation by the courts.

Other sources of law-making

At the end of this lengthy account, the existence of other sources of law-making will be mentioned only briefly.

Local and regional government

Local Government has long had power to make by-laws—in effect a form of tertiary legislation (*see above Box 3.2*)—since by-laws are made under the authority of Acts of Parliament but apply only in the area of the local authority in question. Present discussion about regionalization and the creation in England of bodies of regional government may eventually lead to additional forms of regional legislation.

Under the terms of the Scotland Act 1998 the Scottish Parliament now has the authority to pass legislation in areas within its competence. This is a privilege currently denied to Wales under the Wales Act 1998, though the National Assembly for Wales has power to pass secondary legislation, again within the scope of its areas of competence. There are also independent legislative powers available in Northern Ireland, though they are not available when, as a result of difficulties in the peace process, the institutions of government in Northern Ireland are in suspension.

Other rule-making agencies

A great deal of rule-making is also undertaken by those whose task it is to regulate industries of various kinds: for example the Civil Aviation Authority or the regulators of the privatized utilities.[44] Major new rule-making powers have been conferred on the new Financial Services Authority.[45] The legislative instruments made by these bodies fall outside the conventional institutional framework of Parliament though in most cases are based in legislative authority that has been conferred by Act of Parliament. Following the process of privatization and other initiatives to transfer governmental activity to governmental agencies, this has become an increasingly common practice.

Other international institutions and bodies of international law

We have considered the Council of Europe and the EU in context above. Many other international institutions also have an impact on detailed rules of English law. There are many industries, for example aviation or telecommunications, where at least some of the legislative framework results from the provisions of international treaties. Increasing globalization of economic activity combined with increasing pressure to deal with some of the major issues of the day—the environment, genetic engineering, global warming, international trade—is likely to result in this trend developing.

---

[44] Robert Baldwin, R., *Rules and Government* (Oxford, Oxford University Press, 1995).
[45] Financial Services and Markets Act 2000.

It is also relevant to note the existence of a separate body of Private International Law—in essence rules of English law, designed to assist in the determination of private law rights and entitlements which have an international dimension.

Conclusion

Law-making is a key aspect of modern government. It is theoretically based in democratic principle, though by no means all the sources of law can be said to derive their authority from those principles. Law-making and other normative statements also occur in a variety of formats. This all makes for considerable complexity that has increased enormously in recent years. It is unlikely that the ordinary person in the street is aware of more than a fraction of the legal regulation which in theory might affect her. It is fanciful to claim that ordinary people can be assumed to know the law. One of the challenges that faces the modern world is to explore ways in which new technologies may be used to transform the vast mass of legal information into legal knowledge that can actually be utilized by the ordinary citizen.

Questions for discussion

1. What are the arguments for and against making voting compulsory?

2. Would proportional representation result in fairer electoral outcomes?

3. How should the House of Lords be reformed? Should it become a fully elected body?

4. Should more or less time be spent debating legislative proposals in Parliament?

5. How significant a restrain on law-making powers is the European Convention on Human Rights and Fundamental Freedoms?

6. Is there a 'democratic deficit' in the institutions of the EU? If so, how should it be overcome?

7. Should a Supreme Court replace the House of Lords' judicial function?

Further reading

BIRCH, A.H., *Representative and Responsible Government: an Essay on the British Constitution* (Ann Arbor, Mich., UMI, 1989)

BRAZIER, R., *Constitutional Practice: the Foundations of British Government* (3rd edn., Oxford, Oxford University Press, 1999)

—— Ministers of the Crown (Oxford, Clarendon, 1997)

Cosgrove, R.A., The Rule of Law. Albert Venn Dicey, Victorian Jurist (Chapel Hill, NC, University of North Carolina Press, c1980)

Fine, B., Democracy and the Rule of Law: Liberal Ideals and Marxist Critiques (London, Pluto Press, 1984)

Griffith, J.A.G., Parliamentary Scrutiny of Government Bills (London, Allen and Unwin, 1974)

Harden, I., and Lewis, N., The Noble Lie: the British Constitution and the Rule of Law (London, Hutchinson, 1986)

Hartley, T.C., Constitutional Problems of the European Union (Oxford, Hart, 1999)

—— The Foundations of European Community Law: an Introduction to the Constitutional and Administrative Law of the European Community (4th edn., Oxford, Oxford University Press, 1998)

Marshall, G. (ed.), Ministerial Responsibility (Oxford, Oxford University Press, 1989)

Public Service Committee, Ministerial Accountability and Responsibility: Second Report (H.C.313) (London, HMSO, 1996)

Twining, W., and Miers, D., How to do Things with Rules: a Primer of Interpretation (4th edn., London, Butterworths, 1999)

Vile, M.J.C., Constitutionalism and the Separation of Powers (2nd edn., Indianapolis, Ind., Liberty Fund, c1998)

Zander, M., The Law-making Process (5th edn., London, Butterworths, 1999)

Websites

www.lcd.gov.uk/elections/index.htm (Lord Chancellor's Department elections website)

www.electoralcommission.gov.uk/

www.electoral-reform.org.uk/ (Electoral Reform Society)

www.electoral-reform.org.uk/links/systems.htm (Site providing links to accounts of different voting systems)

www.hansard-society.org.uk/ (Hansard Society—promoting effective democracy)

www.charter88.org.uk/ (Charter 88, campaigning organization for increased democracy)

www.prcommission.org/ (Independent Commission on Proportional Representation)

www.parliament.uk/ (Home page of the UK Parliament)

www.parliament.uk/bills/bills.cfm (Site for bills presented to Parliament)

www.hmso.gov.uk/acts.htm (Acts of Parliament)

www.parliamentary-counsel.gov.uk/ (Parliamentary counsel—statute draftsmen)

www.the-stationery-office.co.uk/ (Government publishers' site)

www.royal.gov.uk/output/Page6.asp (The monarchy today)

www.number-10.gov.uk/output/Page1.asp (Office of the prime minister)

www.ssac.org.uk/ (Social security advisory committee)

www.council-on-tribunals.gov.uk/

www.parliament.the-stationery-office.co.uk/pa/ld/ldjudinf.htm *(House of Lords judgments)*

www.courtservice.gov.uk/judgments/judg_home.htm *(Court of Appeal and other judgments)*

www.wordwave.co.uk/ *(Law reporting site)*

www.bailii.org/ *(British and Irish legal information)*

http://library.ukc.ac.uk/library/lawlinks/default.htm *(Lawlinks—portal to huge range of legal sites)*

www.coe.int/portalT.asp *(Council of Europe portal)*

http://europa.eu.int/eur-lex/en/index.html *(European Commission)*

http://europa.eu.int/cj/en/index.htm *(European Court of Justice)*

www.echr.coe.int/ *(European Court of Human Rights)*

www.bihr.org *(British Institute of Human Rights)*

www.liberty-human-rights.org.uk

www.humanrights.gov.uk *(Lord Chancellor's Department human rights unit)*

www.scottish.parliament.uk/ *(Scottish Parliament)*

www.wales.gov.uk/index.htm *(National Assembly for Wales)*

www.ni-assembly.gov.uk/index.htm *(Northern Ireland Assembly)*

PART II

THE INSTITUTIONAL FRAMEWORK

This Part consists of five chapters. The first (Chapter 4) looks at the contributions made by government departments to the shaping of the English legal system. Primary attention is paid to the Lord Chancellor's Department, but the role of other departments, especially the Home Office, is also considered. The remaining chapters discuss each of the branches of the justice system. The twofold distinction made in most English legal system books between the criminal and civil justice systems is replaced by a more functional classification: criminal justice, administrative justice, family justice, and civil and commercial justice. In each of these chapters a 'holistic' approach is adopted. The focus is not just on what goes on in courts (or other formal adjudicatory bodies), but embraces all those aspects of the justice process which occur outside these formal settings as well as within them.

4

Shaping the institutional framework: The role of Government

Introduction

One way in which the English legal system has changed over the years has been the increasing desire of government to shape and reform the legal system. Central government provides funds not only for running the court services and publicly funded legal services, including paying the salaries and fees of the judiciary, but also for a huge array of other services which are part of or impact upon the legal system. The police, prison and probation services and administrative tribunals are obvious examples. All governments are concerned with keeping levels of public expenditure under control and securing value for money. Inevitably, the involvement of government in the planning of the legal system and the delivery of legal services has grown. Any understanding of the forces of change within the legal system must include analysis of the part played by government. The principal actors considered here are:

- The Lord Chancellor's Department;
- The Home Office;
- The Legal Services Commission;
- Other central government departments.

Lurking behind all of them is the Treasury.

The Lord Chancellor's Department

The Lord Chancellor's Department (LCD) plays the central role in the development of policy relating to the legal system. Uniquely, the chief minister—the Lord Chancellor—is a member not of the House of Commons but of the House of Lords. (This leads to the criticism that his performance is less open to scrutiny by the elected

Members of Parliament sitting in the House of Commons. It has been suggested on many occasions that the LCD should become a Ministry of Justice, led by a Secretary of State based in the Commons.) The LCD is a department that has grown markedly in both size and importance in government. The days (in the 1920s) when its Permanent Secretary—the head civil servant—was able to record that not one item of post had been delivered to the Department are now long gone.

For many years the Department was in some ways seen as a bit 'odd' in the overall government structure. In most government departments, lawyers are used as legal specialists advising on questions of law, drafting bills and regulations and the like, rather than being closely involved in the development of policy. In the LCD the Permanent Secretary—the head civil servant—was required by law to be qualified as a practising lawyer. As a consequence he used to be perceived as slightly different from his counterparts in other departments. In 1997, this rule was abolished. The current appointment, Sir Hayden Phillips, is the first non-lawyer Permanent Secretary.

Principal responsibilities

The principal responsibilities of the LCD fall into two broad categories. First it is responsible for the development of a number of areas of law and social policy that do not obviously fall within the remit of any other government department. In recent years, this portfolio has been increasing. The LCD has long been the lead department in the development of the law relating to the family and property law. More recently, it has taken over responsibility for the development of election and referendum law and human rights. It is responsible for freedom of information, data protection, data sharing and defamation. It also had lead responsibility for a number of constitutional issues, in particular, currently, reform of the House of Lords. Since this book is not dealing with substantive rules of law we shall not consider these functions in detail. But it is worth noting that the LCD has shifted its focus. While the delivery of a service—the justice system—remains its principal function, it now has a much more rounded programme of work.

Secondly, and centrally important to this book, the LCD is responsible for shaping the institutional framework within which the law is practised. It develops policy on:

- procedures in the courts, in the criminal, civil and family justice systems;
- the work and development of tribunals and the administrative justice system;
- the appointment and training of the judiciary, including lay magistrates and other judicial office-holders (such as chairs of tribunals);
- legal aid and the delivery of legal services.

There are hardly any aspects of the justice system that have remained unchanged in recent years. Developments in the civil justice system, following Lord Woolf's report on *Access to Justice*, started in 1999 and are currently the subject of further developments foreshadowed in the White Paper, *Modernising Justice*.[1] Major reform of the criminal justice system is pending, following publication of the Auld committee report[2] and the Government's White Paper on reform of the criminal justice system.[3] Significant reform of the administrative justice system is also in prospect, following publication of the Leggatt review of tribunals.[4] Each of these will be considered more fully in the following chapters.

Reflecting modern trends in government, much of the detailed implementation of these policies is now in the hands of specialist agencies, such as the Court Service, the Legal Services Commission and the Judicial Studies Board (see below). But it is the LCD that shapes the policy.

In short, government injects into the English legal system a dynamism that is often not fully appreciated—both in the sense of its not being understood by those outside the system, and its not being welcomed by those inside. The fact is, however, that many of the images of and pre-conceptions about law and the legal system mentioned in Chapter 1 have been swept away or radically altered by new policy initiatives emanating from the LCD.

The Court Service

One of the most important ways in which the LCD has changed in recent years has been through the creation in 1995 of the Court Service—a governmental agency charged with responsibility for the efficient running of the courts. This development was part of an overall government strategy designed to give greater freedom to those who were running services to do so in a business-like fashion, leaving officials in the departments with responsibility for the evaluation of existing policy and the development of new policy. Its primary task—according to its official literature—is to provide appropriate administrative support to the judiciary. The Court Service is also responsible for promoting and delivering significant policy changes, such as the reforms to the civil justice system considered in more detail in Chapter 8.

In common with other areas of government, the Court Service is now committed to the delivery of defined standards of service to those who come through the doors of the courts—whether as claimants, those defending claims, those appearing as witnesses, jurors, other friends and relatives or general members of the public—standards unheard of only a few years ago. Many of the key tasks required of the Court Service are those of administrative efficiency: dealing with people courteously; dealing with issues expeditiously but fairly; handling matters as economically as

[1] *Modernising Justice: The Government's Plan for Reforming Legal Services and the Courts* (Cm 4155) (London, The Lord Chancellor's Department, December 1998).

[2] *A Review of the Criminal Courts of England and Wales* (London, Stationery Office, 2001); the Halliday Review of Sentencing, *Making Punishments Work: Report of a Review of the Sentencing Framework for England and Wales* (London, Home Office, 2001) is also relevant.

[3] *Justice for All* (Cm 5563) (London, Stationery Office, 2002).

[4] *Tribunals for Users* (London, Stationery Office, 2001).

possible and seeking to reduce costs; and—in the civil courts—recovering from parties to proceedings the costs associated with the provision of court services.[5]

The Court Service is also engaged in a major programme of administrative reform, including investment in computerization and new information technologies.[6] This is not complete and will take some time yet. But the implications, not only for the more efficient running of the existing system, but also for introducing fundamental change into the operation of the system are enormous. Computerization should help with very practical issues such as the listing of cases for hearing, and, more broadly, tracking the progress of cases through the system to ensure that they are not subject to unnecessary delay.

Increasingly sophisticated telecommunications and information technologies should also allow for routine proceedings taking place without the need for personal attendance at court. Professional lawyers could thereby be relieved from the need to waste time attending court on purely procedural matters, parties to proceedings could similarly be allowed to 'attend' court from a distance. The Court Service recently launched its XHIBIT service, a website that provide up-to-date information about the progress of criminal cases listed in three courts in Essex. In addition, it has started a pilot 'Money Claim Online' service that enables persons to bring an action for debt using the internet.

No doubt the presence of parties will still be required during trails; but a great deal of routine procedural work does not require attendance, indeed where to do so wastes resources. Similarly experiments are currently underway to enable more evidence to be presented through video links, thus making it easier for witnesses, who may be unable or reluctant to attend a particular court, to appear.

New forms of electronic data collection also have great potential for reducing the amounts of paper that physically have to be brought to court for major trials. Use of legal databases will also considerably improve the library facilities available in courts to the judiciary—outside the principal courts these are often woefully inadequate.

As a result of these and other developments, the Court Service is also taking a strategic look at the location of its court buildings and their configuration. New modes of court working will entail new forms of court design, in particular to take advantage of the opportunities created by the increased used of technology. (*See Box 4.1.*)

Magistrates' Courts and the Magistrates' Courts Service Inspectorate

The relationship between policy development and policy implementation in the magistrates' courts is more complex. The LCD provides the policy framework.[7] Implementation of the Magistrates' Courts Service currently takes place at the level of

---

[5] Many of these service standards are set out in the Court Service's Charter: see www.courtservice.gov.uk/fandl/menu_chart.htm.

[6] The Modernisation of Courts and Tribunals Programme. The details can be found at www.courtservice.gov.uk/info/reps/mcc_report.pdf.

[7] The law on magistrates was consolidated into the Justices of the Peace Act 1997.

Box 4.1 A model for civil and family justice: the LCD vision

Users of the civil and family courts are confronted with courts that are only open from 10 am to 4 or 4.30 pm, when they may need access to services before the start of the working day or at its end. Transactions are conducted wholly in writing, which excludes many people, slows proceedings down and ignores the potential of other service channels such as the internet. Fees must be paid by cheque or in cash, and other modern payment methods are refused. Court buildings are located where they are largely on the basis of historical accident, and take decades to reflect changing demographics such as the development of new towns. Judges are dependent upon paper files that are easily mislaid, while solicitors and barristers have the use of computerized case-management systems and electronic files. Technology in the courtroom is currently very limited.

Where do we want to be? A new model
We have developed an alternative model which will increase access, reduce social exclusion, enhance judges' case-management role, and improve the use of technology in the courtroom. The main features are:

- *Primary hearing centres*

They will be the principal venues for civil and family hearings. They will be based mainly in existing county and combined court centres in towns and cities across England and Wales. They will deal with most types of hearings, and provide a full range of counter services. They will have high quality facilities and support the use of in-court technology such as video-conferencing, electronic presentation of evidence and digital audio recording. Primary hearing centres will be the centre of local listing management, and the base for casework of family and specialist jurisdiction cases.

- *Local hearing venues*

Some cases will be heard in local hearing venues. These venues will improve access to hearings through the use of existing county courts, partnerships with magistrates courts or hired facilities. A counter service will be provided from local hearing venues on sitting days. Local hearing venues will not be courts in the traditional sense, in that they will not be the base for administration, which will be completed in business centres. Some local hearing venues will sit every day and will have judiciary and staff on site supporting the hearings. Other venues will be for occasional hearings, in some cases only once or twice a month, and in these instances judges and staff will travel to the venue from the nearest primary hearing centre.

- *Technology*

We will introduce electronic files, records and diaries. The electronic file will replace the paper file and existing IT systems. It will include copies of all of the documents filed in each case, details of the steps taken and copies of orders and other court-produced documents. The electronic file will be available from all locations regardless of where the case is being heard or administered. The case-management system supporting the electronic file will automate many of the processes that currently required staff intervention. The electronic diary will be a computerized record of all hearings and available appointments. Information about court hearings will be available on the internet.

• *Business centres*

Business centres will be where the majority of administrative work is carried out. Much of this work will be automated. Business centres will provide back-office support to hearing centres, and will administer all aspects of undefended civil cases. Each business centre will be the focus for all customer contact, whether by letter, telephone or e-mail. The electronic file and diary will link the business centre to the court and the judge.

• *Electronic service delivery*

The internet, telephone, digital TV and video-conferencing will provide access to a range of information and services. Not all services can be provided by the internet, such as those requiring the production of original documents or evidence. In other circumstances internet services may not be appropriate because of the sensitivity of the proceedings, such as in some family cases. We will however use the internet to provide easily accessible information about family services, and links to various support agencies such as those in Community Legal Services partnerships.

• *Customer service*

We will provide new ways in which customers may obtain services, advice and information. We will establish channels suited for particular customer groups. Some services will be available by telephone. Customers will also be able to complete straightforward transactions via the internet from their home or business computer or digital TV. We will enable practitioners to file documents electronically from their offices. We will work with advice agencies and practitioners to provide mediated access to more complex or sensitive services where legal or procedural advice is most appropriate.

• *Field-based enforcement*

We will create a new structure for the county court bailiff service focused solely on enforcement. The enforcement service will be a field-based organization supported by regional support offices, and by technology that provides the bailiff with the electronic warrant and levy slips.

• *Payments*

We will develop services to remove the processing of payments from the courts to bank and building societies. We will also provide alternative payment methods for regular customers and credit and debit card transactions for other users.

Source: LCD September 2002

the local magistrates' court and is the responsibility of Magistrates' Courts Committees (MCCs). And magistrates' courts are at present paid for by local government, which is then reimbursed by a grant from the Lord Chancellor's Department. Here, as with the rest of the court system, there has been a great deal of rapid change. (For the different types of magistrates' courts, *see Box 5.9.*)

First, magistrates' courts boundaries have been realigned so that they match those of the Crown Prosecution Service and the police. As a result, the number of MCCs has been significantly reduced (from 105 to forty-two), so that these committees become responsible for the management of magistrates' courts on the basis of larger geographical areas.[8] In addition, the Government has created a new magistrates' courts authority to cover the entire Greater London area.[9]

Day-to-day management of the courts is now entrusted to justices' chief executives,[10] a new statutory appointment. They have taken over many administrative responsibilities from justices' clerks, whose principal responsibility is to advise lay JPs on matters of law and procedure.[11]

The Government has also changed the basis on which magistrates are empowered to deal with cases. Magistrates are appointed to 'commission areas' and may deal only with cases arising in their commission areas. The Government has also aligned the boundaries of commission areas so that in general they match those of the MCC areas. This should secure greater efficiency with better use of court personnel, magistrates and premises. There are also powers to transfer cases between commission areas in exceptional circumstances.[12] Further major changes are in contemplation, following the commitment of the present Government to a major overhaul of the criminal justice system.

Proposals announced in the Queen's speech in November 2002 will, if brought into effect, make further structural change, with all criminal courts—the Crown Court and magistrates' courts—being brought into one organizational structure. (*See Box 4.2.*)

In addition to these structural changes, the government has set common performance standards covering a variety of practical things such as reducing delays, ensuring that there are separate waiting areas for victims, witnesses and defendants and improving access for those with physical disabilities. The government is anxious that MCCs should, where possible and practicable, use the same systems and common services.

Monitoring of the outcomes of service delivery by MCCs is achieved by the Magistrates' Courts Service Inspectorate (MCSI), a statutory body established in 1994.[13] Its first complete review of all MCCs found many examples of good practice in the delivery of service, but also worrying variations in performance—for example, fine enforcement. In some cases the MCSI found a disappointingly negative response to proposals for greater efficiency. In part this is the result of a lack of adequate infrastructure, in particular information technology. The co-ordinated computer system, Libra, will not be available throughout England and Wales until 2004. In part there is still a lack of understanding of how MCCs are currently expected to function—more like the management board of a company—which involves monitoring of the performance of their courts against defined targets and other performance indicators.

---

[8] Access to Justice Act 1999, s. 74.   [9] *Ibid.*, s. 83. See www.glmca.fsbusiness.co.uk/.
[10] Justices of the Peace Act 1997, s. 40.   [11] *Ibid.*, s. 45.
[12] Access to Justice Act 1999, s. 80.

[13] The Police and Magistrates' Courts Act 1994; the empowering provision is now found in the Justices of the Peace Act 1997, s. 62(3). See www.mcsi.gov.uk. The scope of the Inspectorate's work has now been extended to cover the Children and Family Court Advisory and Support Service (CAFCASS); it also hosts the Criminal Justice Joint Inspectorates' Secretariat which brings together a number of related inspectorates.

Box 4.2 The Courts Bill 2002

The Courts Bill is designed to implement key proposals in Sir Robin Auld's *Review of the Criminal Courts in England and Wales*, 2001.

Unifying administration of the criminal courts. Sir Robin recommended that the present division of responsibility for administration of the courts between the Court Service and Magistrates' Court Committees should be abolished. Clause 1 of the Courts Bill proposes that the Lord Chancellor should have a general statutory duty to administer the Supreme Court, the county court and the magistrates' court. This function will be delegated to a new executive agency, headed by a chief executive. Thus the present Court Service will be replaced by the new agency; Magistrates' Courts Committees will be replaced by Court Administration Councils, designed to represent local community links in court administration issues (clauses 4 and 5). With unification of administration will come unification of funding. Justices' chief executives will be replaced by officers designated by the Lord Chancellor.

Jurisdiction of lay magistrates. The present division of England and Wales into commission and petty sessions areas will be abolished and be replaced by the 'local justice area'. While lay magistrates will be assigned to a local justice area, they will be appointed to a single national jurisdiction. This should enable more flexible use of JPs in the future.

Judges. Further flexibility in the deployment of judges will be made possible. District judges (magistrates courts) will be given some powers of a Crown Court judge. Judges of the higher courts will be given all the powers of JPs.

HM Inspectorate of Court Administration will replace and build on the current HM Magistrates' Courts Service Inspectorate; it will also report on the performance of CAFCASS. For the first time, the work of the Crown Court will be subject to inspection.

Procedural Rule Committees. For the first time a Criminal Procedure Rule Committee will be established, as will a Family Procedure Rule Committee; these will mirror the work of the Civil Procedure Rule Committee in the civil justice system.

Recruitment

Recruitment of lay magistrates is undertaken, not by the MCCs, but by another set of committees which operate at the local level, the Lord Chancellor's Advisory Committees. They undertake a continuous programme of identifying possible candidates (in some areas through the placing of advertisements in the local press); shortlisting; interviewing; and making recommendations to the Lord Chancellor, who makes the final decision. Considerable efforts are made to ensure that there is a reasonable age spread, a good gender balance, representation of ethnic minority groups, and a representation of people with different political beliefs. Indeed, potential candidates are specifically asked about their political affiliations, not to screen out those who might be in opposition to the government of the day, but in order to try to ensure that a good spread of opinion—reflecting the wider society—is recruited to the Bench. Following the publication of a Consultation Paper in October 1998, the present Lord Chancellor has accepted that this may not be the best way to achieve the right mix of personnel and is looking for an alternative mechanism, possibly based on occupational groupings. The difficulty of devising such an alternative means however has led him to the conclusion that, for the time being at least, the use of political affiliation will continue.[14] The process of recruitment is far more open and founded on the principles of equality of opportunity than was the case some years ago.

Notwithstanding these changes, there can be difficulty in recruiting people in the younger age ranges, as employers may be resistant to their staff taking off the not inconsiderable amounts of time required to be a magistrate. The self-employed may find it hard to devote the required amounts of time to this work, particularly when their businesses are still developing. In some areas of the country, there have been difficulties in attracting sufficient numbers of volunteers of the right quality, able to take on the commitments of the role, both to be trained and actually to sit in court. This has led to worries that the part-time lay justices are not as valued by government as they once were to deliver a localized system of criminal justice, and that there may be moves towards appointing more full-time salaried judges. This view, if widespread, would seem highly exaggerated. There are currently around 28,500 lay justices (2001 figure) as against just over 100 district judges and 150 part-time district judges (formerly called stipendiary magistrates) (2001 figures); it seems unlikely that the lay magistracy will suddenly disappear.

Many of the changes noted above are very controversial, certainly at the local level. There is considerable *esprit de corps* in magistrates' courts. Many lay magistrates do not welcome changes in organization that they feel lead to reduced identification with a particular court or location. Nevertheless, the programme of change currently being implemented and still to come must strike a balance between the delivery of justice at the local level and the need for as much administrative efficiency as possible. It cannot be ignored, however, that at least one reason why the Government likes the system is that the lay justices are all unpaid. Whether and for how long this tradition of public service will survive into the twenty-first century is at present a matter for speculation. Should recruitment difficulties get worse and demands for payment become more regularly heard, then the case for the retention of the lay bench may well weaken.

Judicial Studies Board

The Judicial Studies Board (JSB) is another part of the English legal system that has developed significantly in recent years. For a long time, many judges assumed that they knew all that there was to know about law and legal process, and that therefore judicial training was unnecessary; some regarded it as impertinence to suggest

---

[14] LCD Press Announcement, 329/99, 25 October 1999.

otherwise. Notwithstanding this complacent view, there has long been an acceptance that some judicial training was needed. As early as the 1960s, judicial conferences were convened to try to tackle the particular issue of inconsistency in sentencing practices by the judiciary.

The scope of training for the judiciary was put on a more normal footing in 1979 with the creation of the Judicial Studies Board. Over the last twenty-five years the Board has grown in size and stature and now delivers a very considerable programme of judicial training, not only to judges sitting in criminal trials, but also those handling civil trials, and to the chairs of a wide range of tribunals. It also sets the framework for the training of magistrates.

In delivering its programmes, the JSB provides both *induction* courses, which must be taken before a judge begins to sit, and *continuation* courses, which are offered on a three-yearly cycle. In addition to these regular programmes, the JSB also arranges special programmes. For example there were special programmes to introduce the judiciary to the Human Rights Act 1998 prior to its coming into force in October 2000; and to introduce Lord Woolf's reforms to the civil justice system, on how the new system would work. Most controversial was the programme, in 1995–6, to provide ethnic awareness training to the judiciary—an issue which arose from perceived differences in the ways in which people from different ethnic groups might be treated in the courts.[15] (Following the Stephen Lawrence case, this remains an issue of very great importance for the work of the courts, as well as other actors in the legal system.[16])

Besides course provision, the JSB also provides written guidance on the running of trials in *Bench Books*—looseleaf volumes of information that judges keep beside them for easy reference while performing their judicial functions. It has recently produced its first CD Rom for training purposes. Through its Equal Treatment Advisory Committee (formerly the Ethnic Minorities Advisory Committee) it has been developing advice and training for judges to ensure that parties to proceedings in courts or tribunals feel they have been treated equally and not subject to any form of discrimination.

In addition, the JSB has sponsored one or two more practical books, notably the *Guidelines for the Assessment of Damages in Personal Injury Cases*, designed to ensure greater consistency in reaching awards for damages in personal injury cases. It also produces a journal.

Finally, in situations where the resources of the JSB are unable to provide training direct, it nevertheless sets the framework within which judicial training should take place. The clearest example of this occurs with the magistrates. The Magistrates Committee of the JSB does not provide training to JPs directly, but sets the curriculum for such training, which is the delivered at the local, MCC, level.

[15] Hood, R., in collaboration with Cordovil, G., *Race and Sentencing: a Study in the Crown Court: a Report for the Commission for Racial Equality* (Oxford, Clarendon Press, 1992).

[16] Macpherson of Cluny, Sir William, *The Stephen Lawrence inquiry Report* (Cm 4262) (London, The Stationery Office, 1999).

The development of the role of the JSB is a fascinating example of the evolution of policy and its implementation. It has not developed out of high-profile Parliamentary debate or the enactment of special legislation. Rather, senior officials in the LCD, working with influential members of the judiciary, came to see this as an important facet in the management of a modern judicial system. Pockets of resistance among the judiciary—which undoubtedly existed ten or fifteen years ago—have been replaced by an acceptance, reflected in professional life more generally, that continuing education is a proper, indeed essential, part of professional development. Newly appointed judges now expect training; and those in post acknowledge the need for opportunities to reflect on their work.

This is not to say that the model so far developed is perfect. The amount of training which English judges receive is still modest. Unlike the situation in some other jurisdictions, there is no university law school which offers a specialist post-graduate diploma or degree in judicial science. There is always more that can and should be done. Nevertheless, the development of professional judicial studies has been one of the most significant developments in the English legal system in the past two decades. It has not attracted the public attention that it deserves.

The Law Commission

The Law Commission was established by Act of Parliament in 1965 to keep the law of England and Wales under review.[17] It is the most important standing body devoted to questions of law reform. Though independent in character, it falls within the overall responsibility of the LCD. The Commission is chaired by a High Court judge, currently Mr Justice Toulson. He is assisted by four other commissioners, who in turn are assisted by teams of lawyers and research assistants and a small secretariat.

In carrying out its functions it does not attempt to review all the law all the time. Rather it determines, on a regular basis, programmes of work it intends to carry out. (At any one time, the Commission will be engaged on between twenty and thirty projects, at different stages of development.) The programmes of work, which are approved by the Lord Chancellor, comprise two principal elements:

- projects—which come from within the Commission; and
- references—work which the Commission is specifically asked to undertake by government departments.

In addition, the Commission seeks to *codify* areas of law that have become extremely complex, and to *repeal* legislation that is no longer of practical use.[18] The current eighth programme contains projects on criminal law (including review of the law of fraud); commercial law (including work on illegal transactions); property and

---

[17] There is a separate Law Commission for Scotland.
[18] Since 1965, over 5,000 measures have been removed from the Statute Book as a result of this work.

trusts law; and housing and administrative justice (including a review of the law on renting homes).

Codification. In most countries whole areas of law are contained in a single code rather than, as in England, being divided between the common law, which is derived from decisions of judges over the centuries, and statute law enacted by Parliament. It has always been the Commission's objective that English law should similarly be governed by a series of statutory codes, to make the law more accessible to the citizen and easier for the courts and litigants to understand and handle. For instance, in family law much of the Commission's work has resulted in the production of what is in effect a code, though contained in a series of separate Acts of Parliament.

More particularly, since 1968 the Commission has had in hand a project to produce a criminal code, such as exists in almost every other country in the world. Indeed in 1989 the Commission published a Draft Criminal Code, but it was not brought into legislative form. The present Government has, however, recently announced that, as part of its major reform of the criminal justice system, new emphasis should be given to the creation of a criminal code. It is possible that this major Commission project will finally come to a successful conclusion.

Its mode of work is to start by careful analysis of the existing law, including, where relevant, consideration of how other countries have dealt with the issue in question. It then drafts a preliminary consultation paper setting out a statement of the existing law, explaining why that area of law needs reform, and indicating its preliminary views on how the law might be reformed, on which it seeks comments from members of the public. Having analysed those comments, the Commission then develops its ideas into recommendations for the reform of the law. It will usually commission the drafting of a bill designed to capture the outcome of these policy formulations.[19]

However, the mere fact that this stage in the law-making process has been reached by no means guarantees that the bill so drafted becomes law. It still has to go through the Parliamentary process discussed in Chapter 3. And no further progress can be made if Parliamentary time cannot be found. About two-thirds of the Commission's proposals for reform have reached the statute book.

Research

Unlike many other of the large-spending departments, the LCD had until recently a very poor record for research. Specific policy-related research projects were commissioned from time to time. But policy initiatives too often derived from anecdotal evidence, pressure from individual influential judges or groups of judges, powerful professional bodies such as the Law Society and the Bar Council, or the ideas or even prejudices of government ministers or Members of Parliament. It is only over the last three to four years that there has been within the LCD a defined research secretariat

---

[19] One of the particular features of the Law Commission is that Parliamentary Counsel are seconded to it for the purpose of drafting commission bills.

with control over a (modest) budget dedicated to the development of specially commissioned policy-related research. Initially all the research was carried out by academics or other research agencies on a research contract basis.[20] More recently the Department has supplemented this effort by the creation of an in-house research unit.

Although the size of this research effort does not compare with, for example, that of the Home Office or the Department of Social Security, the LCD is at last seen as engaging in a process familiar in other government departments.

It must be right in principle to attempt to develop policy that is going to affect large numbers of people's lives on the basis of hard information rather than soft anecdote. The present Government is very properly committed to the principle of 'evidence-based' policy development. This is very important for the central government, and one that it may be anticipated will develop further in the coming years.

The Home Office

The Home Office is the other major player shaping the institutional framework of the English legal system. It has a central role in relation to the development of the criminal justice system. The detail of this is considered further in Chapter 5. Much of the drive for increased efficiency within the criminal justice system, leading to significant changes to the ways in which criminal processes operate, derives from Home Office initiatives. It is the Home Office that has promoted a number of measures designed to make the police force more efficient, for example by the creation of the National Criminal Intelligence Service and the National Crime Squad.[21] (One of the key features of policing in England and Wales is that there is no national police force, but a number of police forces operating in counties. Arguments in favour of the creation of a national police force are met by the counter-argument that that would lead to too great a centralization of police power.) Its most recent measures have also sought to give some policing functions to civilian staff working within the police force.[22]

Unlike the LCD, which has a relatively focused portfolio of activity, the Home Office has an exceptionally wide remit. In addition to the criminal justice system, the Home Office also takes a lead responsibility in relation to a number of other issues which have an important impact on law-making and the role of law in England and Wales. These include: crime reduction; immigration and nationality; drugs prevention; race equality and diversity, including anti-discrimination legislation; and a number of community issues including volunteering.

One of the challenges that those whose job it is to manage government face is to try to ensure that government presents a more or less coherent view of the world.

---

[20] The LCD has been responsible for opening up significant relationships with the academic and research world, which have benefited both the Department and the research community. The role of the Socio-Legal Studies Association in these developments has been crucial.

[21] Police Act 1997.   [22] Police Reform Act 2002.

'Joined-up government' is, however, much harder to achieve in practice than the outsider might think. Departmental cultures are a very strong influence on the development of policy and practice, and there can be significant turf wars between different government departments. While there are constant calls for better co-ordination between different parts of the government, these are not always delivered in practice, or not without substantial political impetus. In the context of the English legal system, the Home Office/LCD interface is one where the need for co-ordination is crucial. A very important recent development has been the creation of the criminal justice system portal (see websites at the end of this chapter), which draws together information about the various actors in the criminal justice field. Even here, arrangements are not always as co-ordinated or as harmonious as they should be.

Legal Services Commission

Government has also played a crucial role in shaping the delivery of legal services. This is another topic considered in more detail later (Chapter 10). The changing framework for the development of policy and provision of legal services may be noted here.

A statutorily based legal aid scheme, which paid fees to lawyers to provide legal services to the poor or those of moderate means, was first introduced in 1949, with the passing of the Legal Aid Act 1949.[23] Initially the scheme was modest in scope, covering only legal representation in civil cases. Gradually however, during the 1960s and 1970s, the scheme was extended to cover the provision of legal representation in criminal trials; the provision of legal advice and assistance generally, and more specifically for those detained in police stations.

Throughout this period, the LCD made the policy, but the delivery of that policy was through the Law Society. Advice on how the scheme might be improved was offered by the Lord Chancellor's Advisory Committee on Legal Aid and Advice. In addition a number of increasingly influential external pressure groups sought to argue for changes to the scheme, principally through extensions of the scheme. The role of the Legal Action Group was particularly significant.

During the 1980s, voices were increasingly heard that the administration of legal aid by the Law Society—in effect the lawyers' trade union—was not wholly proper. Although the Law Society's legal aid work was wholly separate from the normal functioning of the Law Society, there was a danger that the legal aid scheme might be perceived as being run primarily for the benefit of lawyers, rather than members of the public.

---

[23] There was a long history of initiatives prior to this development. An excellent account is in Abel-Smith, B., and Stevens, R., with the assistance of Brooke, R., *Lawyers and the Courts: a Sociological Study of the English Legal System 1750–1965* (London, Heinemann, 1967).

In 1989, fundamental reform of legal aid was introduced when the administrative role of the Law Society was ended and transferred to the Legal Aid Board.[24] During the 1990s, the Legal Aid Board developed a number of fundamentally different practices relating to the delivery of legal aid services. For example, the Board introduced a scheme for the franchising of firms of solicitors, whereby they had to demonstrate defined levels of expertise and practice management in relation to the provision of legal aid—in effect, they had to promise to deliver a quality service.

The importance of this development can hardly be overstated. One of the greatest challenges which the Law Society faced in the 1970s and 1980s was devising means to ensure that all members of the legal profession were in fact up to the job of providing quality legal services. The Law Society was unable to achieve this, but—within its defined parameters—the Legal Aid Board did so; it proved very uncomfortable for many practitioners.

As a result of the passing of the Access to Justice Act 1999, the Legal Aid Board was abolished and replaced by the Legal Services Commission, which has responsibility for two new schemes: the Criminal Defence Scheme and the Community Legal Service. More detail is provided in Chapter 10. While the concept of 'legal aid' was formally abolished, the new framework builds on the pre-existing legal aid scheme. The changes being made are evolutionary rather than revolutionary in character. But a number of important new principles, not least that certain 'lay agencies' may be able to attract public funding for the provision of certain types of legal services, reinforce the importance of the Legal Services Commission in shaping legal services delivery in the English legal system.

Other government departments

The impacts of other government departments on the English legal system are less focused than the examples given above but are nonetheless considerable. Their influence emerges most clearly in considering the shape and extent of the administrative justice system (Chapter 6 below). The development of tribunals, inquiries, ombudsmen, other mechanisms for the resolution of complaints is driven by initiatives from a large number of different government departments.

It is here, perhaps, that the incoherence of government can be most clearly seen. For example, a policy in relation to the development of a tribunal sponsored by one department may be quite at odds with that being developed by another department. Basic questions, about the management of tribunals; the role of clerks within tribunals; the appointment of the personnel to tribunals; whether or not they should be full-time; whether or not they should be paid, and if so how much, are all answered differently by different departments. Indeed, unlike the situation with the criminal,

---

[24] Legal Aid Act 1988, Part II.

family and civil justice systems, there has been no tradition of government even trying to develop a coherent strategy for the administrative justice system.

At one level lack of coherence may be a good thing. It enables different practices and processes to be tried. The administrative justice system has provided a test-bed for experimenting with different types of dispute resolution procedure. It may also be argued that each part of that system has a specific task to do, and that therefore there is no need for any overarching framework. Nevertheless, the LCD has asserted increasing leadership in the area. The first stage of this culminated in the appointment of Sir Andrew Leggatt to review tribunals. The lack of coherence in the tribunal system was one of the major factors which influenced his recommendation that there should be a unified tribunal service; it seems likely that this will be taken forward by government. This will represent another major structural change to the legal system.

Other structural issues

Despite the pace of change, there are still many important outstanding issues on which there is much current debate.

A Ministry of Justice? The most fundamental issue is whether primary responsibility for the administration of justice should remain, as at present, in the Lord Chancellor's Department, or whether, as is common in many other countries, there should be created a Ministry of Justice, with a minister directly accountable to the House of Commons.[25] The retention of the Lord Chancellor as head of the justice system may seem rather anachronistic, notwithstanding reform of the House of Lords currently in progress. On the other hand, there may be advantage in separating the operation of the courts and the work of the judiciary from day-to-day party political debate.

It should be possible for practices and procedures to be developed, even with the Minister for Justice becoming accountable to the House of Commons, to ensure the continuation of the fundamental principle of the independence of the judiciary, while at the same time making the operations of the legal system subject to greater Parliamentary accountability. It is arguable that the efficiency of the system might be enhanced by greater interest from Members of Parliament.

Regulation of the profession. Another of the unresolved issues is the extent to which the LCD should be responsible for standards of professional service delivery by practising lawyers. One of the claims of any professional organization is that their members should be able to regulate such standards themselves. But there has been increasing criticism that self-regulation of the legal professions is not working satisfactorily. Currently the Law Society's Office for the Supervision of Solicitors, which deals with complaints against solicitors, has been the subject of fierce attack, not only from politicians but also from other consumer organizations, leading ministers to

---

[25] This has been achieved in the Scottish Executive: see www.scotland.gov.uk/who/dept_justice.asp.

suggest that government may have to intervene. In both the Courts and Legal Services Act 1990 and the Access to Justice Act 1999, the Government took powers to intervene in the regulation of the practising legal profession. (See further below, Chapter 9.)

The proper extent of this intervention is extremely controversial. It is important that the legal profession is 'independent'. Too close a regulation of professional activity by government can lead, and in other countries has led, to pressure on lawyers not to undertake work that government would not like to see undertaken. On the other hand, one of the ways in which the public today expects governments to act is through the creation of frameworks to guarantee the quality of goods and services. This may be the basis for a way forward—government setting a framework for quality control, but leaving it to others to implement and police that policy. (To an extent the Legal Services Commission has begun to tackle this issue, at least in relation to the provision of publicly funded legal services.)

The appointment of judges. The appointment of judges is another controversial area.[26] Again significant developments have occurred in recent years. (*See Box 4.3.*)

Box 4.3 Appointment of judges: the review of Sir Leonard Peach, 1999

In 1999 the Lord Chancellor invited Sir Leonard Peach to review the process of judicial appointments and selection of QCs. He noted that many of the LCD practices had, in recent years, developed in accordance with the best personnel management practice. Thus most judicial appointments were advertised; proper job descriptions and person specifications had been developed; and there was a very comprehensive system of feedback, on request, to unsuccessful candidates.

In Sir Leonard's view the most controversial aspect of the process was the consultation process. He thought this required a visibility it currently did not have, to ensure that candidates could have confidence that information about them was well founded, and not based on hearsay. To improve the situation Sir Leonard recommended:

- that better value from the consultations would be achieved by a redesigning of the consultee forms;

- that candidates should provide more information by way of self-appraisal; and

- that there should be greater opportunity for those who were perhaps not well known in the main judicial centres to nominate consultees, whose views should automatically be sought.

Sir Leonard did not recommend, as some had argued, that the process should be removed from the LCD. Instead he suggested the creation of a post of *Commissioner for Judicial Appointments*, who would both provide an ombudsman facility for both disappointed individuals and organizations, and undertake a regular audit of applications on a sample basis of current procedures. These would be used to inform recommendations for improvements in process.

---

[26] Justice, *The Judiciary in England and Wales: a Report by Justice* (London, Justice, 1992).

He agreed with the current practice that all appointments to full-time judicial office should be preceded by a period as a part-time judge. He strongly recommended that appointments as (part-time) Deputy High Court Judges—who form the pool from which appointments to the highest judicial office are usually made—should be subject to the same formal process of appointment as other part-time judicial appointments. He also recommended that an experiment in self-appraisal for certain (part-time) Deputy District Judges be extended to all part-time judicial appointments. Sir Leonard anticipated that full-time judges would become more drawn into personnel-related issues, such as appraisal and mentoring, which might require specific training from the Judicial Studies Board.

One of the very serious issues he addressed related to equal opportunities, both for women and for members of the ethnic minorities. He made a number of suggestions in this context: for example:

- that advocacy experience should not be an essential element in court appointments; rather that experience of the trial and litigation process would be regarded as helpful; and

- that the LCD should be more pro-active in encouraging applications from different groups, for example by encouraging the spread of mentoring and work-experience schemes.

He made a specific recommendation that a disability which might prevent a person serving as judge until the normal retirement age should not be a bar to appointment.

Sir Leonard also made a number of more practical suggestions. For example, noting that judicial appointments was a big administrative task (in 2000–1, the LCD received over 3,600 applications, held over 1,800 interviews, and made over 750 appointments) he suggested that better use could be made of 'reserve lists'—of those who had been approved in principle but for whom a vacancy was not currently available. He thought this might lead to speedier appointments, particularly where—as sometimes happened in tribunals—vacancies could arise at fairly short notice, reflecting changes in patterns of tribunal use.

The criteria for appointment, which were once secret, have been in the public domain for at least fifteen years.[27] Most judicial appointments now follow the publication of advertisements inviting applications for judicial appointments. More recently, an annual report on the process has started to be published. This has been supplemented by the first report of the Commission for Judicial Appointments. (*See Box 4.4.*) There is much more transparency in the system than there was a few years ago. And there can be no doubt that, when it comes to making appointments, successive Lord Chancellors have appointed to judicial office those with an extremely robust independence of mind and outlook.

[27] See websites for the link to the latest edition of these guidelines.

Box 4.4 The Commission for Judicial Appointments

One of the recommendations of Sir Leonard Peach was that a new commission should be established to review the process of making judicial appointments. The commission was created in 2001, and published its first report in October 2002.

The Commissioners' functions were set out in the Judicial Appointments Order in Council 2001. The appointments within the Commissioners' remit are judicial appointments (including Queen's Counsel) made by, or on the recommendation of, the Lord Chancellor, except the Lords of Appeal in Ordinary (the Law Lords) and the heads of Divisions. The appointment of lay magistrates and General Commissioners of Income Tax are not within the Commission's remit.

The Order in Council sets out the following functions for the Commissioners:

(1) The Commissioners shall, in the manner they consider best calculated to promote economy, efficiency, effectiveness and fairness in appointment procedures, exercise their functions with the object of maintaining the principle of selection on merit in relation to relevant appointments.

(2) The Commissioners shall review appointment procedures to establish whether relevant appointments are being made in accordance with the principle of selection on merit.

(3) The Commissioners may investigate any complaints arising out of the application of appointment procedures as may from time to time be made to them.

Although the Commission noted that much had been done to make the appointment process more transparent, it also stated:

In our view applicants for judicial appointment need to understand:

- the criteria against which their applications will be assessed;

- the processes by which their applications will be assessed;

- the weight placed on different aspects of their applications;

- the role played by consultees, in particular automatic consultees, in the assessment process;

- the identity of those who will be consulted; and

- the process by which consultees' comments will be taken into account.

Consultees need to understand:

- their role in the appointment process;

- the criteria against which applications will be judged;

- the importance of relating their comments to the criteria; and

- the process by which their comments will be taken into account.

Lack of understanding of these processes may lead to allegations of secrecy and fuel suspicion about the integrity and fairness of the process. We are aware that the Lord Chancellor's Department already publishes guidance to applicants and consultees for all competitions, and subjects the application forms and guidance to frequent review. We have already had some input into this process. However, the evidence we have seen so far suggests that there is still work to be done.

Failure to do this might lead to a perception of unfairness.

The Commission also noted that there needed to be a clear audit trail for each application, so that the LCD was clear exactly what happened in each case; and that the processes should not be subject to undue delay.

For the future, the Commission has stated it will do more work on the part played by consultees in the process; that it will be looking at the concept of 'merit' in making judicial appointments; and will consider any special factors that may exist in the appointment of High Court judges.

Nevertheless, there is still criticism that too much of the process—the development of files about individuals and the use of those files—is too secret. It is said that, in particular, this has the effect of limiting opportunities for appointment to the Bench of women and of members of ethnic minority groups. While there have been changes in the balance of judicial appointments, trends which are bound to increase in the coming years, demands for more change, and in particular for the creation of a Judicial Appointments Commission separate from the LCD are currently loud and will not be silenced by the Peach report or the other developments that have happened. (*See Box 4.5.*) While movement towards a new appointment system outside the LCD will not be rapid, it may be guessed that it will eventually come.

Box 4.5 Recent changes to the judicial appointments system

On publication of the Commission for Judicial Appointments' first report, the Lord Chancellor announced that there had already been a number of developments in the judicial appointments system. These included:

- a pilot assessment centre for appointments to Deputy District Judge (magistrates and civil) and Deputy Queen's Bench Master;

- abolishing the system of appointments to the High Court Bench by invitation only and allowing all suitable candidates to apply;

- removing lower age limits for most appointments and removing upper age limits for those applying for professional judicial offices. The retirement age for part-time judges has been restored to 70 from 65, except for Recorders and Deputy District Judges;

- reviewing and improving terms and conditions for part-time judges;

- introducing salaried part-time appointment to the District Bench;

- involving judicial and lay members in the selection of candidates for interview as well as the interviews themselves;

- amending appointment criteria in the light of the 1999 report of the Joint Working Party on Equal Opportunities;

- stipulating that any allegation of misconduct or any serious criticism about a candidate must be specific and will be disclosed to the candidate for response;

- providing formal feedback for unsuccessful candidates;

- confirming publicly that homosexuality is not a bar to appointment;

- confirming that advocacy experience is not a prerequisite for judicial appointment;

- extending appraisal and mentoring schemes for District Judges (Civil);

- introducing 'work shadowing' of judges for potential applicants;

- improving application and consultation forms and guidance; publicizing criteria and appointments procedures on the LCD website and on video;

- publishing the *Judicial Appointments Annual Report* since 1999;

- researching factors that affect (especially) women and ethnic minority lawyers in deciding whether to apply to be judges;

- opening opportunities to become Recorders to blind people;

- introducing part-time sitting in concentrated 'blocks' to help those who have had career breaks for family or other reasons;

- consulting the professions and other interested parties on possible improvements to the appointments processes for High Court, Circuit Bench and Recordership.

Questions for discussion

1. What are the arguments for and against the creation of a Ministry of Justice?

2. Should there be a national police force?

3. Should the process of recruitment to the lay magistracy be changed?

4. Is judicial training desirable? How might it be developed?

5. To what extent should the government prescribe practice standards for practising lawyers?

6. Should an independent Judicial Appointments Commission be created to make all judicial appointments?

Further reading

ABEL-SMITH, B., and STEVENS, R., *In Search of Justice: Society and the Legal System* (London, Allen Lance, 1968)

ANDREW, SIR ROBERT, *Review of Government Legal Services* (London, HMSO, 1989)

BEAN, D. (ed.), *Law Reform for All* (London, Blackstone, 1996)

LORD CHANCELLOR'S DEPARTMENT, *Modernising Justice: The Government's Plans for Reforming Legal Services and the Courts* (Cd 4155) (London, Stationery Office, 1998)

MALLESON, K., and BANDA, F., *Factors Affecting the Decision to Apply for Silk and Judicial Office* (London, LCD, 2000)

POLDEN, P., *Guide to the Records of the Lord Chancellor's Department* (London, HMSO, 1988)

STEVENS, R., *The Independence of the Judiciary: The View from the Lord Chancellor's Office* (Oxford, Clarendon Press, 1993)

WOODHOUSE, D., *The Office of the Lord Chancellor* (Oxford, Hart Publishing, 2001)

Websites

www.lcd.gov.uk/ *(Lord Chancellor's Department home page)*

www.criminal-courts-review.org.uk/ *(The Auld review of the criminal courts)*

www.tribunals-review.org.uk/ *(The Leggatt review of tribunals)*

www.courtservice.gov.uk/mcol/information.htm *(Money claims online)*

www.courtservice.gov.uk/xhibit/pilot1.htm *(The Xhibit experiment)*

www.lcd.gov.uk/magist/magistfr.htm *(Information about magistrates courts)*

www.lawcom.gov.uk/ *(Law Commission)*

www.jsboard.co.uk/ *(Judicial Studies Board)*

www.lcd.gov.uk/research/introfr.htm *(LCD research)*

www.homeoffice.gov.uk/rds/index.htm *(Home Office research)*

www.ukc.ac.uk/slsa/index.htm *(Socio-legal Studies Association)*

www.homeoffice.gov.uk/ *(Home Office home page)*

www.cjsonline.org/home.html *(Criminal justice system portal)*

www.legalservices.gov.uk/ *(Legal Services Commission)*

www.justask.org.uk/ *(Legal Services Commission)*

www.lcd.gov.uk/judicial/appointments/jappinfr.htm *(LCD Judicial appointments procedures)*

www.lcd.gov.uk/judicial/judcomrep02.pdf *(Commission for Judicial Appointments, Report 2002)*

www.lcd.gov.uk/judicial/ja_arep2002/index.html *(Judicial appointments, report 2002)*

www.lcd.gov.uk/judicial/judapp.htm *(Judicial appointments statistics)*

www.lcd.gov.uk/judicial/womjudfr.htm *(Judicial appointments statistics—women)*

5

The criminal justice system

Introduction

As indicated in Chapter 2, criminal law is central to the relationship between law and society. It seeks to regulate behaviour; it provides sanctions against those who break those rules. It is intimately linked with key social-policy objectives, such as the maintenance of law and order and preservation of the peace, security of the individual and the protection of property. It is also linked to other objectives, especially the protection of human rights and individual freedoms. Indeed, one of the great difficulties law-makers face when thinking about the development of rules of criminal law and criminal procedure is how to achieve a proper balance between the provisions of the criminal law and the preservation of liberty and the freedom of the individual. Furthermore, the boundaries of the criminal law change over time. They are not always set by the outcome of purely rational debate and argument; they also reflect the preferences, prejudices even, of politicians. The criminal justice system is that branch of the English legal system in which the criminal law is administered.

Any idea that the criminal justice system can be understood simply by looking at the work of the criminal courts can be quickly disabused by considering the wide range of agencies involved. They include:

- the police service;
- the Crown Prosecution Service;
- the Serious Fraud Office;
- other investigating/prosecuting authorities;[1]
- magistrates' courts;
- the Crown Court;
- the appeal courts;
- the Criminal Cases Review Commission;
- the prison service;
- the national probation service for England and Wales;

[1] For example, the Inland Revenue or the Health and Safety Executive; *see Box 5.5.*

- the Criminal Defence Service;
- the Criminal Injuries Compensation Scheme for victims; and
- other victim and witness care services.

Altogether, the criminal justice system affects large numbers of people.[2] It is a substantial employer. It consumes a great deal of public money: around £12bn a year (or £200 for each man, woman and child). Over half (£7.5bn) goes on policing, followed by the Prison Service (£1.8bn), criminal legal aid (£0.9bn) and the Probation Service (£0.5bn). These sums are not trivial; yet there is always pressure to spend more. Calls for increased expenditure have to be set in the context of these figures. Opportunities for doing things more cheaply need to be identified as well. The efficiency of the criminal justice system—to ensure that its social objectives are met, while at the same time keeping control of expenditure levels—is, as in other areas of social policy, a constant challenge for government.

The criminal justice system has been the subject of much political controversy, many official inquiries and considerable change. To give just a few examples: a Royal Commission on Criminal Procedure reported in 1981; a further Royal Commission on Criminal Justice reported in 1993; and a new review of the criminal courts was published in 2001, together with a major review of sentencing policy. Nearly every year there is new legislation on some aspect of the criminal justice system. Reform of the criminal justice system is a key element in the present Government's legislative programme.

Some argue that the system is loaded in favour of those accused of criminal activity and against 'the interest of society at large'. Others point to the serious miscarriages of justice that have occurred over the years and the need to protect the individual from wrongful involvement in the criminal justice system. The pace and scope of these changes pose serious and difficult questions about what the limits of government intervention should be. In the pages that follow, each part of the system is considered. First, though, we consider the social theories that underpin the criminal justice system.

Theories of criminal justice

Just as the social functions of the criminal law may be seen to be quite diverse, so too are the different social theories or models that underpin the criminal justice system.[3] From the criminological literature, a number of 'models' of the criminal justice system may be identified. These include:

---

[2] A longitudinal study carried out by the Home Office shows that 34% of *all* males born in this country in 1953 had, by 1993, received at least one conviction for a criminal offence of a more serious nature; the figure for females was 8%. Reported in Taylor, R., *Forty Years of Crime and Criminal Justice Statistics, 1958–1997* (London, Home Office, Research and Development Section, 1999).

[3] The following is derived from the excellent book by King, M., *The Framework of Criminal Justice* (London, Croom Helm, 1981).

(1) The *due process* model, in which the primary social goal may be said to be 'justice', and where there is an emphasis on fairness, and the rules needed to protect the accused against error and to restrain the exercise of arbitrary power;

(2) The *crime control* model, in which the primary social goal is punishment, and where the focus is on ensuring that the police are able to obtain convictions in the courts;

(3) A *medical model* in which the emphasis is on the rehabilitation of the offender, giving decision-takers discretion to achieve this;

(4) The *restorative justice* model, in which the emphasis is on getting the offender to recognize his or her responsibility in committing the offence and to make amends to the victim;

(5) The *bureaucratic model* in which the emphasis is on the management of crime and the criminal, and the efficient processing of offenders through the system;

(6) A *status passage* model, in which the emphasis is on the denunciation and degradation of the offender, involving a shaming of the offender, reflecting society's views of the offender;

(7) A *power model* in which the emphasis is on the maintenance of a particular social/class order, which reinforces the values of certain classes over others.

None of these models offers a uniquely correct interpretation of the criminal justice system. The attractiveness of each model will vary, depending on the person looking at the system. The defence lawyer or the defendant will take a different view from the policeman or the prosecutor, the victim, or the Home Secretary. Thinking about these models, however, both highlights the tensions and conflicts that—perhaps inevitably—exist in this complex sector of the justice system. It also helps to identify the assumptions that are all too often left unstated in considering developments in the criminal justice system. The reader will wish to reflect, in the light of these models, on how recent developments in criminal justice fit into the models thus identified.

Understanding the criminal justice system

To gain some overall understanding of the criminal justice system, it is necessary to break the total structure into more manageable parts. The approach adopted here is to look at the system in three stages:

- pre-trial stages;
- trial stage; and
- post-trial stages.

Each of these stages is further subdivided.

Pre-trial stages

Before any alleged criminal gets anywhere near a courtroom, a number of very important preliminary steps will be taken, each of which may affect the outcome of the case, and indeed whether a case ever reaches court at all. The following analysis of the stages that an allegation of criminal activity may go through before a trial is reached provides a structure that will not occur in practice as neatly as this; but it should help the reader see the overall shape of the criminal justice system more clearly.

The committing, reporting and recording of crime

It may be obvious that the first step in any criminal process is that some criminal act should have been *committed*. By itself that will (save in the most exceptional circumstances) not be sufficient to launch any kind of criminal process. Unless the offence is *reported* to the authorities, either by the victim or by some other person who has seen the incident or has come to realize that some criminal activity has taken place, no further action will follow. (On criminal statistics, *see Box 5.1*.)

Box 5.1 Criminal statistics[4]

One technical point needs to be made in this context. Most press reports about levels of crime are based on data published by the police of incidents of crime reported to and recorded by them. There are at least two problems with these data as a measure of levels of criminality in the community.

First, as is the case with all data, their value is dependent on the quality of the input. I do not suggest that the police deliberately fail to enter data correctly, but there is always the possibility of error in data collection. And some reporting practices may distort patterns of criminality. The thief who steals a crate of milk bottles from outside a front door may be recorded as having stolen one item (the crate); or twelve items (each individual bottle). In statistical terms this is a very considerable difference. There is also some pressure to relate crime figures to arguments for resources. If it is thought more resources will be available to fight crime if trends are upwards, this may—even if only subconsciously—lead to an increasing trend in the figures; if success in reducing crime were to be rewarded this might equally encourage a downward pressure on figures.

Secondly, the figures relate to reported and recorded crime. Many factors influence reporting and recording. For example, if insurance companies insist on theft from cars or property being reported this may lead to an increase in the rate of recorded crime; conversely a relaxation in their practices may lead to a reduction in recorded crime.

---

[4] These are prepared by the Home Office and published annually by The Stationery Office.

It is not argued here that the figures for recorded crime do not reflect trends in criminality in the community. But one should be cautious about drawing the simple conclusion, as is usually done in the media, that published statistics of recorded crime represents 'the crime figures'. It is more complex than that.

Corroboration of these points is found in the *British Crime Survey*,[5] in which a sample of the population is interviewed about its experience of crime as well as the criminal justice system. Although this survey by no means covers the totality of the population, the sample of over 40,000 people is drawn on the basis of accepted practices for creating social survey databases. The conclusions to be drawn from the *British Crime Survey* is that a very different picture of criminality and the individual experience of crime emerge as compared with the picture presented by the *Criminal Statistics*.

The agency to which most crime is reported is the police. But many other agencies also have criminal law enforcement responsibilities. For example:

- local authorities have responsibilities for areas like environmental pollution and public health;
- central government departments have responsibilities for investigating a wide variety of potential criminal activity—for example social security benefit fraud, tax evasion and other types of fraudulent commercial activity;
- health and safety agencies have duties to prosecute breaches of health and safety legislation (for example unlawful emissions of radioactive material);
- in very rare circumstances, an individual him- or herself may commence a criminal prosecution.

Indeed, although the police are the largest single player, the total number of criminal offences committed each year which are dealt with by bodies other than the police exceeds the total offences reported to the police. Nonetheless, for present purposes we concentrate on the role of the police.

Research shows quite clearly that, if the victim of a crime is unwilling to report a crime and to push the police to investigate it, then in all save the gravest situations no effective further action will be taken in relation to that alleged offence.[6] The initial act of reporting is crucial.

Furthermore, if the police are perceived as being unsympathetic in any particular context, then this will reduce the likelihood of alleged offences being reported. For example, some years ago the police were perceived—whether rightly or not—as being unsympathetic to female victims of alleged rape. The police took this criticism seriously and made strenuous efforts to demonstrate that this was not the case. In so far as the criticism had validity, the police determined to change their practices. At the

---

[5] This is also undertaken by the Home Office. The survey, established in 1982, reported irregularly until 2000. Since 2001 it has reported on an annual basis.

[6] Cretney, A., and Davis, G., *Punishing Violence* (London, Routledge, 1995).

time it could be predicted that the number of reported rape cases would increase. This has indeed happened over recent years. It may well be that the increase in numbers of reported rapes is the result of more rapes occurring. But at least some of the increase is likely to be attributable to a more realistic pattern of reporting and recording, which brings more cases to the attention of the authorities.

Another example is domestic violence. There is a widespread assumption that the police are reluctant to get involved in domestic issues. Whether or not this perception is correct does not much matter. But it is very likely that, as a result of these percep-tions, the number of cases of domestic violence known to the police is considerably smaller than the total number of incidents that actually take place.

Even if an alleged offence is reported, the police may not think that there is suf-ficient information to justify the *recording* of the alleged incident. If the matter is not recorded, no further action will be taken.

Finally, even if a crime is both reported and recorded, no effective further action will necessarily result. Many reports of petty theft, for example, are not taken further by the police—they do not have the resources to carry out the required investigations.

The investigation stage—police powers

Once a crime has been reported to the relevant agency (still using the police as the main example) the next stage is the investigation. In the case of major incidents this will involve the consumption of considerable resource with large numbers of police spending a lot of time on an investigation. In less important cases, the investigation stage may be extremely cursory. (There will be cases where the conceptually distinct processes of reporting and investigating will in practice be blurred. The police may gain intelligence that a criminal act is being planned. This will lead to the investigation of the matter in advance of the commission of the offence. If the offence is actually committed, the preliminary intelligence gathering may also result in the gathering of sufficient evidence to justify the arrest of the person or persons concerned and their being charged with the commission of an offence.)

For the criminal investigation bodies to be able to do their work, they need special powers. In the case of the police, their powers were the subject of major reform in 1984, with the enactment of the *Police and Criminal Evidence Act 1984* (PACE). The statutory powers of the police are accompanied by important *Codes of Practice*, which should also be observed by the police.[7] A joint Home Office/Cabinet Office review of the codes was undertaken in the summer of 2002, with the results published in November 2002.[8] This concluded that the codes played an important part in the

---

[7] There are six Codes of Practice: Code A on Powers of Stop and Search; Code B on Search and Seizure; Code C on Detention, Treatment and Questioning of Persons; Code D on the Identification of Persons; Code E on Tape Recording. A sixth code, F, on Visual Recording of Interviews was issued in May 2002. The codes have also been adapted to apply to immigration officers in their work.

[8] *Pace Review: Report of the joint Home Office/Cabinet Office of the Police and Criminal Evidence Act 1984* (London, Home Office, 2002).

criminal justice process, but that, nearly twenty years after the coming into force of PACE they could be updated. In the short term a new code A will come into effect on 1 April 2003; interim revisions to the other codes are also likely to come into effect in 2003. There may be more fundamental redrafting of the codes at a later date. The review also pointed to a number of broader issues relating to police powers, some of which would require further legislation.

The principal powers enabling the police to carry out their functions are:

• The power to stop and search;
• The power to arrest;
• The power to detain;
• The power to question;
• The power to enter and search premises.

The precise order in which these powers are used in any particular case will naturally depend on the circumstances. The extent of police powers, how they are interpreted and applied by the police, and the balance between those powers and the liberty of the individual are constant sources of controversy.

Stop and search

The powers of the police to stop and search people or vehicles are contained in section 1 of the Police and Criminal Evidence Act 1984. The law provides that a constable must have reasonable grounds for believing that, by exercising his/her powers, stolen goods, or an offensive weapon, or a knife or other bladed or sharply pointed article, or articles adapted for use in burglary, theft or obtaining by deception, or a vehicle that has been taken without authority will be found.

These general powers are supplemented by other powers to stop and search to be found in other specific Acts of Parliament—e.g. relating to terrorism, drugs, firearms or alcohol at sporting events. The Criminal Justice and Public Order Act 1994, section 60, also created an extensive power to stop and search 'in anticipation of violence'. However this power may not be exercised unless a police superintendent has authorized its use in a particular locality.

In exercising these powers, the police are required to follow procedures set down in section 2 of PACE, which, among other things, requires the officer to give his/her name, state why the search is taking place, and record that the stop and search has occurred (unless this is not practicable).

The language of the legislation gives considerable room to the individual police officer to decide whether or not the conditions for carrying out a stop and search are met. The exercise of the power has been controversial, in particular because of evidence that black people are more likely to be stopped and searched than whites. (*See Box 5.2.*) This is an issue which the Home Office now keeps under regular review. (*See Box 5.3.*)

Box 5.2 Stop and search in London

This is one of the most controversial of all police powers, not so much for the power itself as for the manner of its operation. The criticism is frequently made that, in exercising these powers, the police tend to focus particularly on the young, and more particularly on black youth. This has very considerable implications for race relations and the effective policing of many urban areas.

The use of stop and search powers in London was the subject of an important research report in 1999.[9] This seemed to demonstrate that there is a link between the exercise of the power of stop and search and levels of criminality in the community. In particular, it was found that the majority of arrests for possession of offensive weapons and going equipped to steal were the result of the exercise of stop and search powers. There was also a link between stop and search and arrests for crimes relating to drugs.

The report found that there were problems in the ways in which the powers were used, but that in general their use was supported by the public at large.

As regards the impact of arrests on particular ethnic groups, taking the Metropolitan Police area as a whole, the impact of the use of the power on different ethnic groups was less than previously thought. 88 per cent of all searches were in the 13–37 age group, and the ratios of those stopped and searched was 1.6 black to 1.0 white; however in particular areas of ethnic concentration, the figures look rather different. The report argues therefore that basic data on resident populations can be seriously misleading.

In short, there was evidence that if the police take a 'softly, softly' approach to stop and search, levels of crime rise. The conclusion drawn was that, while the power is an important one, it is one that must be used sensibly and with care.

Arrest

Broadly there are two types of arrest—with warrant, and without warrant.

- An arrest *with warrant* takes place under the authority of a warrant issued by a magistrate. A warrant may be issued after information has been given to the magistrate, on oath, that the person named has or is suspected of having committed an offence.

- There are a number of powers to arrest *without a warrant*. PACE section 24 gives the police (and other members of the public) power to arrest without warrant persons who have committed or are suspected of committing an 'arrestable offence'.[10] PACE section 25 also gives a power to arrest without warrant where 'general arrest conditions' are met.[11]

---

[9] FitzGerald, M., *Final Report into Stop and Search* (London, Metropolitan Police, 1999).

[10] This is defined as an offence, such as murder, where the penalty is mandatorily fixed by law, or for which a person may be given a prison sentence of five years or more: in short the most serious offences. There are also a number of offences, e.g. indecent assault on a woman, which, though not meeting these criteria, are defined as 'arrestable'—PACE s. 24(2).

[11] The 'general arrest conditions' include: that the name of the relevant person cannot be ascertained; or

Box 5.3 Race and the criminal justice system, 2001: summary of main findings

In 2000/2001:

Population estimates for 1999–2000 derived from the Labour Force Survey indicate that 2 per cent of the population aged 10 and over in England and Wales were of black ethnic origin, 3 per cent of Asian origin and 1 per cent 'other' ethnic groups.

686,000 stops and searches were recorded on persons by the police under a range of legislation, including the Police and Criminal Evidence Act (PACE), of which 10 per cent were of black people, 5 per cent Asian and 1 per cent 'other' ethnic origin. Police forces varied widely in their numbers for recorded stops and searches. Published research by the Home Office has indicated that resident population figures give a poor indication of the population observed in public places when and where police carry out searches, and therefore do not provide a good basis for assessing ethnic biases in officer search practice. However, these statistics remain important in describing the overall experiences of stop and searches among ethnic minority communities with black people seven times more likely to be stopped and searched than white people.

Compared with 1999–2000, the number of recorded stops and searches fell by 14 per cent for white people but rose by 6 per cent for black people and 3 per cent for Asians in the Metropolitan Police Area (MPA). In England and Wales (excluding the MPA) the falls were greater with an average fall of about 18 per cent for white people and 6 per cent for Asians but a rise of 4 per cent for black people. For both the MPA and England and Wales as a whole, the object for stops and searches remained similar in both years, although showing wide variations in practice between police forces.

Source: Home Office 2002

In addition, there are a number of specific powers to arrest without warrant under particular Acts of Parliament, e.g. the Mental Health Act 1983. Finally there is a common law power to arrest where a breach of the peace is taking place or is reasonably anticipated.

For an arrest to take place without a warrant, the person making the arrest must make it clear, by words or action, that the person arrested is under compulsion. The person arrested must be informed of the ground for the arrest, either at the time of arrest or as soon as possible thereafter, for example where it is not practicable to provide the information before the person to be arrested tries to run away. There is no legal power simply to detain persons for questioning without first making an arrest.[12]

that a name or address is not thought to be real or satisfactory; or that the constable has reasonable grounds to believe that arrest is necessary to prevent the person causing damage to himself or to others or to property; committing an offence against public decency; or causing unlawful obstruction of the highway; or to protect a child or other vulnerable person.

[12] In practice, this does happen. When persons are said in a news bulletin to be 'helping the police with their inquiries', this is an indication that they have not been arrested, but nonetheless 'persuaded' to attend the police station 'voluntarily'.

An arrest is the first stage in a process that may eventually lead to a criminal trial. Research suggests that, despite the legal framework created by PACE, a very large number of arrests lead to no further action being taken, which raises the question of the extent to which police practice on arrest conforms to the legal rules relating to arrest.

Detention

Once a person has been arrested, that person may be detained in a police station to enable further investigation (including questioning of the person) to be carried out. One of the principal changes brought about by PACE was that a detailed set of statutory provisions was put in place to regulate the time for a person could be detained in custody. Under Part IV of the Act, arrangements must be made for a police officer, known as the 'custody officer', to keep the detention under review. The police have, in general, twenty-four hours in which they must either charge the arrested person with an offence, or release the person, either with or without bail. Exceptionally, authorization for detention without charge for up to thirty-six hours may be given.

Once charged the person may be further detained but must be brought before a magistrates' court 'as soon as practicable'. The magistrates will decide whether the person can then be released on bail or remanded in custody.

Part V of PACE[13] sets out detailed provisions for the treatment of those who have been detained. Usually, a person detained is entitled to have someone informed of that fact, and to have access to legal advice, which gives the right to consult privately a solicitor at any time. There are powers to delay these rights where this is thought necessary, e.g. to prevent evidence being destroyed. The statutory rules and Code also set out in detail the physical conditions in which people should be detained; these include details about the provision of drinks and refreshment.

Questioning

The power to question suspects detained by the police is the subject of detailed guidance in Code C. The police regard the power to question as crucial, since in their view questioning often leads to the suspect providing a confession, which in turn leads to considerable savings later in the criminal process, as many of those confessing will plead guilty.

There are two particular problems: 'induced' confessions; and false confessions.

Induced confessions are, as the name implies, confessions that have arisen from the police offering 'incentives' to confess—for example, early release of a suspect on bail, the suggestion that a confession may lead to less serious charges being made against the alleged criminal or that in some other way the outcome will be less serious than it would otherwise be. Such inducements can colour the veracity of the confession.

---

[13] Supplemented by *The Code of Practice for the Detention, Treatment and Questioning of Persons by Police Officers* (Code C) (London, HMSO, 1995).

Rules of evidence which operate in court are designed to ensure that induced confessions are not made, by preventing the evidence obtained from them from being presented in court. Many police practices, for example the tape recording of interviews or the requirement to issue a formal caution to those who may be charged with an offence, are designed to eliminate improper police behaviour. It seems unlikely that the police will never seek to 'induce' a confession, for example in a location where there are no tape recorders. Furthermore the present form of the 'caution'[14] provides some incentive to people to make statements at an early stage.

False confessions are more problematic. Contrary to common sense and expectation there have been cases where a person being questioned by the police has confessed to a crime that he has not in fact committed. This can arise from the considerable pressure people are under when detained in a police station. This was one of the issues which led to the establishment of the Royal Commission on Criminal Evidence and Procedure in 1979.[15]

Entering and searching premises

The last general power available to the police (and indeed other crime investigation agencies) is the power to enter and search premises for evidence, and where relevant to seize that evidence. Many specific Acts of Parliament give power to grant warrants to the police for particular purposes, for example, investigating drugs offences, or theft. Section 8 of PACE creates a general power enabling magistrates to grant warrants to search for evidence relating to a serious arrestable offence. As with other police powers, these statutory provisions are supplemented by a Code of Practice.[16] Certain types of material are excluded from this provision, for example: items subject to legal privilege[17] and certain other categories of excluded material.[18]

There are also circumstances where the police are empowered to enter and search premises without a warrant: for example to arrest someone suspected of committing an arrestable offence or to save life and limb or prevent serious damage to property.[19]

Comment

There can be no doubting the powers that the police have over the ordinary citizen. The range of powers, considered in outline above, may be seen as a sensible code,

[14] 'You do not have to say anything. But it may harm your defence if you do not mention when questioned something which you later rely on in court. Anything you do say may be given in evidence.' This form of words provoked much criticism when introduced, as it was argued that it undermined the right of silence, one of the principal sources of procedural protection for the accused.

[15] See Irving, B., *Police Interrogation: A Study of Current Practice* (Research Study No 2 for the Royal Commission on Criminal Procedure) (London, HMSO, 1980).

[16] *Code of Practice for the Searching of Premises by Police Officers and the Seizure of Property found by Police Officers on Persons or Premises* (Code B) (London, HMSO, 1995).

[17] Principally communications containing legal advice from a professional legal adviser to his/her client.

[18] For example personal records and journalistic records. There is a procedure whereby a circuit judge may be asked to make an order granting access to such material or, in an extreme case, to grant a warrant to search for this sort of material: PACE s. 9 and Sch. 1.

[19] PACE s. 17.

enabling the police go about their business of investigating crime and catching suspects. Nevertheless, there are always concerns, backed by specific examples of police
malpractice, which demonstrate that the police act beyond the powers given to them.
This in turn means further controls on police behaviour to prevent the exercise of
powers beyond the legally prescribed limits are essential.

Where examples of the planting of evidence or the use of oppressive questioning
techniques are demonstrated, some critics argue that use of illegally obtained evidence is endemic to police practice. Others, including the police themselves, argue
that such abuses are simply the result of individual 'rotten apples', and that, so long as
steps are taken to remove them, the basic activities of the police are undertaken within
both the letter and the spirit of the law.

The principal sanction for the police failing to act within the scope of their legal
powers is that any evidence obtained improperly may not be able to be given in court.
The police are aware that during the investigative/information-gathering stage these
rules of evidence will be applied should a case reach court and be contested. These
rules should shape the ways in which evidence is obtained by the police. Failure to
follow these rules can result in the evidence improperly obtained being declared
inadmissible by the trial judge. (But, as is noted later, the law of evidence gives judges
considerable discretion whether or not evidence should be excluded.) In addition,
failure to follow the Codes of Practice can result in disciplinary proceedings being
taken against individual police officers.

As in other aspects of professional and public life, there is now much more formal
accountability than was the case some years ago. The overall efficiency of police forces is
the responsibility of Her Majesty's Inspectorate of Constabulary. The creation of the
Independent Police Complaints Commission[20] (replacing the Police Complaints
Authority) has resulted in new mechanisms for individuals to pursue grievances against
the police. In addition, a number of cases are taken by individuals against the police
each year, for example seeking damages for false imprisonment or damage to property.

Suggestions, made by some, that police activity is characterized by wholesale malpractice and corruption do not appear to be justified. Many who have incidental
brushes with the police find they operate strictly according to the book and in a
perfectly proper fashion. However, it is also likely to be the case that there are more
circumstances than those which hit the headlines in which the police do not behave
strictly according to the book. There seems rather less doubt that, when relations
between the police and members of ethnic minority communities are in question, the
police do not always exercise their powers as they should.

Next steps

On completing the first two stages, the police have four choices (*see Diagram 5.1*).
They may:

---

[20] Police Reform Act 2002, Part 2.

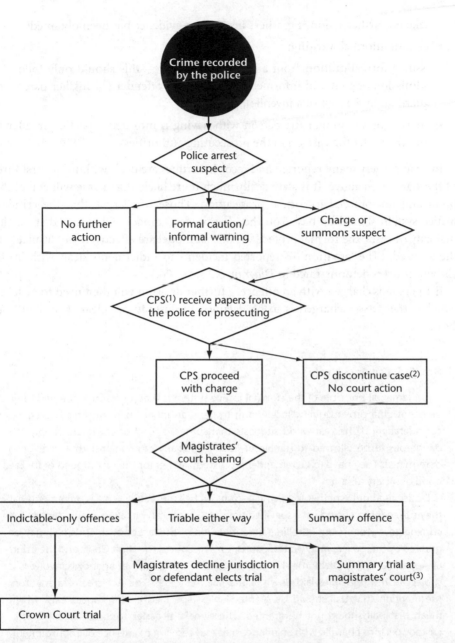

(1) Although the majority of prosecutions are handled by the Crown Prosecution Service, certain offences are still prosecuted by the police, whilst some are by private organizations or government agencies such as the Inland Revenue.

(2) A case will be under continual review, and may be discontinued at any stage before the hearing at the magistrates' court, or the prosecution may offer no evidence. In addition, the charge may be altered up to the final decision of the court.

(3) Magistrates may commit to Crown Court for sentence.

Diagram 5.1 The prosecution process

- take no further action, e.g. where insufficient evidence has been obtained;
- give an informal warning;
- issue a formal caution from a senior police office—this should only follow an admission of guilt and informed consent by the offender (or his/her parents or guardian in the case of a juvenile);[21]
- charge (or summons) the person with having committed a particular offence, and then refer the case on to the prosecuting authorities.

In practice very many reported and recorded crimes are dealt with in the first three of the ways listed above. It is statistically much more likely that a case will end at this point and not proceed to formal prosecution. Those who argue that the criminal justice system should be based on the 'due process' model will realise that, in this majority of cases, the formal protections of that model are effectively not available to the accused. (The 'attrition' of reported incidents to indictments dealt with in the Crown Court is demonstrated in *Diagram 5.2* at p. 106.)

If a person is charged with an offence, a further decision will then need to be taken whether the person charged is to be detained in custody or released on bail. (*See Box 5.4.*)

Box 5.4 Bail or custody

A fundamental principle of the criminal justice system is that a person is deemed to be innocent until proved guilty. It is wrong to deny an innocent person his liberty. Yet consideration of the real world suggests that some accused of crime are simply too dangerous to be allowed to remain at liberty until any case against them has been determined. They have to be remanded in custody, either for their own good or for the good of society at large.

Decisions about whether to release persons on bail (i.e. subject to a requirement that they surrender to custody at a specified time and place) can be taken at any stage in the criminal trial process until the final determination of the last appeal. Thus bail may be granted by the police, magistrates' courts, Crown Courts, the High Court and the Court of Appeal (Criminal Division). The granting of bail, by whichever agency is involved, is subject to the principles laid down in the Bail Act 1976. The Act creates a statutory presumption that bail should be granted unless specified circumstances exist which mean that bail should not be granted. These make it easier to justify remanding in custody persons charged with an offence that may result in a sentence of imprisonment, than those which would not. In some cases, there is no discretion. For example those charged with a homicide offence or rape or attempted rape currently cannot be released on bail if they have a previous conviction for such an offence.[22]

---

[21] 60% of offenders under the age of 18 were cautioned for indictable offences in 1997.

[22] In *Caballero v. United Kingdom*, (2000) 30 EHRR 643, the European Court of Human Rights, following a concession on the point made by the UK Government, held that the automatic denial of bail was a breach of Art. 5 of the European Convention on Human Rights.

In practice the vast majority of those against whom criminal proceedings are taken are granted bail. Nevertheless there are those who argue that bail is granted too readily. In particular, there is disquiet about the numbers of crimes committed by people while they are out on bail. Notwithstanding these fears and the apparent policy of the Bail Act, numbers of those remanded in custody awaiting trial or sentencing or an appeal have increased sharply over the years and have exacerbated the problem of prison over-crowding. This has led policy-makers to consider other options, such as the electronic tagging of defendants so that the authorities can keep track of those persons even though they have not been detained in custody.

The decision to prosecute

Even if a potential criminal investigation has reached the stage where a criminal act has been investigated, and a charge has been preferred against a suspect who has been arrested, or a summons has been issued against a suspect, there still remains the question whether or not an actual prosecution will be taken forward. This decision is taken, not by the police, but by staff employed in the Crown Prosecution Service (CPS). (For other prosecuting authorities *see Box 5.5*.)

Box 5.5 Other prosecuting agencies: the Serious Fraud Office

As noted in passing above, there are many other prosecuting agencies apart from the police. Local authorities, the taxation authorities and the social security authorities are just some of the other public bodies that have the legal powers both to investigate criminal activities and to bring prosecutions before the courts. Limits on space prevent any detailed discussion here.

One particular agency, in relation to which a short note will be provided, is the *Serious Fraud Office* (SFO). This was established by the Criminal Justice Act 1987.[23] Its establishment was designed to increase the capability of the authorities to investigate serious and complex fraud cases. The Director of the SFO, appointed by the Attorney General, works with specially appointed staff. In this area, the investigation and prosecution functions have been kept together. The Director and, by extension, staff have wide powers to require those under investigation (and others believed to have relevant information) to answer questions and to furnish information. The SFO focuses on the most serious fraud cases; other cases are pursued in the normal way through the Fraud Investigation Group within the CPS.

The workload of the SFO is not extensive but is very intense. For example, during the reporting year ending in April 1999, it worked on the investigation or prosecution of ninety-four cases; but the total value of the sums involved was well in excess of £1bn. During the same year, eighteen trials involving thirty-eight defendants were concluded. The principal defendants were convicted in all but one of those trials.

---

[23] Following the *Report of the Roskill Committee on Fraud Trials* (London, HMSO, 1986).

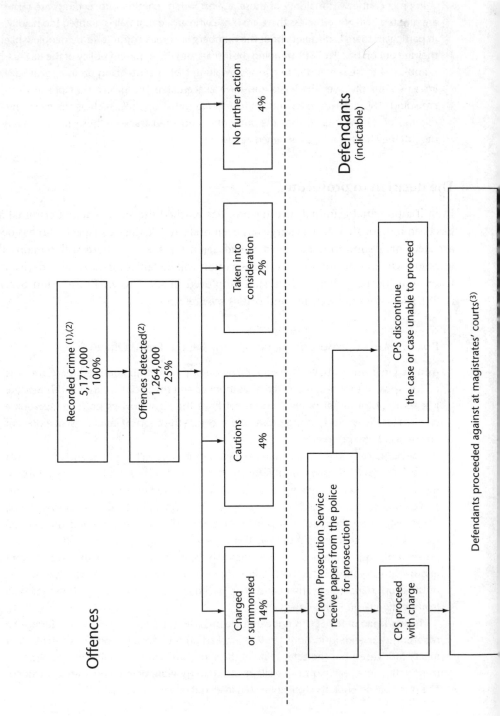

Offences

Recorded crime [1],[2]
5,171,000
100%

Offences detected[2]
1,264,000
25%

No further action
4%

Taken into
consideration
2%

Cautions
4%

Charged
or summonsed
14%

Defendants
(indictable)

Crown Prosecution Service
receive papers from the police
for prosecution

CPS discontinue
the case or case unable to proceed

CPS proceed
with charge

Defendants proceeded against at magistrates' courts[3]

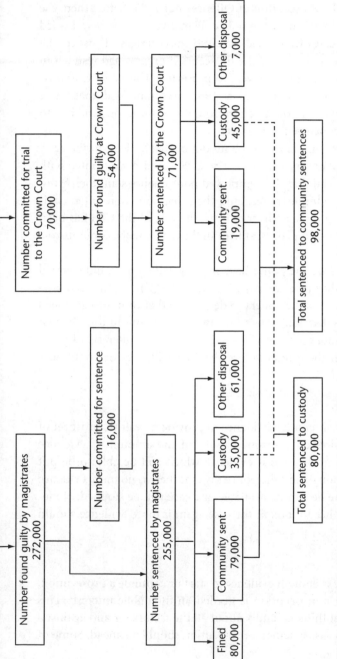

Diagram 5.2 Flows through the criminal justice system, 2000

(1) Covers all indictable, including triable either way, offences plus a few closely associated summary offences.
(2) In the financial year 2000/01.
(3) See Table 6.3 for numbers of proceedings terminated early and defendants discharged at the committal proceedings stage or dismissed.

Source: Criminal Statistics 2000 (Cm 5312, London: The Stationery Office, 2001)

The CPS is a public service, headed by the Director of Public Prosecutions (DPP), and answerable to Parliament through the Attorney General. It was established in 1986, following enactment of the Prosecution of Offences Act 1985. Before then, the decision to prosecute was usually taken by the police themselves.[24] However, this led to the criticism that, in some cases which had involved miscarriages of justice, the interrelation of the investigation process and the prosecution process had resulted in the police inappropriately exercising their powers to prosecute. The Royal Commission on Criminal Procedure, which reported in 1981, recommended that there should be a separation of the investigation function from the prosecution function, to introduce an element of independence into the latter.

This was extremely controversial. There can be no doubt that, at least in the early years, the police in particular were very unhappy. The CPS was also confronted with many public challenges. It was said that they employed poor quality staff; their work was hampered by poor quality administration; and their decisions were often criticized. However, notwithstanding these early criticisms, the role of the CPS has been retained, and there are now fewer complaints, at least in the mass media, about its role in the criminal justice system.

The basic procedure is that, after the police have investigated a crime and charged (or summonsed) the suspect, they pass the papers to the CPS. One of the CPS lawyers—a Crown Prosecutor—reviews the papers to decide whether or not to go ahead with the case. The prosecutor's decision is based on two tests set out in the *Code for Crown Prosecutors*. Is there enough evidence? Is it in the 'public interest' to prosecute? A case has to pass both these tests before the CPS will start or continue a prosecution.

The evidence test

The prosecutor first sees if there is enough evidence to provide a 'realistic prospect of conviction'. This process requires an assessment both of the amount of evidence which is available and also its quality—is it evidence which will be able to be put before a court? If there is not enough and the police say that there is no more evidence or no real prospect of any more becoming available, the case will be stopped. Nonetheless, the CPS will ask the police to look at the case again if more evidence should become available.

The public interest test

If a prosecutor thinks that there is enough evidence to start or continue a prosecution, she will then consider whether a prosecution is needed 'in the public interest'. This means that the prosecutor must think carefully about all the factors for and against a prosecution, and assess in each case whether a prosecution should go ahead. Some of

---

[24] There remain a number of instances where the decision to prosecute remains with the police and other prosecuting authorities. There are also a number of situations in which the decision to prosecute is taken by the Attorney General. The large bulk of decisions to prosecute are however taken by the CPS.

the public interest factors which the CPS takes into account are set out in the *Code for Crown Prosecutors.* For example, a prosecution is likely to be needed if:

- a weapon was used or violence was threatened during an offence;
- the motive for the offence was any form of discrimination; or
- the offence was committed against a person serving the public, such as a police officer.

The CPS is required to act in the public interest, and not just in the interests of one person. Crown Prosecutors must always think very carefully about the interests of the victim of the crime. This is an important factor when prosecutors decide where the balance of public interest lies.

Notwithstanding the general approach of the CPS there are still cases where the CPS comes under heavy criticism, either from the police or from a victim (or her family). Particular problems arise in very emotive cases, which may have attracted considerable media publicity, where therefore there is a great pressure to prosecute, but where the evidence to satisfy the tests sketched out above may just not be there. In making its decisions, the CPS will not always reach conclusions that will attract universal approval.

The CPS employs a considerable number of staff who work in different parts of the country on a regional basis. There is also a group, known as 'Central Casework', which deals with especially important cases, such as deaths in police custody, cases involving the Official Secrets Act or cases involving terrorism.

Monitoring

Because of concerns about the quality of the work of the CPS, an Inspectorate was established in 1996 to monitor the quality and consistency of decision-taking across the country, and to try to ensure the spread of good practice. Initially, the creation of the Inspectorate was the result of executive action; recent legislation has, however, put the existence and powers of the authority onto a statutory footing.[25] Particular incidents may, additionally, be the subject of special inquiry.[26]

Criminal Justice Bill 2002

The Criminal Justice Bill 2002 contains a number of proposals relating to the pre-trial stage. (*See Box 5.6.*) It must be stressed that they had been introduced in Parliament just as the text of this book was being finalized and may not therefore survive in their original form or at all.

---

[25] Crown Prosecution Service Inspectorate Act 2000. This followed a recommendation in the Glidewell Report, *Review of the Crown Prosecution Service* (Cm 3960) (London, The Stationery Office, 1998). The Inspectorate publishes an annual report on its work.

[26] See, e.g., His Honour Gerald Butler QC's report, *Inquiry into CPS Decision-Making in Relation to Deaths in Custody and Related Matters* (London, The Stationery Office, 1999).

Box 5.6 Criminal Justice Bill 2002: proposals on pre-trial issues

Bail

The proposed legislation includes the following provisions in relation to bail:

- When deciding whether to grant bail in respect of an offence which appears to have been committed while the defendant was on bail for another offence, courts will be required to give particular weight to that fact when assessing the risk that (if granted bail) the defendant may commit further offences.

- The right of the prosecution to appeal to the Crown Court against a decision by magistrates to grant bail is to be extended to cover all imprisonable offences, and not just those carrying a maximum penalty of five years as at present.

- The bill creates a presumption that bail will not be granted for a person who is charged with an imprisonable offence, and who tests positive for a specified Class A drug and refuses treatment (the three 'criteria')—unless there are exceptional circumstances in a particular case.

Conditional cautioning

- The bill allows for a caution with specific conditions attached to it to be given where there is sufficient evidence to charge a suspect with an offence which he/she admits, and the suspect agrees to the caution.

- It would be for the CPS to decide whether a conditional caution was appropriate, and for the police to administer it.

- If the suspect failed to comply with the conditions, he or she would be liable to be prosecuted for the offence.

Charging

- The bill provides that cases in which the police would now charge a suspect should generally be referred to the Crown Prosecution Service to determine whether proceedings should be instituted, and if so on what charge. Meanwhile the suspect would be released on bail; provision is made for conditions to be attached (with the suspect's consent) to police bail in such circumstances.

- For certain offences and in certain circumstances (to be set out in guidance), it would remain open to the police to charge without reference e.g. minor, routine offences, or cases where it is necessary to bring the suspect before a court to seek a remand in custody (or on bail on conditions to which the suspect has refused to consent).

- Pilot projects have shown that involving the prosecutor at an earlier stage leads to more accurate charges and earlier guilty pleas.

The trial stage

As will already be appreciated, there are many reasons criminal offences do not all result in an offender being brought before the courts. Even when a case is so brought, the public image of what then happens is likely to be far removed from the typical case. The impression given in the news media or in drama series is that prosecutions result in full-scale trials in the Crown Court. The reality is quite different. The vast bulk of criminal trials are disposed of in the magistrates' court, and the vast bulk of them—both in the Crown Court and in the magistrates' court—are determined on the basis of a plea of guilty. The trial is a statistical rarity.

All prosecutions start in the magistrates' court. Whether they finish there depends on how the case is classified. (For classification of criminal cases *see Box 5.7*.) The

---

Box 5.7 Classification of criminal cases

There are four potential classes of criminal case.

1. Offences triable only on indictment. These are the most serious cases, such as murder, manslaughter and rape. If the defendant pleads not guilty, these cases must be tried in the Crown Court, before a jury.

2. Offences triable summarily. These are all offences created by statute, where the statute provides that they are summary offences. These cases must be determined by magistrates, and there is thus no right to trial by jury. There have been some attempts at reclassifying certain offences as summary only, in particular, small thefts; but political arguments about 'taking away rights to a jury trial' have made change difficult.

3. Offences triable either way. These are offences, also created by statute, where the Act provides that they may be dealt with either summarily or on indictment. In such cases, the accused currently chooses how he wishes to be tried, before magistrates or before a jury. Opting for trial in the Crown Court exposes the accused to the prospect of more serious sentences, as the Crown Court has wider powers of sentence than the magistrates' courts, though the latter can commit a case to the Crown Court where they think their powers of sentence are inadequate. (See further below.)

4. Summary cases triable on indictment. In specific cases an accused may have a charge that he has committed a summary offence 'tacked on' to a charge that he has committed an indictable offence. These can now both be dealt with in the same trial in the Crown Court.[27]

---

[27] Criminal Justice Act 1988 s. 40; see also s. 41.

most serious cases—indictable offences—are forwarded ('committed') to the Crown Court for disposal. The vast majority of criminal cases—summary cases—are disposed of in the magistrates' court. Cases which are triable either way, i.e. either summarily or on indictment, are determined in the appropriate court, once a decision on the classification of the case has been made.

The functions of the courts

Criminal trial courts have two principal functions:

- dealing with the case, which includes determining guilt where the defendant has pleaded not guilty, as well as deciding on the correct sentence; and
- ensuring that, so far as possible, the trial is fair.

They may also have to deal with other procedural questions, such as whether or not to grant bail or remand a person in custody. (See above *Box 5.4.*)

Dealing with the case

In cases where an accused person has pleaded not guilty, the court has to hear the evidence, in the light of that evidence reach findings of fact, in the light of those findings determine whether the accused person is or is not guilty of the alleged crime, and, if guilty, pass an appropriate sentence. In the magistrates' courts all these functions are performed by the magistrates. In the Crown Court, the findings of fact and thus the question of guilt are determined by the jury. However, before the jury starts their work, they are provided with a 'summing-up' of the case by the trial judge, an exercise designed to help the jury focus on the issues they have to decide. If a conviction results, then, subject to further pleas in mitigation and reports on the accused from other agencies such as the probation service, sentence is passed by the presiding judge.

Although many think that the function of the court is to determine the truth about the events that have led to a person appearing in court, in practice the function of the trial is rather different. The prosecution must prove 'beyond reasonable doubt' that the accused committed the offence alleged. The function of the defence, therefore, is to throw sufficient doubt on what the prosecution is alleging so that the burden of proof is not established. If the burden of proof is not established, the defendant must be acquitted.

In cases where the defendant pleads guilty, the only issue for the court, again subject to pleas in mitigation made on behalf of the accused and other reports, e.g. from social workers or probation officers, is to determine sentence.

Ensuring the fairness of the trial

Fairness is at the heart of the 'due process' model of criminal justice. A great deal of the law of criminal procedure and evidence is designed to ensure that the accused gets a fair trial. It is, however, in this context that many of the tensions between the 'due process' model and the 'crime control' model may be seen. A number of initiatives have been taken in recent years which have shifted the balance from the former to the latter. The question is whether the balance has now gone too far. The full detail of the relevant law is beyond the scope of this book. However two examples will be briefly considered: evidence and disclosure.

Evidence. The law on criminal evidence is designed to ensure that only relevant material is put before the court and to prevent material being put before the court which would be unfairly prejudicial to the defendant. Among the rules which exclude evidence in a criminal trial are:

- *the rule against hearsay evidence.* In general, only evidence given by witnesses in court is admitted. What others said to a witness cannot be admitted, as the person who made the statement cannot be challenged (cross-examined) about its veracity;

- *the rule preventing the giving of information about a person's past record.* In general, it is not permitted to tell the court about the person's history, particularly criminal record, unless the accused wishes to challenge the veracity of a prosecution witness, say a policeman.

- *the rule relating to 'similar fact' evidence.* The fact that a person may have been involved in some other activity similar to the events in the present case is not usually admitted, since it is seen as not directly related to what the prosecution has to prove in the instant case.

Many of these rules are not absolute, and judges and magistrates have to exercise judgement as to whether the exceptions to the rule operate in the particular case so as to allow evidence that would otherwise not be admissible to be admitted.

The present Government is currently planning to introduce changes to some of these rules of evidence. (For more detail, *see below Box 5.11.*) In particular it is proposed that, in cases where the trial judge thinks it relevant to the case being heard, evidence of previous misconduct will be able to be put before a jury. This proposal, which derives in part from a detailed study of the issue by the Law Commission, is extremely controversial. Lawyers' organizations and civil liberty groups argue that a person should be tried only for the crime for which he has been prosecuted and that to introduce evidence of previous misconduct will undermine the presumption that a person should be regarded as innocent until proved guilty. Those in favour of the proposal argue that such evidence will not be admitted generally, but only where it is relevant to the case in question.[28]

In some circumstances, there are precise rules of law which relate to the admissibility of evidence. For example, where it is proposed to rely on a confession, section 76 of PACE requires the prosecution to demonstrate beyond reasonable doubt that the confession was not made by oppression of the person who made it, or as a result of

---

[28] E.g., the fact that X had convictions for robbery would not be admitted if X was being prosecuted for rape; however evidence that X had been found guilty of other charges of serious assault against women would be.

inducements made to the person giving it which might render the confession unreliable.

Section 78 of PACE also gives the judge/magistrate a general discretion to exclude evidence that would otherwise be admissible and relevant 'where the admission of the evidence would have such an adverse effect on the fairness of the proceedings that the court ought not to admit it'. Evidence obtained by the police in breach of the rules relating to questioning and interrogation can fall into this category.

Disclosure. A separate issue relates to the question of what evidence should be disclosed by the prosecution to the defendant and vice versa. (See *Box 5.8.*) One of the

---

Box 5.8 Disclosure of evidence

The Royal Commission on Criminal Justice was appointed in 1991 against a background of cases where there had been clear miscarriages of justice: the 'Guildford four', the 'Maguire seven', the 'Birmingham six' and the Judith Ward cases are amongst the best known. In addition, the courts in a number of cases had been developing the (then) common law relating to disclosure. The result had been to place increased responsibility to disclose on the police. This provided an opportunity to the defence to mount fishing expeditions to find out what information the police had. The Royal Commission sought to strike a balance between the duties of the prosecution and the rights of the defence. The Royal Commission proposed that there should be a new scheme for disclosure enshrined in statute, accompanied by a Code of Practice or a more detailed statutory instrument.

In May 1995, the then Government published a consultation paper, which led to the Criminal Investigations and Procedure Act 1996, which provides for the following scheme:

a. The investigator (usually the police but not necessarily) is under a duty to preserve material gathered during the investigation and make available to the prosecutor material falling into defined key categories, plus a list of other material which has been acquired;

b. The prosecutor is under a duty to serve on the defence the material on which the prosecutor intends to rely to found her case;

c. The prosecutor is under a duty also to disclose certain material on which the prosecution does not intend to rely, which falls into specified categories or which would otherwise undermine the prosecutor's case. The Act also provides that a list of non-sensitive unused material must also be provided. This is known as the 'primary prosecution disclosure';

d. The defence has to provide sufficient particulars of its case to identify the issues in dispute. Failure to disclose can be the subject of (adverse) comment during the trial. The Act makes this procedure mandatory in trials on indictment, voluntary in summary trials. This is known as 'defence disclosure'.

e. The prosecutor is then required to disclose any additional unused material which would assist the particular line of argument disclosed by the defence—known as the 'secondary prosecution disclosure'.

Any disputes about disclosure are to be resolved by the court in a pre-trial hearing.

The main features of the process are: (i) that it is statute based; (ii) that it puts the responsibility on the prosecution to decide what should be disclosed; (iii) that it requires, for the first time, that the defence should make disclosure of its case before the start of the trial.

The accompanying *Code of Practice* (made under the authority of Part 2 of the Act) requires the appointment, in any criminal investigation, of an 'officer in charge', plus a separate 'disclosure officer' who will be responsible for the administration of the investigation, including the operation of the disclosure scheme. The 'investigator'—the police or other officer carrying out the investigation—is made responsible for retaining material gathered or generated by the inquiry. The disclosure officer prepares the schedule of unused material, together with a list of any sensitive material (e.g. relating to national security or information given in confidence). The disclosure officer must send these schedules to the prosecutor, accompanied by copies of any material relating to the unreliability of witnesses or confessions or containing any explanation by the accused for the offence. Once the defence statement is filed, the disclosure officer is to look at all the files again and draw attention to any which may assist the defence. He must then certify to the prosecutor that, to the best of his knowledge and belief, the duties imposed by the Code have been complied with.

In a recent decision by the European Court of Human Rights, it was held that where the prosecution withheld evidence because it was claimed to be immune from disclosure on the grounds of public interest, the failure to put it before a trial judge so as to permit him to rule on the question of disclosure deprived an accused person of the right to a fair trial.[29]

It will be realized that the effectiveness of these arrangements depends to a large extent on the willingness of the particular individuals, on both the investigation and prosecution sides, to operate the scheme in accordance with the statutory provisions and code of guidance. A recent report by the Crown Prosecution Service Inspectorate[30] gives a disturbing account of routine failures to follow the rules.

most significant causes of serious miscarriages of justice arises when the prosecution withholds evidence which it has acquired during the process of its investigation but which weakens the case which the prosecution is seeking to build against the accused. This was a central issue considered by the Royal Commission on Criminal Justice which reported in 1993. As a result of, though not fully accepting, its recommendations, the former Conservative Government introduced a new legal regime relating to

[29] *Rowe and Davis v. United Kingdom, The Times,* 1 March 2000.
[30] Crown Prosecution Service Inspectorate, *Report on the Thematic Review of the Disclosure of Unused Material* (London, CPS, 2000).

disclosure, contained in Parts I and II of the Criminal Procedure and Investigations Act 1996. Disputes about whether or not documents should be disclosed are also resolved by the court at a pre-trial hearing.

Magistrates' courts[31]

Magistrates' courts have a long history. They have a distinct character in that, although subject to nationally determined guidelines, they currently operate at a local level. They also depend very heavily on volunteer/lay persons to determine decisions. Much of the claim to legitimacy for the magistrates is that benches are composed of persons who come from the community affected by the alleged criminal activity.[32] (For types of magistrates' courts *see Box 5.9*.)

Box 5.9 Types of magistrates' courts

There are two distinct types of magistrates' courts which operate in England and Wales: the *lay justices'* courts, and the *district judge* (formerly *stipendiary*) *magistrates'*[33] courts. Lay justices' courts are made up of (usually) three lay persons (i.e. persons with no specific legal qualifications), known as Justices of the Peace (JPs), who sit and determine criminal cases, with legal advice on their powers given to them by the *Justices' Clerk*, a specially appointed official who is legally qualified. JPs provide their services on a voluntary basis; they receive expenses, for example for travel and subsistence, and, where appropriate, can claim a 'loss of earnings' allowance. Apart from that, however, they are unpaid. By far the majority of magistrates' courts are lay justices' courts.

District judge magistrates' courts are run by district judges, who are qualified lawyers and sit on their own, rather than in panels of three. They used to sit only in those areas of the country designated by the government as appropriate for such courts. As the result of a change in the law, they are now able to sit in any magistrates' court in the country, thus giving court managers greater flexibility in the use of this source of judicial manpower.[34]

Functions

All criminal trials start in the magistrates' courts. In carrying out their judicial function, there are two distinct types of procedure which they control: *committal proceedings* and *summary trials*. In addition they have responsibility for enforcing non-custodial penalties, especially fines.

---

[31] For an introduction to the principles on which magistrates' courts are managed, and on proposals to change that system, see above Chapter 4 pp. 72. The magistrates' court also has responsibilities in certain family matters. These are considered below in Chapter 7.

[32] An independent research report on magistrates was published by the Home Office in December 2000. See Morgan, R., and Russell, N., *The Judiciary in the Magistrates' Courts* (London, Home Office, 2000).

[33] Stipendiary magistrates were renamed District Judges (Magistrates' Courts) by the Access to Justice Act 1999, s. 78.

[34] Access to Justice Act 1999, s. 78 and Sch. 11.

Committal proceedings

These take place where the nature of the case is such that it has to be tried in the Crown Court, either because it must be tried on indictment or the decision has been made, in the case of an offence triable either way, that the trial should be on indictment. The function of committal proceedings is to ensure that the magistrates are satisfied that there is a case for the defendant to answer. It used to be the case that committal proceedings were fully aired in the press and other mass media; but this led to the criticism that such publicity made it difficult to find members of a jury who had not heard about the case. The law was therefore changed; publicity to committal proceedings can be given only where the defendant permits this. It is only very rarely that magistrates find there is no case to answer.

In 2001, just over 80,000 cases were committed to the Crown Court for trial (down from over 91,000 in 1997). Much of this decrease is attributable to a change in procedure whereby accused persons are required to enter a plea—guilty or not guilty—in the magistrates' court.[35] Thus those who would have been sent to the Crown Court for trial and who would then have pleaded guilty were no longer committed for trial to the Crown Court but they are committed for sentence. (On sentencing generally, see further below.)

Summary trials

All other prosecutions are dealt with summarily, that is to say by the magistrates themselves. In 2000 some 1.9 million defendants were proceeded against in the magistrates' courts. The vast majority of prosecutions are dealt with in this way. And the vast majority of these cases (82 per cent) are determined by a plea of guilty, rather than following a trial. Nearly 30 per cent of cases where there was a trial resulted in the case being dismissed.[36]

Committals for sentence

In all cases where guilt is established, whether or not there is a trial, the magistrates have to impose a penalty. The powers of magistrates to impose sentences are strictly limited. However they can commit a case to the Crown Court where they think that their powers of sentence are inadequate. The number of cases referred to the Crown Court has increased sharply in recent years, rising from around 14,800 cases in 1997, to nearly 26,000 in 2001. The reason for this large jump is the procedural change noted above which requires the accused person to indicate how he will plead (guilty or not guilty) before any decision as to which court should hear the case is made.

[35] Criminal Procedures and Investigations Act 1996, s. 49, introducing the Magistrates' Court Act 1980, s. 17A

[36] *Criminal Statistics, 2000* (London, The Stationery Office, 2001).

Fine enforcement

In many cases where the penalty imposed is a fine, the magistrates have to follow this up with enforcement proceedings.

Youth court

When dealing with young offenders, the magistrates' court is technically known as the *youth court.* (See *Box 5.10.*)

Box 5.10 Youth justice

A vast amount of criminal activity is carried out by people, mainly men, at a relatively early age. 'Juvenile delinquency' and measures to try to deal with it—not, it has to be said, with conspicuous success—have been on the policy agendas of governments for many years. There have been major tensions between the desire to prevent juvenile crime and deal with those young persons found guilty of criminal activity, and the desire not to blight young lives unnecessarily by giving them criminal records which may prevent them entering the job market or otherwise disadvantage them.

There have also been fierce debates about where the responsibility for youth crime should lie—with individual offenders, with their parent(s), or with the wider society which is said to fail to provide the educational and employment opportunities that might make them more productive members of society.

The issue was reviewed by government in 1997, in the White Paper *No More Excuses.*[37] This led to two Acts, the Crime and Disorder Act 1998 and the Youth Justice and Criminal Evidence Act 1999. These contain a number of new initiatives which have been put in place, not only to process young offenders (those under the age of 18) through the criminal justice system more quickly, but also to try to demonstrate to them the effect their actions have had on the lives of others.

The Crime and Disorder Act 1998, for example, saw the creation of *youth offending teams*—multi-disciplinary agencies brought together at the local level to devise effective programmes to prevent offending and re-offending by young people. Their work is kept under review nationally by a new board, the *Youth Justice Board.* The Board is also responsible for funding offending prevention schemes.

In addition, the 1998 Act replaced the non-statutory policy whereby police could merely decide to caution a young offender, with a new statutory 'final warning' scheme. The Act provides that once an offender has received this, any further offence will lead to criminal proceedings in court.

When dealing with young offenders, magistrates' courts are technically known as *youth courts.* When sitting as a youth court, magistrates are subject to special procedural rules designed to ensure that cases are dealt with as speedily as possible. Magistrates were also given a special range of sentencing options under the Act of 1998.

---

[37] (Cm 3809) (London, The Stationery Office, 1997).

These include powers to make a *reparation order*,[38] an *action plan order*,[39] a *child safety order*,[40] and a *parenting order*.[41]

For the most serious cases, a new sentence, authorized by the Act of 1998, and introduced from April 2000—the *detention and training order*—provides for a single custodial sentence for all 10–17-year-olds.[42]

In addition, as a result of the Youth Justice and Criminal Evidence Act 1999, magistrates may refer first-time offenders to a *youth offender panel*.[43] This is intended to work with the young offender to establish a programme of behaviour for the young offender to follow. The programme is explicitly based on the theory of 'restorative justice', to ensure that the offender takes responsibility for the consequences of his offending behaviour; makes restoration to the victim; and achieves re-integration into the law-abiding community. Whether these objectives will be achieved is, as yet, too early to determine. It must also be questioned whether the theory of restorative justice is the only theory behind the new programme; other 'justice models'—including the 'crime control' and the 'bureaucratic'—appear to be in play as well.

The Home Office has recently published a *Good Practice Guide for Youth Courts*.[44] This evolved from an experiment in two courts which sought to achieve four key objectives:

- effective engagement with defendants and their parents to probe the reasons for offending and to encourage plans to change behaviour;

- changing courtroom layouts to facilitate better communication;

- making the court process more open by lifting reporting restrictions where appropriate, and exercising discretion to allow others such as victims to attend court;

- giving feedback to sentencers on the outcome of sentences.

The new guide is designed to encourage youth courts to respond positively to such initiatives to counter public perceptions that they were not perceived as delivering effective justice.

---

[38] E.g., requiring the offender to write a letter of apology to a victim; or to clean up graffiti or repair criminal damage.

[39] A three-month programme of community-based intervention combining punishment, rehabilitation and reparation, designed to address specific causes of offending.

[40] Also known as a curfew order, to protect children under the age of 10 from the risk of involvement in crime. This may involve requiring the child to be at home at particular times or to stay away from certain people or places. The Government is currently considering raising the age limit to 16.

[41] Which could require parents to attend counselling and guidance sessions, and to ensure their children attend school.

[42] It replaces the sentences of a *secure training order* and *detention in a young offenders' institution*.

[43] The power to refer is available only in the youth court. A young offender tried in the Crown Court may, however, on conviction be referred to the youth court for sentence in a case where the trial judge regards that as appropriate.

[44] *The Youth Court: Changing the Culture of the Youth Court* (London, Home Office, 2001).

The Crown Court

Jurisdiction and organization

The Crown Court is where the most serious criminal cases—cases tried on indictment—are disposed of. The Crown Court is divided into three tiers located in about ninety centres around the country. These centres are further grouped into six circuits.[45]

- First-tier courts are those in which High Court judges, circuit judges and recorders sit. They have higher levels of security to deal with the most difficult prisoners. The full range of criminal work, together with High Court civil work (see Chapter 8), is dealt with in these courts.

- Second-tier courts are the same, though no civil work is conducted in them.

- Third-tier courts are presided over only by circuit judges or recorders.

The offences dealt with in the Crown Court are themselves divided into four classes, under directions given by the Lord Chief Justice.[46] The aim is that the most serious offences are dealt with by the most senior judges. Distribution of business is the responsibility of the presiding judges—judges specially nominated in each circuit to have responsibility for the efficient running of trial lists.

The Crown Court also has powers to sentence persons convicted in the magistrates' court where the magistrates have decided that their own powers of sentencing are inadequate. In addition, the Crown Court hears appeals from decisions of the magistrates' court.

Workload

Committals for trial. According to the latest *Judicial Statistics,* the Crown Court had just over 80,500 cases committed to it in 2001, a sharp increase on the previous year's figure of 71,000. 75,500 cases were dealt with in 2001, of which just under 28,400 followed a plea of not guilty—i.e. just under 40 per cent. A considerable number of trials were 'cracked trials', i.e. cases originally listed for trial, but where the accused changed his plea from not guilty to guilty, very often on the day of the trial. There were nearly 18,000 cracked trials in 2001.

Of those pleading not guilty to all charges, 66 per cent were acquitted. This represents just over 20 per cent of the total number of defendants dealt with by the Crown Court during the year. Of these, only about a third were acquitted as the result of a verdict of not guilty by the jury; the remaining two-thirds were either discharged by the judge or acquitted on the direction of the judge.

Of those convicted after pleading not guilty 23 per cent were convicted on the basis

---

[45] Midland and Oxford; North Eastern; Northern; South Eastern; Wales and Chester; and Western. The 'Old Bailey' is the name given to the Central Criminal Court in London, a Crown Court in the South Eastern Circuit.

[46] These are set out in *Judicial Statistics 2001* (Cm 5551) (London, The Stationery Office, 2002).

of a majority verdict; the rest were convicted by the unanimous decision of the jury.

Committals for sentence. Around 26,000 committals for sentence were made; just about the same number of cases were dealt with.

Appeals. Nearly 12,500 appeals from magistrates' courts were made, and a similar number were dealt with. Of these, roughly a quarter were allowed, and a similar percentage of cases resulted in a variation of the sentence.

Hearing times. The average hearing times were:

- For not guilty pleas, 2.4 hours;
- For guilty pleas, 1.0 hours;
- For sentence, 0.8 hours;
- For appeals, 0.9 hours.

Comment

- The most obvious point is that, as in the magistrates' courts, full-scale trials following a plea of not guilty are a statistical rarity.
- A significant percentage of those who plead not guilty are ultimately acquitted, though far more are on the direction of the judge rather than by a jury verdict.
- The newspapers may give the impression that cases in the Crown Court take significant amounts of time, particularly where there is a full trial. Although trials take longer than other forms of disposal, on average they last only two and a half hours.
- The 'success rate' in appeals could be seen as raising some questions about the quality of magistrates' decisions, though the total number of appeals is a tiny proportion of the total number of cases dealt with by the magistrates.

Issues in the criminal justice trial system

Charge and plea bargaining

The high level of guilty pleas in both the magistrates' and Crown courts may suggest that the police and prosecution allow only the strongest cases to come before a court. But it may nonetheless seem surprising that in a system where the theory is that all are innocent until proved guilty so few accused actually take advantage of the due process model of criminal justice and submit the evidence presented by the prosecution for testing before either the magistrates or a jury.

Of course there will be cases where the evidence is so overwhelming that a guilty plea is the only sensible option for the accused. But in less clear-cut cases, at least part of the answer to this puzzle arises from the fact that those within the criminal justice system work quite hard, through various forms of bargaining, to ensure that accused persons plead guilty. This saves considerable amounts of court time (as the statistics for average hearing times set out above clearly show) and thus expense and other resources. There are various practices which may occur to assist the accused in deciding what plea to enter.

First, there may be a negotiation between the prosecutor and the defence about the charge to be proceeded with before the courts. If the accused is willing or can be persuaded to plead guilty to a charge which carries a less severe penalty, the prosecution may then decide not to pursue an alternative charge which could arise from the same factual situation, which might attract a more severe penalty.

Secondly, there may be an indication that if a plea of guilty is entered, then, in passing sentence, the judge may reduce the sentence he might otherwise have imposed. Direct negotiations between defence lawyers and judges on sentence, commonplace in the USA, do not take place here. Further, the decision in *R v. Turner*[47] makes it clear that judges may not indicate the sentence they are planning to impose, nor indicate how that sentence might change were the defendant to plead guilty. However, at the end of a hearing, the Criminal Justice and Public Order Act 1994, section 48(2), requires a judge to give reasons for any reduction in the sentence from what would normally be expected for the offence in question taking normal sentencing guidelines into account. It is therefore known that in practice judges allow a discount of between 25 and 33 per cent in cases where the defendant pleads guilty.

The formal legal position on these practices is that undue pressure must not be put on defendants to enter any particular plea, as this may lead the innocent to plead guilty to a crime they did not commit. In other words, such practices do not fit with the due process model of the criminal justice system. The reality is, however, that justice is frequently negotiated, a practice justified by the added efficiency that it brings to the system, thus fitting the crime control model. The extent to which such practices should be condoned is the subject of considerable debate in the criminal justice literature.

Jury trial

A second issue of considerable current importance relates to the use of juries to determine the facts in Crown Court trials. There are three issues which should be considered separately: are juries competent to decide cases? to what extent should the accused be entitled to choose trial by jury in those cases where a choice is open to them? should the classification of indictable offences (for which the right to trial by jury arises automatically) be altered?

The competence of juries. Jury trial is perceived by many as one of the great strengths of the English criminal justice system. There is an enormous literature on the jury, asserting their importance as a defender of civil liberty and a bulwark against oppression by the state. Indeed, the use of juries may be said to legitimate decision-taking in the criminal justice system by enabling decisions to be taken by ordinary lay people. This reinforces the independence of the judicial system in this context and thus

---

[47] [1970] 2 QB 321.

fits with the constitutional separation of the courts from other decision-making bodies.

There have certainly been historically significant, if rare, cases where juries appear, despite the weight of evidence, to have acted on their conscience to protect civil liberty by finding persons not guilty of crimes which may be said to have significant political overtones. The example of the acquittal of Clive Ponting is often cited. Ponting was a former civil servant, accused of offences under the Official Secrets Act 1911 after he had passed to a Member of Parliament confidential documents relating to the sinking of an Argentinian battleship during the Falklands War in 1982. Despite a ruling from the judge that Ponting had no authorization to pass the documents on, and that there was no other lawful justification for his action, the jury acquitted him. It was assumed that the jury had decided that the moral arguments in favour of his doing what he did outweighed the legal arguments that what he did was unlawful.

Important changes to the constitution and functions of juries have been made over the years. Thus the range of persons entitled to sit as jurors is now significantly wider than it was before 1972, when occupation of a house with a prescribed rateable value was one of the criteria for selection.[48] This has led to profound changes in jury composition, certainly in terms of their class composition. Since 1981, selection for jury service has been by random selection using a computer. Perhaps the most significant change occurred in 1967 when the ability of juries to determine cases on the basis of majority verdicts was introduced.[49]

Despite the arguments in favour of jury trial, which have considerable force, little is actually known about how juries function. Direct research into the work of the jury has never been permitted. The only research currently available is through the use of 'surrogate' juries dealing with hypothetical situations.

There have been a number of suggestions that in particular types of case—lengthy and complex fraud trials are given as the prime candidates—juries as traditionally constituted are not best suited to determining facts. This has led to alternative proposals being adopted, for example judges sitting with a panel of lay assessors, or such cases being heard by a panel of judges rather than just a single judge. (There are significant dangers in allowing facts to be found from disputed evidence by a single adjudicator.)

Although some believe that juries are too ready to acquit defendants, there are actually no serious proposals that jury trial should be abolished. Such a step would be seen as politically unacceptable, and as too great a move from the due process model to the crime control model of criminal justice. This is one of the issues which is being raised again in the Government's latest proposals for the reform of the criminal justice system.

Choice of mode of trial. A quite distinct issue, though a matter of considerable

---

[48] Changes were made in the Criminal Justice Act 1972.

[49] See now the Juries Act 1974, s. 17. Majority verdicts are subject to an important *Practice Direction* [1967] 1 WLR 1198, and [1970] 1 WLR 916 which regulates their use. Current data on the use of majority verdicts are given in the text above.

controversy, is the question of who should have the right to choose jury trial in those cases which are triable either way. The present Government originally proposed, following the Royal Commission on Criminal Procedure's report in 1993, that the decision should be made by the magistrates before whom all such cases initially come, and not left to the discretion of the accused. Powerful voices dissented, arguing that such a change would involve a fundamental issue of principle which, once conceded, would further undermine the due process model of criminal justice. It looks as though the Government has decided not to pursue this issue having tried twice in the last few years to get such a proposal through Parliament.

Should the classification of indictable offences be altered? There is a quite distinct argument that the present classification of offences allows some to be tried by juries in situations where this does not seem warranted by the seriousness of the offence. There have been examples of this happening in recent years.[50] There have been other attempts to, for example, reclassify certain types of minor theft as summary offences, thereby denying those accused of them the right to trial by jury. Proposals for change are always countered by the 'thin end of the wedge' argument, that any step in this direction will encourage governments to take further steps in the same direction, thereby reducing the scope of jury trial still further. Nevertheless the latest suggestion from the Government is that the jurisdictional limits of the magistrates' courts should be raised, so that they would be able to deal with a number of slightly more serious offences which currently have to go to the Crown Court for trial or sentencing.

Representation

The Criminal Defender System is discussed below, Chapter 10, p. 263.

Criminal Justice Bill 2002

The Criminal Justice Bill contains a number of very important changes to the rules relating to the criminal trial process. They go to the heart of the present Government's legislative programme, but will generate extensive opposition. The fate of the proposals (summarized in *Box 5.11*) is far from certain at the time of writing.

Sentencing (*see Diagram 5.3*)

In the same way that the criminal justice system as a whole may be seen to depend on a variety of conflicting social theories, so too is sentencing policy and practice based on a variety of conflicting theories. The literature on theories of sentencing is extensive. Ashworth has classified the approaches under five main headings:

- desert (retributive) theories;
- deterrence theories;
- rehabilitative theories;

---

[50] The Criminal Justice Act 1988 reclassified a number of motoring offences as summary only.

Box 5.11 Criminal Justice Bill 2002: proposals relating to criminal trials

1 Disclosure

The Criminal Justice Bill includes a number of amendments to the current provisions which govern the prosecution's disclosure of unused material to the defence before the trial and defence disclosure requirements. These include:

- replacing the existing two-stage disclosure test with an objective single test for the disclosure of unused material, requiring the prosecution to disclose to the defence unused material that has not previously been disclosed and which may be considered reasonably capable of undermining the prosecution case or of assisting the accused;

- increasing the amount of detail that an accused will be required to provide in his/her defence statement which he/she is required to serve before trial, setting out the nature of his/her defence;

- requiring the judge to warn the accused about failures to comply with the defence statement requirement;

- giving the court power to order an accused to give a defence statement to his/her co-accused, with the aim of placing all parties on an equal footing; and

- giving the court power to direct that the jury be given a copy of the defence statement and, if necessary, to direct that the statement be edited to exclude any inadmissible evidence.

The proposed provisions would also require an accused, in advance of the trial, to give the court and the prosecutor a notice giving details of witnesses that he intends to call to give evidence at the trial and disclose details of experts consulted but whom it is not intended to call to give evidence.

2 Evidence of bad character

The proposed reforms would enable judges to let juries hear about a defendant's previous convictions and other misconduct where relevant to the case. The court will be able to exclude evidence of previous misconduct if it thinks that the jury will give it disproportionate weight (in other words, if the relevance of the evidence to the case is outweighed by any prejudicial effect). The starting point will, however, be that relevant evidence is admissible.

3 Reported evidence (hearsay)

The proposals would enable witness statements to be used as evidence, subject to a number of safeguards, where the witness is identified but unavailable to testify or the statement is contained in a business document. The court would have a further discretion to admit hearsay evidence where it would not be contrary to the interests of justice for it to be used. In addition, witnesses' previous statements would become more widely admissible at trial. This will enable witnesses to refer to their statement whilst giving evidence in court and permit greater use of video recorded statements for crucial evidence in serious cases.

4 Double jeopardy—retrial for serious offences

The proposed provisions include an exception to the double jeopardy rule for a defined list of very serious offences where new evidence emerges that strongly indicates that an acquitted person is in fact guilty of that offence, and it is right in all the circumstances of the case for that person to be retried. A number of safeguards would be included in the legislation to guard against the possible harassment of acquitted persons. The DPP's consent would be needed before a suspect could be re-investigated and before an application could be made to the Court of Appeal to quash the acquittal. It would be possible to make only one application for an acquittal to be quashed, so there would be no prospect of repeated re-trials.

5 Judge-alone trials

The proposed legislation would allow trial by judge alone in the following circumstances:

- where the defendant has asked for it, subject to the consent of the court;

- in cases involving complex or lengthy financial and commercial arrangements;

- where there is a serious risk of jury intimidation.

The defendant would be able to appeal against a decision to try a case by judge alone, or against a refusal by the court to grant his request for judge-alone trial.

Where a trial is conducted or continued without a jury, and the defendant is convicted, the judge will be required to give a reasoned verdict.

6 Jury service

The Bill includes provisions to abolish the categories of ineligibility (with the exception of mentally disordered persons and certain groups of convicted persons) for, and excusal as of right from, jury service. This means that certain groups of people who currently must not, or need not, do jury service would, when these provisions are enacted, be required to do it unless they can show good reason not to.

7 Live links

Legislation would enable witnesses to give evidence using TV links from remote locations if this would be more efficient or effective.

8 Prosecution appeals

Provisions in the Bill would introduce an interlocutory prosecution right of appeal against those rulings by a Crown Court judge that have the effect of terminating the trial early before the jury has considered the evidence.

- incapacitative theories; and

- restorative (reparative) theories.

Desert or retributive theories take as their focus the idea that punishment is a natural or appropriate response to crime, at least as long as it is proportionate to the crime committed. It is assumed that a person who commits a crime deserves to be

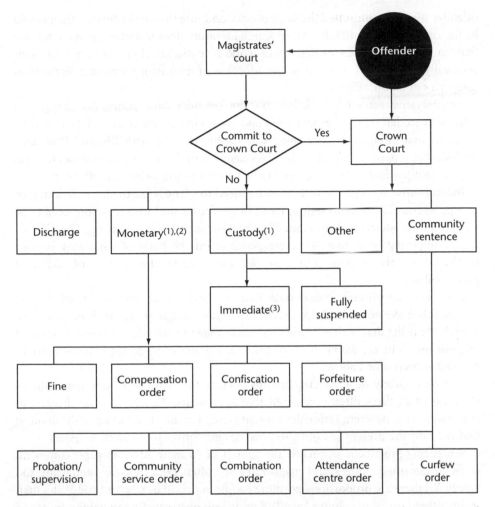

(1) Magistrates' courts and the Crown Court differ in their powers to award monetary and custodial penalties.
(2) May either be the sole penalty or in association with another disposal.
(3) Includes detention in a young offenders' institution and unsuspended imprisonment.

Diagram 5.3 The sentencing process

punished; and that society is entitled to see that retribution is exacted from the offender. The problem of determining whether sentences are in fact proportional to the offence is, of course, a matter on which there can be great room for debate—and often is when the press criticize judges for apparently light (occasionally over-harsh) sentencing.

Deterrence theories offer a slightly different view. Here the perspective is on deterring future offending behaviour by punishing the offender currently before the authorities. Such a theory would then justify harsher penalties being imposed on an offender who has committed the same offence on more than one occasion than would be the case for a first offender. The research literature does not offer great confidence that, in practice, policies of deterrence work. Nonetheless they are very important politically, and indeed have led to the adoption of mandatory sentences for certain categories of repeat offenders.

Rehabilitative sentencing focuses on the offender and efforts to change his behaviour so that he can become a full and productive member of society. It may be assumed that offenders are in some way unable to cope with life and thus need professional support to change. It involves elements of diagnosis and treatment; it also implies that particular decisions need to be tailored to the individual offender.

Incapacitative sentencing focuses on the need to identify particular individuals or groups who are likely to do serious harm in the future, and who therefore need to be removed from society ('incapacitated') to prevent such harm occurring. The difficulties of imposing what may be severe penalties on the basis of what may happen in the future are obvious, but arise, for example, in the context of convicted paedophiles.

Restorative approaches concentrate more on the victim and the need for the offender to make amends to the victim. Restorative justice shares with rehabilitative models the belief that such outcomes will encourage the offender to change his way of life, but the focus on the victim is distinctive. The use of these approaches in youth justice has been noted above.

The wide variety of sentencing options open to the criminal courts demonstrates elements of all these often very conflicting approaches. As with general theories of criminal justice, different rationales for sentencing practice need to be understood so that not only the present law but also possible alternatives to it can be assessed.[51]

Sentencing practice is frequently the subject of (usually adverse) press comment, often ill-informed. Judges and magistrates are often criticized for sentencing too lightly. Yet there are proportionately more people in prison in England and Wales than in any other European country, save Turkey. Prison overcrowding remains a source of very considerable tension in the criminal justice system, with judges being told both to impose severe sentences where necessary and not to send people to prison unless absolutely essential.

The range of penalties has grown in recent years. In particular new forms of 'community sentence', in which the offender is obliged to undertake some form of reparative work in the community and for the victim, have been introduced. (For some basic facts on current sentencing outcomes *see Box 5.12*.)

The present Government commissioned a major review of sentencing which was published in 2001. Many of the recommendations made in it are now incorporated in the provisions of the Criminal Justice Bill 2002. As before, the summary of the main

---

[51] The powers of the courts to sentence offenders were consolidated in the Powers of Criminal Courts (Sentencing) Act 2000; they have already undergone further revision and will undergo more change once the Criminal Justice Bill 2002 becomes law.

Box 5.12 Sentencing: some basic facts[52]

1,423,700 offenders were found guilty in 2000 of indictable and summary offences.

In magistrates' courts 31 per cent of those sentenced summarily for the more serious triable-either-way offences were fined, 31 per cent given a community sentence, 20 per cent sentenced to a conditional or absolute discharge, and 10 per cent to immediate custody. The rest were otherwise dealt with.

In the Crown Court, 64 per cent of those sentenced for indictable offences were sentenced to immediate custody, 26 per cent to a community sentence, 2 per cent were fined, and 3 per cent received an absolute or conditional discharge.

Use of the fine following conviction for indictable offences in the magistrates' courts fell to 31 per cent (down from 43 per cent in 1992).

Use of community sentences following conviction in the magistrates' court increased to 155,500 (31 per cent); in the Crown Court such sentences were used in about 26 per cent of cases.

106,000 persons were sentenced to immediate custody in 2002, the highest figure since 1928.

issues (*see Box 5.13*) comes with the health warning that their precise outcome cannot at the time of writing be known.

The post-trial stages

Appeals[53]

Those convicted in magistrates' courts can appeal to the Crown Court, either against conviction or against sentence. Similarly appeals from the Crown Court can be made to the Court of Appeal (Criminal Division).

In 2001, there were nearly 12,600 appeals from the magistrates' courts to the Crown Court. Of these, 44 per cent were allowed.

The Court of Appeal dealt with 7,449 applications for leave to appeal, of which 5,497 were against the sentence imposed. About 2,000 of these applications were granted. Of the appeals actually determined by the full Court of Appeal, 30 per cent of appeals against conviction were allowed, and 66 per cent of appeals against sentence were allowed.

---

[52] Data from *Criminal Statistics 2000* (London: The Stationery Office, 2002).

[53] Data from Home Office Statistical Bulletin 3/98, reported in Barclay, G. C., and Tavares, C. (eds.), *Information on the Criminal Justice System in England and Wales* (London, Home Office, Research, Development and Statistics Directorate, October 1999).

Box 5.13 Criminal Justice Bill 2002: sentencing

Purposes and principles of sentencing. The Bill would set in statute the purposes of sentencing to protect the public, act as punishment, reduce crime (including to deter, incapacitate, reform and rehabilitate) and promote reparation. It would also make explicit the principles that should determine the seriousness of an offence and the severity of the resulting sentence.

Magistrates' sentencing powers. The Bill would extend magistrates' sentencing power from six to twelve months.

Sentencing Guidelines Council. The Bill would provide for the establishment of a Sentencing Guidelines Council, replacing the present Sentencing Advisory Council, which would be tasked with drafting and promulgating a consolidated set of sentencing guidelines to be taken into account by all criminal courts.

Deferred sentence. The Bill would require more of the offender on a deferred sentence. He may have to complete undertakings in the community as set by the court.

Generic community sentences. The Bill would create a single community sentence under which all of the options currently attached to the different community orders would be available.

Custody minus. A short prison sentence of between two and thirteen weeks can be suspended for up to two years while requirements in the community which are set by the court are undertaken. If the offender breaches any of the activities or requirements, the custodial term is activated, and the sentence becomes one of custody plus. Committing a further offence during the entire length of suspension would also count as breach.

Intermittent custody. The Bill would create a new sentence of intermittent custody (modelled on the structure for custody plus—see below) in which the custodial period can be served intermittently. The licence period, complete with requirements set by the court, is served in between the custodial periods and beyond (if applicable).

Custody plus. This sentence would consist of a custodial period of between two and thirteen weeks, followed by a period of at least six months served in the community on licence within an overall sentence envelope of less than twelve months. Some of the options under the generic community sentence are available as licence conditions.

Sentences of over twelve months. For offenders serving a sentence of over twelve months (apart from the sentences for dangerous offenders outlined below) release would be automatic at the halfway point and they would remain on licence until the end of the sentence. The Prison and Probation Services would set a number of requirements in addition to be followed during the licence period.

Sentences for dangerous offenders. The Bill would introduce a new scheme for the sentencing of dangerous adults. Offenders who have committed a specified sexual or violent offence and have been assessed as dangerous would get one of two new sentences for dangerous offenders or a discretionary life sentence. Release from all of these sentences would be at the discretion of the Parole Board. The most dangerous offenders who continue to pose a risk to the public may be kept in prison for an indeterminate period.

Sentence enforcement. Enforcement of community orders is to be strengthened by giving the court stronger options in the case of breach. This Bill makes recall to custody an executive decision, rather than having to be approved by the Parole Board as currently. The Parole Board would scrutinize all recall decisions to ensure they are fairly taken.

Sentence calculation. The existing method of calculation based on the principle of single-terming would be simplified and replaced with a set of clear provisions for calculating the time served in custody where several sentences are passed. The method for deducting time spent on remand from the custodial part of the sentence to be served would also be simplified by the Bill.

Powers of review. Under the new suspended sentence, the court will have the powers to review the progress of the offender if it chooses, and alter the requirements accordingly. The aim is to increase the court's involvement in the outcome of the sentences it hands down.

Criminal Cases Review Commission

One of the most serious challenges facing the criminal justice system is ensuring that miscarriages of justice do not occur. Notwithstanding the opportunities for appeal and the outcomes from appeal, there may always be cases where the full facts have not emerged at trial or on subsequent appeal, possibly because there have been failures by the police or prosecution to put evidence before the court.

The Criminal Cases Review Commission was established in 1997.[54] It will usually consider only those cases that have been through the normal judicial appeal process. It started undertaking casework at the end of March 1997; by the end of March 2002 it had received over 4,800 applications. Of the cases accepted for review, which is a small percentage of the total, only 162 had been referred back to the Court of Appeal. Reviews are conducted by Case Review Managers. There is serious concern that levels of work and insufficient staff numbers are leading to unacceptable delays in processing applications.

Decisions on the outcome of the work of the Case Review Managers are taken by the Commission. The Commission has fourteen members, appointed from a variety of backgrounds. Any decision to refer a case back to the Court of Appeal must be taken by a committee of at least three members.

The function of the Commission is to consider whether there would be a real possibility that a conviction, finding of fact, verdict, or sentence would not be upheld by the court, were a reference back to be made. In relation to reviews of convictions,

---

[54] Criminal Appeal Act 1995, Part II. This followed recommendations from the Royal Commission on Criminal Justice, 1993. It has recently had its powers extended to enable it to consider cases where the verdict of 'guilty but insane' was reached: Criminal Cases Review (Insanity) Act 1999. Although this verdict was abolished in the mid-1960s, there is a small number of people whose cases were so determined, who might wish to take advantage of these new provisions. Since 1964 the verdict in such cases is 'not guilty by reason of insanity': Criminal Procedure (Insanity) Act 1964.

there has to be either an argument or evidence which had not been raised at the trial or on appeal, or other exceptional circumstances; in relation to sentencing, again there has to be legal argument or information about the individual or the offence which was not raised during the trial or on appeal.[55]

Parole and the work of the Parole Board

Even though the court may have imposed a custodial sentence in a particular case, this does not mean that the convicted person will serve the whole period of the sentence. Sentences are subject to review by the Parole Board. This body has been in operation since 1968.[56] Its primary function is to make risk assessments which will inform decisions whether prisoners can be released back into the community early. While protection of the public is a matter of paramount concern, the Board seeks to enhance the rehabilitative effect of prison in cases where that seems possible. The responsibilities of the Board vary, depending on different types of case.

Determinate sentence cases

Where a convicted person has been sentenced to a fixed term of imprisonment, it is now provided (since 1 October 1992) that a prisoner becomes eligible for parole half-way through his sentence (backdated to include any time spent in custody on remand before the trial).[57] Thus a prisoner sentenced on 2 January 1994, who had also spent six months in custody on remand, became eligible for parole on 2 July 1996—the Parole Eligibility Date (PED).

Six months before the PED, officers of the Parole Board begin gathering the information together to enable a panel from the Parole Board to take an initial decision on whether the prisoner may or may not be suitable for parole. The prisoner will also be interviewed by a Parole Board member. In addition to written reports, the panel is required to take into account *directions* made by the Home Secretary. These give guidance on particular issues on which the panel must be satisfied before finding in favour of the prisoner.

The decision to grant parole is formally one for the Secretary of State. But he has delegated his decision-taking powers to the Board in all cases where the prisoner was sentenced to a period of less than fifteen years.[58]

Whether or not prisoners are released following a Parole Board review, determinate prisoners are automatically released two-thirds of the way through their sentence. However, all those released either after a parole decision or under the automatic process remain subject to supervision by the Probation Service and are subject to

---

[55] A detailed account of the work of the Commission can be found in its *Annual Report* for 2001–2. (London, Criminal Cases Review Commission, 2002).

[56] It was established under the provisions of the Criminal Justice Act 1967.

[57] For those sentenced before 1 October 1992, the date of eligibility for parole arose one-third of the way through the sentence.

[58] Until 1998 the upper limit for Parole Board decisions was sentences for less than 7 years.

recall either for reoffending or for other breaches of the probation supervision until 75 per cent of the period of the sentence has expired. Although the supervision of the Probation Service ends at that point, the remaining 25 per cent of the sentence can be reactivated if the person is subsequently committed for another criminal offence.

The latest Annual Report from the Board records that in 2001–2 parole was awarded in 51 per cent of the 5,514 applications it considered; and that the rate of recall of parolees to custody for committing another offence was only 3 per cent—the lowest in the Board's history.

Life sentences

The Parole Board also has important responsibilities in relation to life sentences. In dealing with them, a distinction is drawn between *mandatory* life sentences, where the judge had no option but to impose a life sentence (as in the case of a conviction for murder), and *discretionary* life sentences, where this was the sentence that the judge decided was appropriate.[59]

The starting point is a decision on *the tariff*. This is the minimum period which the prisoner is to serve. Under the provisions of the Crime (Sentences) Act 1997, the tariff for mandatory lifers is fixed by the Home Secretary taking into account a recommendation of the trial judge. Following an important decision of the European Court of Human Rights,[60] the House of Lords has declared that imposition of the tariff is indistinguishable from sentencing, and thus in effect part of the trial process.[61] Article 6 of the European Convention on Human Rights requires that tribunals deciding criminal trials must be independent of the executive arm of government. Thus the role of the Home Secretary is incompatible with Article 6.[62] The Home Secretary has announced that he will consider the implications of the judgment and introduce legislation in the near future to bring a new judicial system into effect which is compatible with the European Convention. The tariff in other cases is set by the trial judge.

Three years before the expiry of the tariff, the case is reviewed by the Parole Board which considers whether or not a prisoner is suitable to be moved to the more relaxed regime of an open prison.

On the expiry of the tariff, the Parole Board considers whether the prisoner is

[59] This group includes those sentenced under the provisions of the Crime (Sentences) Act 1997, which gives the court power to impose a life sentence where a person has been convicted of a second serious offence. It also includes those under the age of 18 who have been convicted of murder.

[60] *Stafford v. United Kingdom* (Application No 46295/99, 28 May 2002).

[61] *R v. Secretary of State for the Home Department, ex parte Anderson* (25 November 2002). In the same judgment, the Lords also held that a mandatory life sentence for murder was not incompatible with the provisions of the European Convention on Human Rights.

[62] In *R v. Secretary of State for the Home Department, ex parte V and T* [1998] AC 407, the House of Lords held that it was unlawful for the Home Secretary to set a tariff relating to a young person which did not take into account the provisions of the UN Convention on the Rights of the Child. The European Court of Human Rights has now held *T v. United Kingdom, V v. United Kingdom* (1999) 30 EHRR 121 that setting a tariff is a sentencing function which should not be carried out by a member of the executive arm of government but by an independent tribunal.

suitable for release on licence. If release on licence is recommended, the prisoner will still be subject to supervision by the Probation Service, for at least four years. At that point (or later) the Home Secretary may decide that the supervision requirements can be lifted. This power is not affected by the recent House of Lords decision. However, the prisoner remains liable to recall and for the balance of his sentence to be reactivated for the rest of his life, should there be reason for so doing, such as subsequent offending.

If the Parole Board concludes that on the expiry of the tariff, release would not be appropriate, the case is reviewed normally every two years.

Procedure

The process of reaching these decisions does, however, vary. In the case of *mandatory* lifers, the decision-taking process is very similar to that for determinate sentences. Reports are prepared; an interview is held by a member of the Parole Board with the prisoner; and a decision is reached on the papers. Mandatory lifer panels are specially constituted to include a judge and a psychiatrist. Again the panel is required to take into account *directions* prescribed by the Home Secretary. The actual decision is always taken by the Home Secretary; the Parole Board panel can only make a recommendation.

For *discretionary* lifers, the process of review involves the compilation of a dossier of reports. But there is then a fundamentally important difference. An oral hearing (rather like a tribunal hearing) is listed before a discretionary lifer panel of the Parole Board (which includes a judge and a psychiatrist). The prisoner is entitled to legal representation at this hearing. At the conclusion of the hearing, the panel may recommend transfer to open prison conditions, or may in appropriate cases direct release.

The Parole Board considered 956 life sentences cases in 2001–2. Of these, 513 were mandatory lifers. Of this latter group, release on licence was recommended in 17 per cent.

The place of the victim

One of the ways in which the criminal justice system has been transformed in recent years is through increased recognition of the victim of crime. As has already been noted, the position of the victim is fundamental to the whole criminal justice system since, if the victim does not report a crime, no further steps are usually taken in the criminal process. Further, as also noted, the viewpoint of the victim is one of the factors taken into account by the CPS in reaching a decision whether or not to prosecute a case. There are respects in which sentencing policy reflects the impact the criminal activity may have had on the victim. Much of the activity in the youth justice system is designed to make the offender aware of the victim's perceptions of what he has done. The Home Office has sought to bring support for victims (and witnesses) together in its *Victims' Charter* (published in 1997).[63]

Three particular developments may be briefly noted: victim support schemes, the criminal injuries compensation scheme and compensation orders.

Victim support schemes

There are now about 365 local victim support schemes with some 15,000 volunteers offering help to over 1.5 million victims. In the Crown Court, there are another 1,500+ volunteers helping over 120,000 victims and witnesses who have to attend court. These do a great deal of work trying to reassure the victims of crime that they have not been targeted, but are simply the victims of opportunistic criminal activity. They also help victims and other witnesses cope with the stress and strain of appearing in court.

It is argued that more should be done to inform victims about outcomes, particularly where the police or prosecuting authorities determine not to pursue a case which a victim has reported to the police. It is also argued that more information should be provided to victims when a person who has been sent to prison is released. These criticisms are, in the main, accepted, and there will be continued developments in these areas in coming years.

The importance of taking the victim's perspective on the criminal justice system seriously has been emphasized in *A Better Deal for Victims and Witnesses*.[64] There it is noted that public confidence in the criminal justice system has fallen. For example victim satisfaction with the police fell from 67 per cent to 58 per cent in the period 1994–2000; too few victims see 'their' offender brought to justice—only about one in five crimes reported to the police result in the offender being brought to justice; half of all crime is never reported to the police. Many of the proposals in the Criminal Justice Bill, for example relating to bail or the use of video links (see above), are designed to assist victims and other witnesses to give evidence. In addition, a further major development is that, in 2003, a Victims and Witnesses Bill will be introduced. This will, if enacted, put the current Victims' Charter on a statutory footing. It will become possible for people to complain to the Parliamentary Ombudsman if public agencies fail to deliver services to the required standard. And a new independent commissioner for victims and witnesses will champion their cause and seek to maintain the reform momentum.

The Criminal Injuries Compensation Scheme

This has been in operation for many years. This is a state-funded scheme which was revised in 2001 and is administered by the Criminal Injuries Compensation Authority.

---

[63] Currently under review.

[64] (London, Home Office, November 2002). See: www.cjsonline.org/library/pdf/Final%cent20version%20of%20Victims%20Paper.pdf.

In 2000–1, the scheme paid about £113 million compensation to some 37,000 success-ful claimants. (Over 50 per cent of applications were unsuccessful.) The scheme is limited to those victims who have been injured as the result of violent criminal activity directed towards them. Critics point out that other negative consequences of being the victim of crime are not thus compensated.

Compensation orders

In addition to this statutory scheme, it may also be noted that since 1972 the criminal courts have had power to order those convicted of crimes to pay compensation to their victims. These powers have been developed so that there are circumstances in which a compensation order may be imposed as the sole penalty. Since 1988, the courts have been required to consider making compensation orders in defined groups of cases involving death, injury, loss or damage, and to give reasons where an order is not made. And since 1991 the limits on the sums which magistrates may order as compensation have been increased. These developments may be seen as more reparative forms of outcome for the criminal justice system.

A strategic approach to criminal justice?

Underpinning many of the particular facets of the criminal justice system set out above has been the recognition by successive governments of the need for a more integrated approach to dealing with crime. Numerous initiatives have been taken in recent years to try to deliver this. In addition to steps considered earlier in this chapter, two further examples are mentioned here.

First, the *Trials Issues Group* (TIG) brings together representatives of all those working in the criminal justice system to iron out inter-agency difficulties and to improve the working of the system generally. It has been in existence for some nine years and meets monthly. Members of the TIG focus on the practical and operational, rather than the conceptual. It grew out of an acceptance that the participants in the criminal justice system are heavily inter-dependent, that simply apportioning blame for the problems in the system was sterile and that no progress could be made without some give and take. Thus its members are expected to take an objective attitude, to be as co-operative as possible and not to seek to defend their corners come what may.

TIG members are drawn from organizations across the criminal justice system including the Lord Chancellor's Department, the judiciary, the Home Office, Crown Prosecution Service, police, the Magistrates' Association, the Justices' Clerks' Society, the Probation Service, the Law Society and the Bar Council. The TIG has a number of sub-groups which draw in participants from outside the main group in order to work through projects suitable to be taken forward on an inter-agency basis. Examples of previous projects include:

- the development of new-style case files to reduce police administrative forms;
- joint performance management as a means of improving the quality and timeliness of case preparation by the police and prosecution;
- the development of new standards for witness care; and
- introduction of new streamlined procedures for finalizing minor road traffic cases.

The TIG has a permanent projects team drawn from the Crown Prosecution Service, the police, the Home Office and the Lord Chancellor's Department. Its members combine their TIG functions with other duties in their home organizations.

Secondly, the *Criminal Justice Strategy* started with the publication in December 1998 of a Public Service Agreement (PSA) setting out what the public should expect from the criminal justice system.[65] This has more recently been supplemented by a *Strategic Plan for the Criminal Justice System for 1999–2000 to 2001–2002*. The Government has set two aims for the strategy:

- to reduce crime and the fear of crime and their social and economic costs;
- to dispense justice fairly and efficiently and to promote confidence in the rule of law.

It is the second of these that is most relevant to this work.

In relation to this objective, the Government is seeking substantially to reduce times taken for the disposal of cases, particularly those involving persistent young offenders.[66] A number of processes should be available in the next few years, to take advantage of increased investment in IT:[67]

- records initially built in the police station (incorporating information about previous convictions taken from a national database) can be passed electronically to the CPS for decision about prosecuting;
- if the prosecution goes ahead, the file can then be forwarded electronically to the defendant's lawyers;
- the court listing officer uses information—provided electronically—to find a date when witnesses are able to attend court;
- the court's video-conferencing facility is used for deciding preliminary issues, such as remanding in custody without the need for attendance at court;
- requests for pre-sentence reports can be forwarded by e-mail to the Probation Service;

---

[65] Part of the White Paper, *Public Services for the Future: Modernisation, Reform, Accountability* (Cm 4181) (London, The Stationery Office, 1998).

[66] In 1996, the Audit Commission estimated that people under 18 committed 7 million offences a year; the Government argues that dealing quickly with this group will indicate the seriousness with which young offending is regarded.

[67] Electronic case files have been piloted in the Stockport police force.

- information about driving offences can be obtained direct from the DVLA;[68]
- information about a convicted person including previous convictions can be forwarded to prisons to enable a full risk assessment to take place;
- similarly electronic means can be used to assist probation officers, or those taking decisions on parole.

Investment in IT in the criminal justice system is proceeding rapidly.

The combined effect of new legislative measures, not only the Criminal Justice Bill 2002 but also the Police Reform Act 2002 and the new Courts Bill, designed to integrate the management of the magistrates' courts and the Crown Court, is that a substantial body of new legislation will have been put in place within a very short time. These are all evidence of the present Government's intent to improve and modernize the operation of the criminal justice system in the holistic sense considered here. The success of the measures taken by the Government, however well-intentioned, cannot be guaranteed. The challenge will be to enthuse those who deliver front-line services with the same sense of commitment to change.

Questions for discussion

1. What do you think are the primary objectives of the criminal justice system? How far are they consistent?

2. How can the tension between 'due process' and 'crime control' be managed?

3. Do the police have too many/too few powers?

4. Should the rules of evidence in criminal trials be changed?

5. Should the criminal justice system become more 'victim-focused'?

6. What are the primary objectives of sentencing policy?

7. Are too many people sentenced to prison? What are the alternatives to prison?

8. Is it right that the Home Secretary should not have the power to set the tariff for very serious offenders?

9. Can mandatory sentences be justified? Or should sentencers always retain sentencing discretion?

10. Should the rules relating to jury trial be changed?

11. Should it be possible to undertake research into the jury?

---

[68] At present it is estimated that around 170,000 cases are adjourned each year, with all the knock-on consequences of increased costs and delays in other cases, simply because magistrates' courts cannot directly access driving records.

Further reading

ASHWORTH, A., *Sentencing and Criminal Justice* (3rd edn., London, Butterworths, 2000)

—— *The Criminal Process: an Evaluative Study* (2nd edn., Oxford, Clarendon Press, 1998)

AULD, LORD JUSTICE, *A Review of the Criminal Courts of England and Wales* (London, The Stationery Office, 2001)

BALDWIN, J., and McCONVILLE, M., *Jury Trials* (Oxford, Clarendon Press, 1979)

BARCLAY, G., and TAVARES, C. (eds.), *DIGEST 4—Information on the Criminal Justice System* (London, Home Office, 1999)

COLVIN, M., *Negotiated Justice: a Closer Look at the Implications of Plea Bargains* (London, Justice, 1993)

CORNISH, W.R., *The Jury* (Harmondsworth, Penguin, 1971)

GIBSON, B., *Introduction to the Magistrates' Court* (2nd edn., Winchester, Waterside Press, 1995)

HALLIDAY, J., *Making Punishments Work: Report of a Review of the Sentencing Framework for England and Wales* (London, Home Office, 2001)

HOME OFFICE, *Justice for All* (Cm 5563) (London, The Stationery Office, 2002)

HOOD, R., in collaboration with CORDOVIL, G., *Race and Sentencing: a Study in the Crown Court: a Report for the Commission for Racial Equality* (Oxford, Clarendon Press, 1992)

JUSTICE, Committee on the Role of the Victim in Criminal Justice, *Victims in Criminal Justice* (London, JUSTICE, 1998)

McCABE, S., and PURVES, R., *The Jury at Work: a Study of a Series of Jury Trials in which the Defendant was Acquitted* (Oxford, Blackwell for the Oxford University Penal Research Unit, 1972)

—— and —— *The Shadow Jury at Work: an Account of a Series of Deliberations and Verdicts where 'Shadow' Juries were Present During Actual Trials* (Oxford, Blackwell for the Oxford University Penal Research Unit, 1974)

McCONVILLE, M., and BRIDGES, L. (eds.), *Criminal Justice in Crisis* (Aldershot, Edward Elgar, c1994)

—— and WILSON, G. (eds.), *The Handbook of the Criminal Justice Process* (Oxford, Oxford University Press, 2002)

MACPHERSON OF CLUNY, SIR WILLIAM, *The Stephen Lawrence Inquiry Report* (Cm 4262) (London, The Stationery Office, 1999)

MAGUIRE, M., MORGAN, R., and REINER, R. (eds.), *The Oxford Handbook of Criminology* (3rd edn., Oxford, Clarendon Press, 2002)

ROBERTSHAW, P., *Jury and Judge: the Crown Court in Action* (Aldershot, Dartmouth, 1995)

ROYAL COMMISSION ON CRIMINAL JUSTICE (Chairman, Viscount Runciman), *Report* (Cm 2263) (London, HMSO, 1993)

ROYAL COMMISSION ON CRIMINAL PROCEDURE (Chairman, Sir Cyril Phillips), *Report* (Cmnd 8092) (London, HMSO, 1981)

SANDERS, A., and YOUNG, R., *Criminal Justice* (2nd edn., London, Butterworths, 2000)

SKYRME, SIR THOMAS, *The Changing Image of the Magistracy* (London, Macmillan, 1979)

ZANDER, M., and HENDERSON, P., *Crown Court Study* (Research Study No. 19, Royal Commission on Criminal Justice) (London, HMSO, 1993)

Websites

www.cjsonline.org/home.html *(Portal to criminal justice system)*

www.apa.police.uk/ *(Association of Police Authorities)*

www.homeoffice.gov.uk/hmic/hmic.htm *(HM Inspectorate of Constabulary)*

www.homeoffice.gov.uk/pcrg/pacereview2002.pdf *(Review of PACE Codes)*

www.cps.gov.uk/ *(Crown Prosecution Service)*

www.cps.gov.uk/Home/CodeForCrownProsecutors/

www.hmcpsi.gov.uk/ *(Crown Prosecution Inspectorate)*

www.sfo.gov.uk/ *(Serious Fraud Office)*

www.legalservices.gov.uk/cds/index.htm *(Criminal Defence Service)*

www.pca.gov.uk/ *(Police Complaints Authority)*

www.cjsonline.org/citizen/witnesses/service.html *(Witness care service)*

www.cica.gov.uk/ *(Criminal Injuries Compensation Authority)*

www.homeoffice.gov.uk/cpg/nps/ *(National probation service)*

www.homeoffice.gov.uk/cpg/hmiprobhome.htm *(HM Inspectorate of Probation)*

www.hmprisonservice.gov.uk/

www.homeoffice.gov.uk/hmipris/hmipris.htm *(HM Inspectorate of Prisons)*

www.homeoffice.gov.uk/ppoweb/ *(Prisons and probation ombudsman)*

www.youth-justice-board.gov.uk/

www.magistrates-association.org.uk

www.jc-society.co.uk/ *(Justices' Clerks' Society)*

www.statistics.gov.uk/CCI/nscl.asp?ID=5004&x=126&y=15 *(Crime and justice statistics)*

www.archive.official-documents.co.uk/document/cm53/5312/crimestats.pdf *(Criminal statistics for 2000)*

www.homeoffice.gov.uk/rds/bcs1.html *(British Crime Survey)*

www.lawcom.gov.uk/files/lc273.pdf *(Law Commission report on evidence of bad conduct)*

www.youth-justice-board.gov.uk/

www.ccrc.gov.uk/ *(Criminal Cases Review Commission)*

www.paroleboard.gov.uk/

http://natiasso03.uuhost.uk.uu.net/ *(Victim support)*

www.homeoffice.gov.uk/cpd/pvu/viccont.htm *(Victims' Charter)*

www.homeoffice.gov.uk/new_indexs/index_victimsofcrime.htm *(Link to materials on victims)*

www.homeoffice.gov.uk/cpd/pvu/jvuhome.htm *(Justice and Victims Unit, Home Office)*

6
The administrative justice system

Introduction

Although the criminal justice system, discussed in the previous chapter, is institution-
ally extremely complex, the primary focus of the system—on the regulation of forms
of social behaviour, and dealing with those who transgress the rules—is clear. By
contrast, the very concept of 'administrative justice' is controversial, meaning different things to different people. Traditional analyses of the legal system, focusing
exclusively on criminal and civil law, have failed to recognize any separate system of
'administrative justice'. Discussion of administrative justice gets wrapped up in
general discussion of the civil justice system.

In part, this failure to acknowledge a distinct system of administrative justice
reflects the continuing influence of the nineteenth-century writer A. V. Dicey, who
argued that there should not be a separately identifiable body of *droit administratif*
(administrative law). He thought that this would result in public officials and others
who worked for public bodies being given legally preferential treatment and thus
offend against the fundamental principle of the rule of law, that all should be treated
equally before the law.

A hundred years on, the reality is that the state plays a large part in the regulation of
society; there is a vast array of institutions employing individuals who provide public
services on behalf of those institutions. Although there may still not be a conceptually
distinct branch of the law which may be described as 'administrative law', as there is
for example in many of the countries in Continental Europe, understanding the
modern English legal system involves recognizing the concept of 'administrative
justice'.

The primary focus of this chapter is on the range of institutions in which administrative law is practised. First, however, we reflect on the nature of administrative law
and the role it plays in modern society.

The role of administrative law: authority and values

As already noted, one of the features of the twentieth century—and one likely to continue into the twenty-first—has been the significant role of government in developing and implementing a vast range of social policies. Legitimacy for the activities of public officials in implementing those social policies depends on law. Administrative law:

- provides authority for public servants to deliver government policy, whose legitimacy is enshrined in the laws (primary, secondary and tertiary—*see above Box 3.2*) passed through the Parliamentary system;

- authorizes the raising and expenditure of public funds;

- sets limits to the powers of public officials;

- creates the institutional mechanisms for calling public officials to account; and

- provides means for the redress of individual grievances or resolution of complaints by the citizen.

In addition to the functional attributes of administrative law, 'administrative justice' embraces certain *values* or *principles*, which should underpin good administration by state officials, and others who deliver services on behalf of the state. These include: openness (or transparency); fairness; rationality (including the giving of reasons for decisions); impartiality (independence) of decision-takers; accountability; the prevention of the exercise of arbitrary power and the control of discretion; consistency; participation; efficiency; equity and equal treatment.

These underlying values of administrative justice are not wholly consistent one with another. There may be circumstances in which openness may properly yield to confidentiality; where fairness of process may conflict with the efficient reaching of a decision. Each of these values is to an extent contingent upon the context in which it is asserted. One of the challenges for those who govern, and for those who criticize the role of government, is to achieve an appropriate balance between these conflicting objectives.

The details of any particular area of substantive public law (for example the statutory rules relating to the provision of social security benefits) are not for discussion here. Rather the focus is on the mechanisms of accountability which exist to keep officials in check and provide means of resolving disputes when things go (or are alleged to go) wrong. But the reader should reflect on the tensions between the different values in administrative justice in the context of particular administrative activities—for example, the collection of taxes; or the granting of planning permissions; or the payment of social security benefits.

Administrative justice: the institutional framework

There is a great variety of bodies which make up the institutional framework for administrative justice. They include:

- the courts;
- tribunals;
- inquiries;
- ombudsmen;
- complaints procedures.

Each of these is considered below. It will quickly be realized that this is another area in which there has been very rapid development in the last thirty to forty years. It is one of the most dynamic areas of the English legal system.

This way of conceptualizing the framework of administrative justice is not wholly orthodox. Practising lawyers tend to think of 'administrative law' as, in essence, the special process available in the High Court known as *judicial review*. Academic lawyers go beyond this court-focused approach to include in their analyses comments on other mechanisms for the resolution of disputes. But the treatment tends to be somewhat superficial, and even here the balance is normally tilted in favour of the court's role.[1] There are perfectly good reasons for this:

(1) The *qualitative* importance of the law of judicial review is clear. It is the reported decisions of judges in the Administrative Court and above that have developed the jurisprudence of judicial review. The fundamental principles, of procedural fairness and for limiting the exercise of discretionary power by officials, are the creation of the courts. The range of persons permitted to bring proceedings by way of judicial review has been expanded. The numbers of bodies and institutions subjected to the principles of judicial review have been significantly widened. The grounds on which judicial review may be sought have also been developed. Judicial review provides the legal background against which the administrative justice system must operate. This is largely the work of the courts—judges asserting their constitutional function of independence over the executive.

(2) Secondly, it is in the courts that practising lawyers earn good money and develop formidable reputations. With rare exceptions, legal aid is not available to pay for legal representation before tribunals or other dispute resolution/ grievance handling fora. There is therefore little incentive for legal practitioners to get to know about the wider world of administrative justice.

(3) The work of this wider range of bodies is often not the subject of formal

---

[1] There are honourable exceptions: Harlow, C., and Rawlings, R., *Law and Administration* (2nd edn., London, Butterworths, 1997).

published documentation. Thus legal scholars find it hard to access the material needed for a full review of the administrative justice system as a whole.

Nevertheless, concentration on judicial review—a procedure that brings about 4,000 cases before the courts each year—means that other procedures for the delivery of administrative justice are not paid the attention they are due. For example, the Appeals Service, which adjudicates on social security disputes, determined in excess of 285,000 appeals in 2001;[2] immigration adjudicators disposed of over 56,500 immigration appeals in 2001, and the Immigration Appeals Tribunal dealt with another 19,500 appeals;[3] Mental Health Review Tribunals currently deal with around 20,000 cases a year.[4] Many other examples could be given. The large number of ombudsmen that now exist handle thousands more cases in a year. And the variety of complaints procedures available under the general umbrella of the concept of the 'citizen's charter' deal with countless other grievances. *Quantitatively* these other mechanisms are far more significant than the courts. This account seeks to redress the balance.

The reason for making this argument arises, however, not just from a desire to be different. What the administrative justice system—taken as a whole—provides is a vast test bed for the development and evaluation of new procedures:

- decisions being taken on the papers;
- decisions by a single judge;
- decisions by three-(or more-)person tribunals;
- procedures involving the unrepresented and inarticulate.

It is one of the great wasted opportunities that those who have sought in recent years to introduce change into the civil justice system should have paid such scant attention to what goes on in practice in the administrative justice system. It provides a rich source of ideas regarding how things might be done differently. Those who in the past may have looked down their noses at the administrative justice system as 'not being proper courts' should think again. It is here that alternative procedures are to be found, often working extremely well.

The courts

The heart of the administrative justice system is found in the Administrative Court (formerly known as the Divisional Court of the Queen's Bench). This is where the fundamental principles of *judicial review* have been developed, particularly since the

---

[2] Council on Tribunals, *Annual Report, 2001/2002* HC 14 (London, The Stationery Office, 2002), Appendix J; these figures relate to England and Wales only. 42,000 Scottish cases were also heard.
[3] *Judicial Statistics Annual Report 2001* (Cm 5551) (London, The Stationery Office, 2002).
[4] Council on Tribunals, n. 2 above.

mid-1960s.[5] The essence of judicial review is straightforward. Public officials must act within the constraints of the law. If they do not the courts will declare a decision to be unlawful. In general the judges limit themselves to this; they will not usually substitute their own decisions for that of the original decision-taker.

The primary tasks of the judges in a judicial review case are:

- *To interpret statutory provisions.* There are many situations, particularly when a new piece of legislation has been passed, when the law may need clarification. Deciding the limits of the law, and whether or not a person acted within the law or outside it, is one of the tasks of the judges.

- *To control discretion.* In some situations the legislation has been drafted in a deliberately vague fashion, in order to give officials some flexibility in the application of the law to the particular case. Where a statute states that the minister 'may' act in a certain way or reach a 'reasonable' decision, these are examples of the granting of discretionary power. In this context the judges have developed the principle that the exercise of discretion must not be 'unreasonable'.[6]

- *To determine the validity of secondary legislation.* The courts have resisted the temptation to decide, as does the Supreme Court in the USA, that particular items of legislation are unlawful, though it has recently been decided that they should do so if an item of British legislation is contrary to the law of the EU.[7] However, the courts have long asserted the power to declare secondary legislation unlawful, on the basis that the statutory instrument was beyond the powers of the minister as established by the primary Act of Parliament.[8]

- *To determine the fairness of procedures.* The courts have also been determined to develop fundamental principles of fairness in the lower courts, in other tribunals and in a range of other contexts in which decisions affecting the citizen are made. Where these principles apply, the person must know the basis of the case against her, and have an opportunity to be heard.

- *To prevent bias.* In addition, the judges have insisted that adjudicators in the courts and other fora must not be 'biased', in the sense that they must not have a personal interest in the outcome of any particular case.

Judicial review has not just developed in a vacuum. It is a response to the fact that people no longer accept official decisions as easily as they once did. The reasons for this are complex: better public education; a more 'consumerist' society; the development of this type of legal activity by legal practitioners. But government has also

---

[5] Woolf, Lord and Jowell, J. (assistant editor Le Sueur, A.P.), *Judicial Review of Administrative Action* (5th edn. of book originally written by Prof. S. A. de Smith) (London, Sweet & Maxwell, 1995).

[6] *Associated Provincial Picture Houses Ltd v. Wednesbury Corporation* [1948] 1 KB 223.

[7] *Factortame v. Secretary of State for Transport (No. 2)* [1991] 1 AC 603.

[8] *R v. Secretary of State for Trade and Industry, ex parte Thomson Holidays*, The Times, 12 January 2000; and *R v. Secretary of State for the Environment, Transport and the Regions and Another, ex parte Spath Holme Ltd* [2000] 1 All ER 884.

expanded its activities. It seeks to regulate large tranches of human activity. It is not surprising that the use of judicial review, or the threat of such use, should now be part of the 'politics' of modern public administration.[9]

One of the outcomes of the developments of judicial review has been that there has been an increased use by pressure groups of the courts for testing the validity of legislation or its interpretation. 'Test cases', or as it is known in the USA 'cause lawyering', have become a part of contemporary legal practice.[10] The coming into force of the Human Rights Act 1998 in October 2000 has provided a new focus for such work as challenges about the compliance of legislation and policy with the European Convention on Human Rights are made.

Tribunals

The adjudicative fora in which the vast majority of disputes between the citizen and the state get resolved are known collectively as tribunals. Some, such as the General Commissioners of Income Tax, trace their history back to the late eighteenth century. But the vast majority are the creation of the twentieth century, reflecting the increasing involvement of the state in the lives of its citizens.

For the first twenty to thirty years of that century, there was considerable concern about the use of tribunals as a mechanism for the resolution of disputes. It was argued that only courts had the constitutional authority to perform this function. It was, perhaps, one of the advantages of the lack of a written constitution that, despite this claim, there was no written constitutional principle that *required* all dispute resolution bodies to have the status of 'court'. In fact, the development of tribunals was a pragmatic response to the problems caused for the court system when, at the end of the nineteenth century, jurisdiction to deal with disputes arising under the Workmen's Compensation Acts was given to the county court. This had the result of completely drowning those courts in work, thereby preventing them from dealing efficiently with other business. When the National Insurance Act 1911 was passed, creating the first social security benefits, appeals against decisions were not to the courts, but to a tribunal, the sportingly named *Committee of Referees* with a further right of appeal to the equally sporting *Umpire*.

Criticism of the use of bodies other than the courts for resolving disputes led to fierce criticism, not least from the then Lord Chief Justice, Lord Hewart, who in 1929 published his famous polemic *The New Despotism*. This resulted in the establishment of the Committee on Ministers' Powers, under the chairmanship of Lord Donoughmore, which in 1932 reported that, in its view and subject to safeguards,

---

[9] On the 'tactical' use of judicial review see Bridges, L., Meszaros, G., and Sunkin, M., *Judicial Review in Perspective* (London, Cavendish, 1995).

[10] Prosser, T., *Test Cases for the Poor: Legal Techniques in the Politics of Social Welfare* (London, Child Poverty Action Group, 1983); Sarat, A., and Scheingold, S., *Cause Lawyering and Professional Responsibilities* (New York, Oxford University Press, 1998). See also the work of the Public Law Project (website at the end of this chapter).

tribunals were a necessary if not desirable part of the fabric of the English justice system.

The issue was revisited after the Second World War when, in 1955, a further committee under Sir Oliver Franks was established, in the wake of a scandal known as the Crichel Down affair, to review tribunals and inquiries. The report of his committee was published in 1957. By this time many more tribunal systems were in existence. Franks accepted that, subject to basic principles of openness, fairness and impartiality, tribunals should be accepted as a part of the adjudicative structure. Since that time, there has been no serious discussion about the need for tribunals. Indeed, their number has continued to grow (alongside other institutional developments, to which we shall come below). The position of tribunals is even more secure following the enactment of the Human Rights Act 1998, since Article 6 of the European Convention on Human Rights requires the existence of courts or tribunals to determine a person's civil rights.

There are currently at least eighty different tribunal systems in existence. They come in a bewildering variety of forms.

Structure

Some are 'two-tiered' tribunal systems. For example in social security, appeals go first to the Appeals Service,[11] which may consist of three, two or one members— depending on the type of case. From there a case may go, with leave and on a point of law only, to the Social Security Commissioners. The Commissioners usually sit on their own, but for the occasional difficult case they may sit in a tribunal of three. There is a similar structure with employment tribunals, with a second tier appeal to the Employment Appeal Tribunal consisting of three people: a judge and two lay assessors. In immigration, cases are heard at the first tier by an immigration adjudicator sitting on his/her own. There may then be an appeal to the Immigration Appeal Tribunal which usually comprises three people (though this practice is changing). In all these cases, there is the possibility of further challenge on a point of law in the courts.

Other tribunal systems are 'one-tier': examples include the Mental Health Review Tribunal, the Valuation Tribunal and the Rent Assessment Committee. In other words, there is only one level of appeal or review within the statutory framework. Any further challenge has to be direct to the courts.

Personnel

Although the label 'tribunal' may imply a body of three people, as has already been noted in passing, some are made up of fewer than three people; one-person tribunals are becoming increasingly common as government departments seek to cut the costs of administrative justice. Other tribunals may have more than three persons involved, particularly tribunals which deal with matters relating to the National Health Service.

[11] See Social Security Act 1998.

Qualifications

Most tribunal systems these days have legally qualified chairmen. But this is not universal—for example General Commissioners for Income Tax who determine tax cases, and Valuation Tribunals, which determine property values, operate with only lay persons on the tribunal. In such cases it is usual for the clerk to the tribunal to be legally qualified (rather like the Justices' Clerks who assist benches of lay magistrates).

In other tribunal systems, there is more professional expertise sitting around the table. Most commonly there is legal expertise; but, where relevant, there may be a valuer or an accountant or a doctor. In cases where the tribunals operate with professionally qualified adjudicators, whether lawyers or other professionals, the clerk will perform more of an administrative or clerical role, not giving advice to the tribunal.

Process

Tribunals operate under a bewildering variety of procedures. Some take evidence only on oath or after affirmation, given by the witness or party to the proceedings; others do not use the oath. Some sit in courtrooms—or rooms set out like courtrooms. Others are established in much more informal contexts, such as school rooms or hotel rooms. Some large tribunal systems manage their own tribunal accommodation; others have to rent or borrow space as occasion demands. (It is remarkable—given the extent of the administrative justice system, and the numbers of tribunals it comprises—that towns do not have 'administrative justice centres' to match the criminal court centres and civil court centres that are commonly found.)

Many tribunal systems make extensive efforts to deal with appellants who—as the result of a lack of availability of legal aid—either have to represent themselves or have to rely on lay advocates. The social security appeal system, for example, prides itself on its 'enabling role'. Unlike the adversarial approach of the courts, where the judges tend to take a back seat while the argument, for and against, is presented by advocates for both sides, members of tribunals take a more interventionist role, seeking to draw relevant information from the parties by appropriate questioning. It is in this variety of forensic methods that much of the potential innovation of the tribunal system is to be found, and from which the courts—if they knew what went on in the best-run tribunals—might have much to learn.[12]

It is sometimes suggested that tribunals offer 'informal' as opposed to 'formal' justice. This gives the wrong impression, certainly if 'informal' implies a lack of organization or discipline. The primary advantage of a tribunal as opposed to a court is that there is a lack of rigidity of process, though the person running the tribunal must have a very clear grasp of what the issue to be decided is. If this is clear, the precise order in which people speak will not matter, so long as everyone has their say.

---

[12] Mr Justice Lightman argued, in a lecture to the London Solicitors' Litigation Association on 9 November 1999, that the judges in the ordinary courts should adopt a more interventionist approach. This merely reflects what has long happened in many tribunals.

The relevant information can thereby be obtained which should allow the tribunal to come to a fair and proper decision.

Management

Management of tribunals also varies enormously. Many systems have presidents who operate at national level, often through a regional structure—for example social security, employment and the Special Educational Needs and Disability Tribunal. These tribunal systems tend to be well organized, with comprehensive programmes of training for members and chairmen, monitoring and evaluation of performance and the use of other modern management techniques.

In other cases, such as Education Appeal Committees, the tribunals are organized at the local authority level, with very little central direction. Others operate on a regional basis; they include mental health, rent assessment and valuation. These tribunal systems tend to be less advanced in the development of training programmes and the use of other management techniques, and seem less well resourced for the tasks they are required to perform.

Reporting of decisions

A final respect in which tribunal systems differ relates to the ways in which important decisions get reported. Many of the two-tier systems have the means of publishing significant decisions from the upper tier. Some of these reports are published commercially—as in the case of employment cases; other are published regularly by the government department in question—such as immigration reports, or tax cases. Others appear on a more hand-to-mouth basis, such as the reported decisions of the Social Security Commissioners. Other tribunal systems have no formal reporting mechanisms.

Reforming the tribunals system

Within the tribunals system there is currently much debate about change. A number of tribunals have either undergone or are undergoing reviews that will change the way they operate. At the same time, the wide variety of structure and process poses an obvious bigger question: is this 'system' with all its variation the best way of running this part of the administrative justice system? Would there be scope for greater efficiency if there were to be some restructuring? Or do the individual procedures— developed to deal with particular sets of issues—provide the most efficient method of delivering a service to the public?

These were among the questions that the Lord Chancellor, in May 2000, asked Sir Andrew Leggatt[13] to consider as part of a major review of tribunals. The subsequent report, *Tribunals for Users: Ones System, One Service*, was completed in March 2001 but not published until August 2001. It set out a long list of detailed proposals for rendering the present tribunal system more coherent. A short summary of the key principles can be found in *Box 6.1*.

---

[13] A retired judge of the Court of Appeal.

6.1 Leggatt Review of Tribunals: key points

'In the 44 years since tribunals were last reviewed, their numbers have increased considerably and their work has become more complex. Together they constitute a substantial part of the system of justice in England and Wales. The object of this review is to recommend a system that is independent, coherent, professional, cost-effective and user-friendly. Together tribunals must form a system and provide a service fit for the users for whom they were intended.

So they have to be rationalised and modernised; and this Review has as its four main objects: first, to make the 70 tribunals into one Tribunals System that its members can be proud of; secondly, to render the tribunals independent of their sponsoring departments by having them administered by one Tribunals Service; thirdly, to improve the training of chairmen and members in the interpersonal skills peculiarly required by tribunals; and fourthly, to enable unrepresented users to participate effectively and without apprehension in tribunal proceedings.

There is only one way to achieve independence and coherence: to have all the tribunals supported by a Tribunals Service, that is, a common administrative service. It would raise their status, while preserving their distinctness from the courts. In the medium term it would yield considerable economies of scale, particularly in relation to the provision of premises for all tribunals, common basic training, and the use of IT. It would also bring greater administrative efficiency, a single point of contact for users, improved geographical distribution of tribunal centres, common standards, an enhanced corporate image, greater prospects of job satisfaction, a better relationship between members and administrative staff, and improved career patterns for both on account of the size and coherence of the Tribunals Service. It should be committed by Charter to provide a high quality, unified service, to operate independently, to deal openly and honestly with users of tribunals, to seek to maintain public confidence, and to report annually on its performance.

The independence of tribunals would best be safeguarded by having their administrative support provided by the Lord Chancellor's Department. The Lord Chancellor's policy responsibilities do not give rise to tribunal cases. He has extensive experience of managing courts, and already appoints most tribunal members. He is also responsible for the administration of the Judicial Studies Board, through which the training of judges is supervised, and the training of tribunal members should be furthered. As a Minister he is answerable to Parliament, and so to the public, for the proper functioning of our system of justice. He is uniquely well placed to protect the independence of those who sit in tribunals as well as of the judiciary, through a Tribunals Service and a Tribunals System analogous with, but separate from, the Court Service and the courts.'

Source: Review of tribunals, Overview

Publication of the report caused considerable consternation in the corridors of Whitehall. Government departments came to see that implementation of the review's proposals would involve some ceding of their current portfolio of functions to another department, never an attractive prospect. Rather than simply accepting the review's conclusions, the Lord Chancellor's Department—on the day the review report was published—also put out a consultation paper designed to allow for a further round of discussion within government about how the principles Leggatt espoused might be introduced. The White Paper setting out the Government's conclusions on this exercise is, at the time of preparing this edition, still awaited. Current indications are that, contrary to what many observers feared, the opportunity for rendering the tribunal system more coherent will be seized; the degree to which this will be done and the speed with which it will be done are both currently unclear.

Inquiries

The historically conceptual distinction between a tribunal and an inquiry was that, whereas a tribunal usually had statutory authority to reach a final decision which, subject to any right of appeal, determined the dispute before it, an inquiry gathered information, in the light of which a government minister would decide the issue.

In practice, this distinction has become somewhat blurred. Mental Health Review Tribunals, for example, when dealing with mental patients who have been detained in a mental hospital as a result of a court order, can only make a recommendation to the Home Secretary that a patient should be released from hospital; it is the Secretary of State (or his officials) who takes the final decision. So too in the sphere of the inquiry, many inquiries now result in a decision being reached, rather than a report to a minister which would form the basis for a decision.

Planning inquiries and related procedures

The principal use of the inquiry as an institution in the administrative justice system is now found in the context of the planning process. In a geographically small country with a substantial population, it has long been accepted that the state has an interest in determining how land should be used. The planning process seeks to balance the competing interests relating to land use of urban dwellers, rural dwellers, industrialists, scientists, the pursuers of leisure interests, the providers of transport systems and other utility providers (gas, electricity, water), to give just some examples.

The bulk of planning decisions are taken by local authorities, acting as local planning authorities. Strategically key decisions—for example over the siting of a new airport—may be 'called in' for determination by the Secretary of State within central government.

Once a planning decision has been reached, rights of appeal are provided. Whereas in other contexts a tribunal has been established to deal with appeals, in the planning context appeals are dealt with by way of inquiry, supplemented by two additional procedures: written representations and hearings. All these procedures are dealt with by a special team of decision-takers, known collectively as the Planning Inspectorate. Originally, planning inspectors did not reach decisions in planning appeals; they held inquiries and in the light of their findings made recommendations to the Secretary of State in the central government. These procedures were 'inquiries' in their original sense. As a result of changes in the law, planning inspectors now have the authority to make the final determination in all save the most complex or important cases, where they still make recommendations to the Secretary of State. In the majority of cases, the functions of the planning inspectorate are indistinguishable from the functions of a tribunal.

As noted, planning inspectors have three mechanisms for reaching determinations:

* written representations;
* hearings; and
* inquiries.

Statistically, the inquiry is the least frequently used mode for determining planning appeals.[14]

* *Written representations* are, as the name implies, a means of dealing with an appeal purely through written representations. This is the speediest and cheapest of the procedures and is particularly suitable for the determination of relatively small matters, e.g. an extension to a dwelling.

* *Hearings* involve the appellants and the local planning authority in a hearing before a planning inspector, but the process is consciously 'low-key'. Planning inspectors are trained to run hearings proactively to try to avoid the need for the use of expensive legal representation. The inspector shapes the hearing by assisting the parties to identify the issues that need to be addressed. Typically, the hearing is used in cases slightly more significant than those dealt with by written representation, but not as large scale as those going to inquiry.

* *Inquiries* are much more formal. They are used primarily for major planning issues. (Inquiries are also used to determine the shape of local planning authorities' local plans—which provide the background against which individual planning applications are decided.) Inquiries involve hearing a wider range of persons with an interest in the decision—for example, environmental groups or trade associations—than written representations or hearings. Procedurally they are more formal, with the parties usually using barristers or solicitors to represent their interests. Inquiries can take a very long time; the public inquiry into the Fifth Terminal at London Heathrow Airport took over five years to complete.

Particular and ad hoc inquiries

In addition to planning inquiries, which are held on a regular basis, many other

---

[14] In 2001–2, 10,714 planning appeals were determined by written representations; 2,920 by hearing; and only 937 by inquiry: *Council on Tribunals Annual Report, 2001–2002* (London, The Stationery Office, 2002).

particular forms of inquiry are put in place as the need arises, for example, inquiries into serious rail accidents or other disasters.

The government may also use an ad hoc inquiry to deal with the aftermath of a particular incident. Recent examples include the inquiry into events at the Bristol Children's Hospital, or the Scott inquiry into the Arms for Iraq affair. The Council on Tribunals has issued advice on matters that government should take into account when establishing such ad hoc inquiries.[15] Local authorities and other public bodies may also establish inquiries into a range of issues, as they arise.[16]

Review

Another form of process for the redress of grievance is review, whereby officials within the department that has taken the initial decision are required to review that initial decision to see whether or not it is correct or should be revised. The reviewer may in some cases be the initial decision-taker; in others the reviewer is another official, usually more senior in the hierarchy. Reviews may seem to lack the independence that characterizes an appeal to a tribunal or an inquiry.[17] But they do provide an easy and quick means of rectifying a decision where something has clearly gone wrong. Reviews are found in two basic forms: the formal and the informal:

- *Formal* reviews are those which are required by law to be carried out. In some cases, as with Child Benefit Appeals or Disability Benefit Appeals, statutory review was a preliminary stage which all appeals had to go through before the decision could reach a tribunal.[18] In other cases, such as review of decisions relating to the Social Fund, there is no tribunal process available at all—all appeals go through the review process.

- *Informal* reviews are those that are not required by law but which officials nonetheless carry out as part of their routine administrative procedures. In the case of social security appeals, for example, any appeal by a social security claimant against a decision of the Benefits Agency triggers an internal official review to check whether the decision appealed against is or is not correct. There is evidence that more cases are revised in favour of claimants at this stage than at the appeal stage.[19]

Reviews as a feature of the administrative justice system have been the subject of

---

[15] Council on Tribunals, *Advice to the Lord Chancellor on the Procedural Issues arising in the Conduct of Public Inquiries set up by Ministers*, July 1996 (published as an appendix in the *Annual Report, 1995–1996*). (HC 114, 1995–1996) (London, HMSO, 1996).

[16] For discussion of some of the issues that can arise in relation to such inquiries see Law Commission, *Publication of Local Authority Reports* (CP 163) (London, The Stationery Office, 2002).

[17] A view that would certainly be challenged by the Social Fund Commissioner who runs the Independent Review Service.

[18] This type of formal review has now been abolished and replaced by *informal* review: Social Security Act 1998.

[19] See Baldwin, J., *et al.*, *Judging Social Security* (Oxford, Clarendon Press, 1992).

considerable criticism. In the same way that, in the context of criminal justice, decisions by the police to deal with suspects administratively—e.g. by issuing a caution—are criticized for undermining the 'due process' model of criminal justice, so too is review seen as undermining the 'due process' model of administrative justice. Thus Sainsbury argues strongly that the review process is objectionable in principle, in that there cannot be independence where reviews are conducted essentially within the organization that made the initial decision. He also objects to review on the practical ground that, by introducing another layer of decision-taking, this may have the effect of denying claimants the right to appear before a tribunal to hear their case—at least in situations where review is a preliminary to appeal before a tribunal.[20]

Against this, others suggest that models of administrative justice should be based not just on due process but also on other principles, such as cost-effectiveness and efficiency. This might result in the conclusion that review is not so objectionable. Rather, review is a pragmatic and sensible way of ensuring that mistakes are corrected without the expense and delay of a tribunal hearing, and can be organized so as to meet the objection that they lack independence.[21] In addition, when well organized, review has all the hallmarks of independence and due process in any event.[22]

While the theoretical objections can perhaps be overstated, the review mechanism—in its various guises—will undoubtedly remain in the repertoire of the dispute resolution procedures of the administrative justice system, and should thus be seen as a part of that system. The question is not so much whether review should be part of the system at all; rather, consideration needs to be given to those cases where review is appropriate and those where it is not.

Practical experience suggests that the primary reason decisions taken by officials are often found to be wrong is not that the official has misunderstood the law to be applied to the case in question, but that the factual information on which the decision is based is in some respect wanting. It should therefore make sense to find ways of getting at the relevant facts other than by the relatively expensive and long-drawn-out process of a tribunal hearing. In this context, review may be a valuable procedure. However, if the way in which the review works is that no effort is made to see whether new evidence is forthcoming, or that those who may have a case to take to a tribunal become so disheartened that they fail to pursue their claims in full, then the review may not be fulfilling a helpful role in the repertoire of administrative justice procedures.

---

[20] Sainsbury, R., 'Internal Reviews and the Weakening of Social Security Claimants' Rights of Appeal' in Richardson, G., and Genn H. (eds.), *Administrative Law and Government Action* (Oxford, Clarendon Press, 1994).

[21] Harris, M., 'The Place of Formal and Informal Review in Administrative Justice' in Harris, M., and Partington, M. (eds.), *Administrative Justice in the 21st Century* (Oxford, Hart, 1999).

[22] Scampion, J., 'New Procedures' in *ibid.*

Ombudsmen

The Parliamentary Ombudsman

The Ombudsman concept was introduced into the UK from Scandinavia in 1967. The first Ombudsman was and still is formally known as the 'Parliamentary Commissioner for Administration' (PCA), though she now describes herself as the *Parliamentary Ombudsman.* Following devolution, she also holds the posts of *Scottish Parliamentary Commissioner for Administration* (the Scottish Commissioner)[23] and *Welsh Administration Ombudsman.*

The Ombudsman's function is to investigate complaints and allegations of *maladminstration* in central government departments which may result in injustice. She also has important functions to deal with complaints about failures by government departments to provide information about their work, contrary to the *Code of Practice on Access to Official Information.*

Two particular features of the Parliamentary Ombudsman's jurisdiction should be noted. First, members of the public are not entitled to complain directly to the PCA;[24] they must get their complaint referred to the Ombudsman by a Member of Parliament (in Scotland, a Member of the Scottish Parliament). MPs are not actually obliged to refer cases on, if they think they can deal with the matter themselves. The reason for the existence of this filter is that, when the Ombudsman concept was introduced, there were those who argued that it might undermine the primary responsibility of Parliament and its members to call ministers (and their officials) to account. The 'MP filter', as it is known, was not part of the original Scandinavian Ombudsman concept, where direct access by the public was permitted.

Secondly, the Parliamentary Ombudsman cannot order that any particular consequence should follow a finding of maladminstration. She can only 'persuade' a government department, for example, to pay compensation to an aggrieved citizen. Again, in other countries, the Ombudsman has power to enforce his decisions.

The Health Service Ombudsman

Since first established, the jurisdiction of the Ombudsman has broadened considerably. The same person also holds the three separate posts of Health Service Ombudsman for England, for Scotland, and for Wales. As Health Service Ombudsman she investigates complaints about failures in National Health Service (NHS) hospitals or community health services, about care and treatment, and about local NHS family doctor, dental, pharmacy or optical services. Any member of the public may refer a complaint direct—i.e. not necessarily through a Member of Parliament —to one of her offices, though normally only if a full investigation within the NHS complaints system has been carried out first.

[23] This is distinct from the Scottish Public Service Ombudsman, who investigates allegations of maladministration in a wide range of Scottish public services: www.scottishombudsman.org.uk/.

[24] There is now an exception: complaints to her as Welsh Administration Ombudsman do not have to be referred though a member of the Welsh Assembly.

Besides investigating and, where appropriate, redressing grievances, the Ombudsman sees her function as also to improve the quality of administration. She thus endeavours to ensure that her reports contain general guidance on good practice from which government departments may learn. Summaries of her investigations are published regularly and are also now available on the internet. She also produces an *Annual Report* which is submitted to the Select Committee of the House of Commons, to the Scottish Parliament or to the National Assembly for Wales, as appropriate. The Select Committee regularly sees the Parliamentary Ombudsman, as well as senior civil servants from departments that have been criticized by her. Thus Parliament is kept informed about the Ombudsman's work and the impact it has had on government departments.

Local government ombudsmen

The ombudsman concept has been extended to local government. There are now three local government ombudsmen covering all local authorities in England, plus one each for Wales and Scotland. They investigate complaints against principal councils (not town, parish or community councils) and certain other bodies in England, Scotland and Wales. By law, some kinds of complaint cannot be considered. Examples are personnel complaints and complaints about the internal running of schools.

As with other ombudsmen, the objective of the local government ombudsmen is to secure, where appropriate, satisfactory redress for complainants and better administration by local authorities. Indeed, since 1989, they have had power to issue advice on good administrative practice, drawing lessons from the cases they have handled. To date, six guidance notes have been published: on setting up complaints procedures; good administrative practice; council housing repairs; local authority members' interests; the disposal of land; and remedies when things have gone wrong.

The Government has started a process of review of these public sector ombudsmen with a view to seeing whether there should be any restructuring of the present arrangements or any changes to their procedures or powers. The outcome of this has not been finalized, though the Government is committed in principle to change, including the eventual removal of the 'MP filter'.[25]

Others

A more recent development is that, increasingly, Ombudsman or Ombudsman-type offices are being created which are much more specialist in nature. For example, in areas of particular relevance to this book, there is now a *Legal Services Ombudsman* with powers to investigate complaints about services provides by lawyers; the *Police Complaints Authority*, which—as the name implies—deals with complaints against

---

[25] See *Review of the Public Sector Ombudsmen in England*, www.cabinet-office.gov.uk/central/2000/ombudsmenreview.pdf (April 2000); *Review of the Public Sector Ombudsmen in England: A Consultation Paper*, www.cabinet-office.gov.uk/central/2000/consultation.pdf; and written evidence of Chris Leslie MP to the Select Committee on Public Administration, 31 January 2002 (HC 563-i, 2001–2002) (London, The Stationery Office, 2002).

the police; a *Prisons and Probation Ombudsman*, who deals with complaints about the prison and probation service; and the *Independent Housing Ombudsman*, who deals with complaints against (primarily) registered social landlords (formerly called Housing Associations).

The rise of private sector ombudsmen

Over the last fifteen years or so, a peculiarly British phenomenon has emerged. A considerable number of private sector industries have set up their own sector-wide ombudsman schemes to deal with those customer complaints that cannot be resolved within a particular company. These schemes include the Estates Agents Ombudsman, the Banking Ombudsman, the Insurance Ombudsman, and the Building Societies Ombudsman. By contrast with the PCA and the other public sector ombudsmen, where the levels of complaints has been relatively low, many of these private sector ombudsmen have had large caseloads to deal with. They offer a 'mass-market' dispute resolution procedure, as opposed to the more 'Rolls-Royce' work of the PCA.[26]

As a result of the Financial Services and Markets Act 2000 a Financial Services Ombudsman scheme has brought together many of these private schemes, and now operates under statutory rather than industry-determined powers.

Process

A common feature of all ombudsmen's procedures is that they operate on what might be described as an 'inquisitorial' or 'investigative' basis. The complaint is made; the relevant ombudsman's staff investigates the complaint, taking further evidence both from the government department or other agency concerned and the complainant. In the light of the investigation a conclusion is reached on whether or not there was in fact maladministration. Many investigations result in a finding that the department or agency in question behaved perfectly responsibly, and the complainant was being unreasonable. Where there was a finding of maladministration, there is comment on whether the response of the department was appropriate. Many findings of mal-administration lead to no more that the writing of a letter of apology, which is often all that the complainant wanted in the first place. Usually there is no possibility of an oral hearing (though the Pensions Ombudsman is required to offer this).

The European Ombudsman

In addition to developments in England and Wales, the Ombudsman concept now also extends to the work of the European Union. The creation of a European Ombudsman was approved in the Maastricht Treaty; the statute giving him his authority was agreed in 1994. He took up office 1995 and has been issuing annual reports on his work since 1996.

He operates on the basis of *The European Ombudsman Implementing Provisions*; the

---

[26] Williams, T., and Goriely, T., 'A Question of Numbers: Managing Complaints Against Rising Expecta-tions' in Harris, M., and Partington, M. (eds.), *Administrative Justice in the 21st Century* (Oxford, Hart, 1999).

first set of these dated October 1997, have been replaced by a new set, effective from January 2003. These not only set out in general terms the principles on which the Ombudsman will carry out his work, but also list the various powers he has when determining cases: these include the possibility of making 'critical remarks', where no more general conclusions can be drawn from the case under investigation, and the making of a 'report with draft recommendations', where it appears that some more general lessons may be learned.

In addition, and unlike the national ombudsmen in England and Wales, the European Ombudsman has a very broad power to instigate his 'own-initiative inquiries'. One fruit of this, to date, has been the preparation of a set of draft recommendations, which have been put both to the European Commission and to the European Parliament and Council of Ministers, relating to the adoption of a *Code of Good Administrative Behaviour*. His reason for doing this was the result of reflecting on many of the individual complaints he had received, which indicated that maladministration might have been avoided had clearer information been available about the administrative duties of Community staff towards its citizens. The code has now been approved by the European Parliament and published.[27]

The Citizens' Charter/Service First

Another development in the field of administrative justice, and one that has not attracted the attention it deserves, was the introduction of the concept of the Citizens' Charter, now 'rebadged' as *Service First*. In contrast with the Ombudsman, where the concept has moved from the public sector to the private, the Citizens' Charter concept has gone the other way. Private sector ideas about standards of customer care and service delivery, and modes of responding to failures in those standards, have been brought into the public sector.

Though the initial introduction of the Charter, in 1991 by the government of Mr Major, was seen as rather gimmicky, it has provided another impetus to promoting service standards in the public sector, through the concept of the 'Customers' Charter' and the related 'Chartermark' awards, and for dealing with customer complaints.[28] In May 1999, the British Standards Institute published a British Standard (BS 8600:99) dealing with the effective management and handling of complaints.

As part of the New Charter Programme, nine principles for public service delivery have been promulgated. They include:

- setting standards of service;
- being open and providing full information;
- encouraging access and promoting choice;

---

[27] March 2002. See www.euro-ombudsman.eu.int/code/pdf/en/code_en.pdf.

[28] The Service First website, part of the Cabinet Office website, provides links to the complaints procedures of nearly 50 central government departments and agencies; this does not include any of the health service or local government procedures.

- treating all fairly;
- putting things right when they go wrong;
- innovating and improving.

These principles provoke two immediate reflections. First, it seems surprising that those engaged in the delivery of public services should need to be provided with such a set of principles at all. They seem to be obvious and rather common sense in content. However, if it is the case that those who deliver public services do not already satisfy these principles, then no harm can be done by issuing them, and indeed as they develop some considerable good may flow from them. Secondly, and more specifically, although most public sector activity is bounded by rules of law which empower officials to take action, there is no mention of the need for officials to obey the law in performing their administrative tasks.

To date, not all the initiatives that have been taken are necessarily as effective as might be wished. Some of the customer charters[29] set standards of service that do not appear to be particularly demanding. But other targets—for example, relating to the time for dealing with matters or responding to queries from the public—have become tougher in recent years. In so far as the concept of administrative justice embraces issues relating to the proper and efficient delivery of service standards, then this is another development which, for all its current limitations, should be regarded as significant in the administrative justice system. *Service First* should certainly be better understood by students of the administrative justice system.

Other complaints-handling bodies

It might be thought that, with the creation of ombudsmen to deal with issues at a high level and with the more recent development of a wide variety of complaints resolutions procedures in individual government departments, there were now adequate means for the redress of citizens' complaints. In fact, other bodies and procedures have been created with more specific remits than the ombudsmen's but more general authority than an internal complaints procedure. It is possible to give only examples here:

- The *Adjudicator* investigates complaints from people and businesses about how the Inland Revenue (including the Valuation Office Agency), Customs and Excise and the Contributions Agency of the Department of Social Security have handled their affairs. The Adjudicator does not look at issues of law or of tax liability, because there are tribunals which resolve these problems. But she does look into excessive delay, mistakes, discourtesy of staff and the use of discretion.

- The *Independent Case Examiner for the Child Support Agency* investigates

---

[29] Again the *Service First* website provides links to a number of these—currently in excess of 40 can be taken directly from the web.

complaints about maladministration by the Child Support Agency, when clients are dissatisfied with the outcome of the Agency's internal complaints service.

- Similarly the *Independent Complaints Reviewer to HM Land Registry* investigates complaints about the Land Registry. Her role is to establish whether there has been maladministration on the part of the agency in the conduct of matters giving rise to complaints. These include failure to meet standards of service, quality, speed and performance. Where appropriate she makes recommendations aimed at putting matters right for an individual complainant and improving Land Registry services in the future.

Other bodies include the *Subsidence Adviser* who considers the ways in which the Coal Authority and private mining companies handle claims for mining subsidence damage, and the *Waterways Ombudsman* which deals with complaints against British Waterways, where internal complaints have failed.

'Collective' administrative justice—regulators of privatized utility providers

Another context for the resolution of disputes arises from the privatization of the main utility providers—water, gas, telecommunications, for example. Following privatization, the provision of services by state monopolies was, in the main, replaced by private monopolies. New regulatory offices—including OFWAT, OFGEM and OFTEL—were established to regulate these new industries to prevent abuse of market power in the setting of prices, and to create the conditions in which other suppliers might come into the market to provide the competition essential for consumer protection. These regulatory offices have also had some responsibility for the development of procedures for dealing with individual customer complaints and complaints from others wishing to enter particular market sectors.[30]

This is not the place to consider the work of these industry regulators in detail. But their existence does need to be noted and the fact that they too now play a part in the overall framework of administrative justice.

'Private' administrative justice—regulation of the professions

A final area in which the presence of institutions of administrative justice may be said to exist is in the regulation of the professions. Here private bodies, such as the Law Society (for solicitors) or the General Medical Council (for doctors) exercise statutory powers relating to the regulation of their professions, designed to enhance the quality of service provision and the protection of the public. In carrying out these functions, they and other professional regulators tend to operate through varying forms of

---

[30] The complaints-handling work of these bodies has been discussed in detail by McHarg, A. T., 'Separation of Functions and Regulatory Agencies: Dispute Resolution in the Privatised Utilities' in Harris, M., and Partington, M. (eds.), *Administrative Justice in the 21st Century* (Oxford, Hart, 1999).

tribunal, before which the doctor or lawyer is required to appear to answer the case against him or her.

This is a little-researched[31] and thus poorly understood part of the administrative justice system. But again its existence should be noted in any overview of that system.

Overview of the administrative justice system

The Council on Tribunals

The best established of the bodies which keep the administrative justice system under review is the Council on Tribunals. Created in 1959 under the authority of the Tribunals and Inquiries Act 1958, the Council has the statutory responsibility to advise and report to the Lord Chancellor. Its primary function is to consider and keep under review the work of the tribunals and inquiry systems under its jurisdiction; to comment on drafts of procedural regulations, on which the Council must be consulted; and to deal with such other matters as may be referred to it.

It has over the years interpreted its remit broadly, and indeed government departments have used it more broadly than this. For example, the Council is regularly consulted on proposals to establish new tribunals or to introduce changes to existing tribunals, for example by changing their procedural rules or by expanding the range of cases which may go before the tribunal.

In addition the Council has prepared a number of reports relating to general issues about the operation of tribunals and inquiries: for example, in 1991 it produced a major analysis (currently under revision) of the procedural rules that might be adopted by tribunal systems.[32] In 1997 it produced a report on the independence of tribunals, reasserting the importance of this fundamental principle in the operation of tribunals.[33] In 2002 it produced the first *Framework of Standards for Tribunals.*[34]

A particular feature of the *modus operandi* of the Council is that it has, in the vast majority of the tribunal systems under its authority, a statutory right to attend hearings. Members of the Council make around 120 visits a year to different tribunals and inquiries in all parts of the country. Members produce reports for consideration by the Council on what they have seen, which provide a powerful source of information about both good and bad practice in the system.

As a result of these visits many items of concern to the Council have emerged, which have been translated into proposals for change, for example:

---

[31] For an honourable exception see Smith, R. G., *Medical Discipline, The Professional Conduct Jurisdiction of the General Medical Council, 1858–1990* (Oxford, Oxford University Press, 1994).

[32] *Model Rules of Procedure for Tribunals* (Cm 1434) (London, HMSO, 1991).

[33] *Tribunals: Their Organisation and Independence* (Cm 3744) (London, The Stationery Office, 1997).

[34] London, Council on Tribunals, 2002.

- the need for training of tribunal chairmen and members;
- the importance of the role of the clerk and administrative support generally in ensuring the smooth running of tribunals;
- the need for an adequate level of resource to enable the work of the tribunals to be done effectively.

The *Annual Reports* of the Council provided a rich repository not just of information about developments in the administrative justice system, but also of the principles and practices which should be adopted in that system. The obvious limitation of the work of the Council is implicit in its name; its focus is limited to the tribunals and inquiry system over which it has been given a supervisory function. Nevertheless, the Leggatt review of tribunals saw the Council as a key part of the administrative justice system and recommended that its role should be enhanced.[35]

The British and Irish Ombudsmen's Association (BIOA)

Ombudsmen are another very important part of the administrative justice system. As this mechanism for dispute resolution has developed, BIOA was founded in 1995. Its principal purpose is to ensure that only those bodies that subscribe to certain procedural standards use the label 'ombudsman'. In particular, ensuring that ombudsmen in the private sector of the economy, who were privately financed, are truly *independent* of their paymasters, is an important function for BIOA. It has also undertaken other activity, such as developing principles for the training and procedures to be adopted by individual ombudsman systems. One feature particularly worthy of note—and which it is surprising does not exist in other parts of the English legal system—is the link with our neighbouring common law jurisdiction, Ireland. (Though not strictly relevant to this book, there would be advantage in thinking of other areas of the justice system where there might be opportunities for the British and the Irish to learn from each other.)

Need for a new overview body?

As will be realized from the coverage in this chapter, there remain other areas of the administrative justice system which fall outside the remit either of the Council on Tribunals or the BIOA. For this reason there have been calls for some more wide-ranging body or institute which might keep the administrative justice system, taken as a whole, under review. For example in Australia there is an Australian Institute of Administrative Law, with a wide membership drawn from throughout that great continent.

In the British context, there have been similar calls for the creation of a body which might take on the role of looking at the administrative justice system in the holistic

---

[35] Ways in which the Council is adapting to this challenge are set out in its recent *Annual Reports*.

sense indicated above; to explore the extent to which there may be gaps in provision or over-provision; to argue for the provision of sound statistical information to provide proper management information about the development of administrative justice and so on.

More specifically a number of developments are occurring which, in the context of individual tribunals or other dispute resolving fora, may seem justifiable but which need to be seen in the round. For example, there is considerable pressure in a number of tribunal systems to move from three-person to one-person tribunals; there is pressure to do as much decision-taking as possible on the papers only without hearings; there are very considerable resource pressures which have led to the reduction or even withdrawal of essential administrative services, such as the provision of clerks; provision of training is still very patchy; the use of accommodation for tribunals and other fora is often less efficient than it should be.

The Human Rights Act 1998 and the Freedom of Information Act 2000 have considerable potential for making an impact across the administrative justice system.

These are the sorts of structural issue that should be kept under general review, which under present arrangements does not happen. The fact that the Lord Chancellor's Department is now asserting much greater leadership in this area is a very important new development. But, as with the Select Committee on the Parliamentary Commissioner for Administration, it would also help if a Select Committee of the House of Commons were to take a more specific interest in the structure and workings of the administrative justice system as a whole.

Audit and quality control

The discussion of administrative justice so far has focused on the wide variety of fora, ranging from the courts to informal complaints-handling procedures, available to the individual citizen, dissatisfied with some aspect of public administration. There are now many avenues for challenging the legality of a decision, or the use of a discretionary power, or the process by which a decision was made.

Other mechanisms have also been introduced to try to ensure quality of performance and the provision of good public services which provide value for money. As Ison has argued, if officials get the initial decision right, then the consumers of public services should be better satisfied and have less need to use the myriad appeal and complaints mechanisms outlined above.[36] (Indeed, one of the criticisms that can be made of many of these processes—the ombudsmen are perhaps an exception—is that there is rather little institutional commitment to the idea of considering what *general* lessons might be drawn from the resolution of the *individual* appeal or complaint. Indeed, the very process of encouraging disputes to be resolved on an individual basis

---

[36] Ison, T., 'Administrative Justice: Is it Such a Good Idea?' in Harris, M., and Partington, M. (eds.), *Administrative Justice in the 21st Century* (Oxford, Hart, 1999).

may disguise structural questions which, if addressed by the government department or other agency, might have prevented the problem arising in the first place.)

Among the alternative techniques now used to try to achieve these more general objectives are:

- the use of audit to ensure that value for money in the provision of public services is achieved;

- the use of inspectorates to ensure the quality of service provision;

- the provision of benchmarking statistics to provide baseline data against which performance by public sector agencies may be measured; and

- the conclusion of public service agreements, designed to encourage the modernization of service delivery, support proposals for reform and increase accountability by the setting of clear aims and objectives.[37]

The time has come to consider the importance of the application of these techniques to the administrative justice system.

Questions for discussion

1. Are tribunals properly seen as part of the English legal system?

2. Can tribunals ever be truly 'user-friendly'? How can those who cannot afford representation before a tribunal be best assisted to make their case?

3. What are the arguments for and against keeping tribunals as three-person bodies?

4. Should there be a direct right of access by members of the public to the Parliamentary Ombudsman?

5. Should all ombudsmen be able to award compensation for proven maladministration?

6. Are there too many avenues for complaint when things go wrong?

7. Is there a need for a new body to review the whole of the administrative justice system?

8. What other mechanisms are there to review administrative action and control the power of state officials?

---

[37] See *Public Services for the Future: Modernisation, Reform, Accountability* (Cm 4181) (London, The Stationery Office, 1998).

Further reading

BRIDGES, L., MESZAROS, G., and SUNKIN, M., *Judicial Review in Perspective* (London, Cavendish, 1995)

GENN, H., and GENN, Y., *The Effectiveness of Representation at Tribunals: Report to the Lord Chancellor* (London, Queen Mary College, Faculty of Laws, 1989)

HARLOW, C., and RAWLINGS, R., *Law and Administration* (2nd edn., London, Butterworths, 1997)

HARRIS, M., and PARTINGTON, M. (eds.), *Administrative Justice in the 21st Century* (Oxford, Hart, 1999)

LEWIS, N., and BIRKINSHAW, P., *When Citizens Complain: Reforming Justice and Administration* (Buckingham, Open University Press, 1993)

RICHARDSON, G., and GENN, H. (eds.), *Administrative Law and Government Action* (Oxford, Clarendon Press, 1994)

SMITH, R.G., *Medical Discipline, The Professional Conduct Jurisdiction of the General Medical Council, 1858–1990* (Oxford, OUP, 1994)

WOOLF, LORD, and JOWELL. J. (assistant editor Le Sueur, A.P.), *Judicial Review of Administrative Action* (5th edn. of book originally written by Prof. S. A. de Smith) (London, Sweet & Maxwell, 1995)

Websites

www.publiclawproject.org.uk/

www.law.cam.ac.uk/ccpr/home.htm *(Cambridge University Centre for Public Law)*

www.courtservice.gov.uk/tribunals/tribs_home.htm *(Mini-portal to tribunals currently under the control of the Lord Chancellor's Department)*

www.lcd.gov.uk/rlinksfr.htm#part22 *(Longer set of links to different tribunal and tribunal-related sites)*

www.appeals-service.gov.uk/

www.courtservice.gov.uk/tribunals/ossc/court02.htm *(Social Security Commissioners' decisions)*

www.employmenttribunals.gov.uk/

www.employmentappeals.gov.uk/ *(Employment Appeals Tribunal)*

www.iaa.gov.uk/ *(Immigration Appeals Authority)*

www.irs-review.org.uk/ *(Independent review service of the social fund inspectorate)*

www.doh.gov.uk/mentalhealth/mhrtreport.pdf *(Report on Mental Health Tribunals; the tribunal does not currently have a website)*

www.housing.odpm.gov.uk/structure/rap/ *(Rent assessment panels)*

www.tribunals-review.org.uk/ *(The Leggatt review of tribunals)*

www.planning-inspectorate.gov.uk/

www.bioa.org.uk/ *(British and Irish Ombudsmen's Association—portal for links to most ombudsman sites)* www.ombudsman.org.uk/ *(Parliamentary Commissioner for Administration and Health Service Ombudsman)*

www.doh.gov.uk/complaints/index.htm *(NHS complaints procedure)*

www.lcd.gov.uk/foi/foidpunit.htm *(Lord Chancellor's Department: Freedom of Information and Data Protection Division)*

www.parliament.uk/parliamentary_committees/public_administration_select_committee.cfm *(Select Committee of the House of Commons with responsibility for reviewing the reports of the PCA)*

www.lgo.org.uk/ *(Local Government Ombudsman)*

www.olso.org/ *(Legal Services Ombudsman)*

www.pca.gov.uk/ *(Police Complaints Authority; to be replaced by the Independent Police Complaints Commission)*

www.ppo.gov.uk/ *(Prisons and probation ombudsman)*

www.ihos.org.uk/ *(Independent Housing Ombudsman)*

www.financial-ombudsman.org.uk/ *(Financial Services Ombudsman)*

www.adjudicatorsoffice.gov.uk/ *(Adjudicator's Office—deals with range of complaints relating to taxation, national insurance contributions)*

www.ind-case-exam.org.uk/ *(Independent Case Examiners—deals with complaints of maladministration against the Child Support Agency)*

www.bioa.org.uk/BIOA-New/OtherComplaints.htm *(Long list of sites for other complaints procedures)*

www.cabinet-office.gov.uk/servicefirst/2000/Complaints/links.htm *(Another list of bodies responsible for handling complaints)*

www.euro-ombudsman.eu.int/code/en/default.htm *(European Ombudsman)*

www.euro-ombudsman.eu.int/lbasis/en/statute.htm *(European Ombudsman Statute)*

www.euro-ombudsman.eu.int/lbasis/en/provis.htm *(European Ombudsman implementing provisions)*

www.ofgem.gov.uk/ *(Office of Gas and Electricity Markets)*

www.oftel.gov.uk/ *(Office of Telecommunications)*

www.ofwat.gov.uk/aptrix/ofwat/publish.nsf/Content/navigation-homepage(ofwat) *(Office of Water Services)*

www.council-on-tribunals.gov.uk/

7

The family justice system

Introduction

The role of law in regulating family relationships is particularly controversial. Some argue that the law should have little part to play; how people structure their lives is essentially a matter of private choice and personal morality. Others argue that 'society' has a legitimate interest in the arrangements that people make, particularly where children are involved, since it is in these arrangements that the foundations for the continuity of society are laid. Current trends suggest that law is likely to become more rather than less involved in family matters, particularly if a broad view is taken of the scope of family policy and the arrangements that might be needed to underpin that policy. (*See Box 7.1.*)

For present purposes, the principal functions of the law relating to the family may be defined as:

(1) To define the rules for the validity of marriage;

(2) To prescribe the bases on which marital relationships may be brought to an end through divorce or nullity;

(3) To deal with the consequences of divorce and other relationship breakdown, in particular questions of responsibility for children, financial support and the division of property rights;

(4) To provide a framework for the protection of children;

(5) To provide a framework for dealing with issues of domestic violence.

The last two of these items are not dependent on the existence of a marriage; the first two are. The third is largely dependent on the existence of a marriage, though there is limited though complex involvement of the law on the breakdown of *de facto* relationships.

The extent to which the law should be involved in the regulation of *de facto* relationships is currently the subject of considerable debate. For example there is fierce argument about the extent to which, if at all, the provisions for distributing property on the breakdown of a marriage should or should not apply to (heterosexual) *de facto* relationships where parties have lived together as a family, but without formally getting married. Equally controversial are questions of the extent to which, if at all,

Box 7.1 *Supporting Families*: the scope of family policy

Lawyers tend to think of the family justice system as the place where issues are resolved when things have gone wrong with a relationship. In November 1998 the Government published a Green Paper, *Supporting Families*, which made it clear that family policy must be seen much more broadly than that. While purporting to acknowledge the limits of the law, the Government nevertheless stated that it wished to focus on five key issues, where it claimed government can make a difference:

- ensuring all families have access to the advice and support they need;

- improving family prosperity and reducing child poverty through the tax and benefit system;

- making it easier for families to balance work and home;

- strengthening marriage and reducing the risks of family breakdown;

- tackling the more serious problems of family life, such as domestic violence, truancy and school-age pregnancy.

Much of the detail of the Green Paper focused on, for example, developing the role of health visitors and other advice-givers; creating a National Family and Parenting Institute to provide government with advice on best practice; using social security and tax policy to enhance the finances available to families; improving incentives to employers to adopt 'family-friendly' employment policies; enhancing maternity and paternity leave entitlements; tackling issues of social exclusion to ensure that families with problems do not miss out on the opportunities open to the majority. This approach includes dealing firmly with juvenile crime, as well as other issues such as truancy from school. Many of these policies implied the creation of new law or the amendment of existing law.

Despite evidence of the increasing numbers of families created by those in long-term relationships who are not married, the government argued that marriage is the preferred context for bringing up children. It proposed a number of measures to enhance marriage, including:

- Providing couples intending to marry with a clear statement of what their new status means in terms of extra rights and also extra responsibilities;

- Making 'pre-nuptial' written agreements about property legally binding for those who wish to make them;

- Improving arrangements to help people prepare for marriage. This would include a wider role for registrars to give better support to marrying couples; allowing couples more time to reflect before they marry; and requiring both partners to attend the register office to make the first arrangements before marriage;

- Enhancing and modernizing the service provided by registrars, who now perform the majority of marriages in Britain;

- Helping to support marriages in difficulty, including strengthening marriage counselling before divorce;

- Reforming information meetings before divorce to increase the chance of saving more marriages;

- Helping with relationship problems at the birth of a child;

- Encouraging baby-naming ceremonies to help parents make a public, long-term commitment to their children and bring together friends and the wider family.

Despite the Government's assertion that families do not want to be nannied, this seems a pretty detailed list of suggestions.

Nevertheless there are also striking omissions. Nothing was said about the impact on families of bereavement; nor of a partner being sent to prison. More generally nothing was said about the resources that might be needed to set up the proposed institute or to develop the role of health visitors.[1] A summary of responses to the Consultation Paper was published in 1999.[2] The Home Office has a family policy unit to take these ideas forward, but progress to date has not been striking. Current indications suggest that detailed changes to the law are not imminent.

those involved in homosexual relationships might be subject to analogous principles.[3] It seems likely that, in the mid-term, there will be renewed attention paid to the possibility of recognizing the status of long-term relationships outside marriage, though defining when such relationships should be recognized will not be easy.

Social trends

Social statistics[4] demonstrate quite clearly, first, that the link between marriage and the creation of children is not as strong as it was twenty-five years ago. In 2000, over one third of all live births occurred outside marriage. Even so around 80 per cent of those births were registered by both parents of the child, and of these 75 per cent were registered by both parents living together at the same address. By contrast the number of births registered by a sole parent has remained relatively constant, at under 10 per cent over the period 1974–2000. While a majority of children (79 per cent in spring

---

[1] The Annual Report of the Home Office for 2001–2002 reports that a grant of about £680,000 was made to the Institute, which has now been established as a charity to work with other family support charities.

[2] Supporting Families: Summary of Responses to the Consultation Paper (London, The Stationery Office, 1999).

[3] An attempt by the Law Commission to develop principles for determining the allocation of property on the breakdown of *de facto* relationships ended when it became clear that any new rules would cause greater injustice than the present (admittedly unsatisfactory) law: see *Sharing Homes: A Discussion Paper* (Law Com 278) (Cm 5666) (London, The Stationery Office, 2002).

[4] *Social Trends, No 32* (London, The Stationery Office, 2002).

2001) live in a couple family, around 22 per cent of children live in a lone parent family. This is three times as many as in 1971.

Secondly, there has been a sharp decline in the incidence of marriage. In 1999 there were 179,000 first marriages, less than half the figure in 1970. Overall (taking into account second and subsequent marriages) there were 301,000 marriages in 1999, the lowest figure since 1917. Of this total less than half were religious ceremonies, though for second and subsequent marriages over 80 per cent were civil ceremonies.

Thirdly, between 1970 and 1999, the number of divorces more than doubled, from around 80,000 to around 165,000. It has been estimated that 28 per cent of children born in England and Wales will be affected by divorce before reaching the age of 16.

Given these social trends, it seems clear that this is an area of law that must develop in response to changing societal attitudes. For example:

- general social attitudes in relation to children born 'out of wedlock' are now wholly different from the situation before the Second World War, and indeed for some time after;

- the stigma on couples living together without being married, very significant two generations ago, is much reduced (though still strong amongst those over the age of 60); and

- the emphasis on the proof of 'fault' as the basis of obtaining a divorce, though not entirely disappeared, is certainly less significant than it was thirty years ago.

Public discussion of how the law on family relationships—whether in marriage or outside—should develop tends to focus on what might be good for the parties to those relationships; much of the Government's *Supporting Families* paper illustrates this point. However, it should not be forgotten that the state has a considerable interest in encouraging relationship stability and responsibility, particularly where there are children. New arrangements for the provision of child support for example (see below, p. 179) were 'sold' by politicians on the basis that they would reinforce parental responsibility for children; but they were also designed to cut the social security bill for maintaining children. Similar observations can be made in relation to the new provisions relating to the division of pension rights on divorce. The more that ex-partners are enabled/required to provide for themselves, the less potential financial liability falls on government.

The bases on which substantive family law should develop in future are beyond the scope of this book. However, three particular issues have emerged in the last twenty years as factors which should influence not only the structure of the family justice system, but also the roles that people who work within that system should perform:

- First, there has been the important realization that if a marriage (or indeed other long-term relationship) does break down, the process of bringing that relationship to a formal end should—wherever possible—reduce the inevitable feelings of stress, rejection, failure that accompany such a process, rather than add to them.

- Secondly, there is now a widespread acceptance, given statutory recognition, that the welfare of the child must be protected wherever possible.
- Thirdly, there is much greater awareness of the problem of domestic violence and other forms of abuse which occur in the family home. There have been a number of legal developments designed both to assist victims of such abuse, and also to send the broader educational message that such behaviour is not acceptable.

These issues have informed much of the institutional development of the family justice system and the attitudes of those who practice within it.

Family justice: the institutional framework

Unlike some other countries, England and Wales has no specialist family court. Rather there is a complex set of arrangements with different courts having a range of powers to determine the different issues that may arise in family law. While the idea of a separate family court structure—often proposed by experts in the field—has not been accepted by the Government, it is nevertheless accepted that, in most areas of family work, the relevant judiciary should ideally be specially suited to the particular tasks it has to perform.

In many instances it is required to undertake specialist training before it can determine family cases, particularly those relating to children. The training embraces not only instruction on the law and legal procedures, but also issues relating to the theories of child development and principles of social work. The difficulty of resolving cases relating to children can hardly be overstated, since the outcome of such cases may be that children are removed from one parent and transferred to another, or are removed from the parent(s) altogether and placed under the care and supervision of others. Judicial training has been designed to ensure that as appropriate decisions as possible are taken.

Children

From October 1991 (when the Children Act 1989 was implemented) there has been a common jurisdiction across all the tiers of the court structure for dealing with issues relating to children. The structure is designed to enable cases to be disposed of at the most appropriate court level. Three levels of courts need to be considered:

- Family Proceedings Courts;
- The County Court;
- The High Court.

Family Proceedings Courts

The lay magistrates who sit in Family Proceedings Courts (as magistrates' courts are called when they deal with family matters) are drawn from specially selected family panels, the members of which have all been trained and receive on-going training. The district judges who sit in family proceedings are also specially trained. In this jurisdiction they sit with lay justices. Family proceedings courts have jurisdiction to deal with both public and private law matters relating to children. (For the distinction between public law and private law cases, see *Box 7.2*.) All public law cases start in the family proceedings court.[5] (Despite their name, family proceedings courts do not deal with divorce.)

This is a busy jurisdiction, with over 14,000 public law applications being made in the family proceedings court in 2001, and nearly 25,500 private law applications being made during the same period.

Box 7.2 Public law and private law cases

In relation to children, an important distinction must be drawn between 'public law' cases and 'private law' cases. *Public law* cases are those brought by public authorities—in particular the social services departments of local authorities—or other agencies such as the NSPCC, which may be seeking orders from the court relating to the care, supervision or emergency protection of children. *Private law* cases are those brought by private individuals, usually the parents of the child, seeking orders relating to the child in the context of a divorce or the separation of the parents.

One of the principal objectives of the Children Act 1989 was to ensure that the voice of the child was heard. To assist in this, in most public law applications, the court will appoint a children's guardian (formerly called *guardian ad litem*) to assist the child, unless the court is satisfied that this is not needed to protect the interests of the child. The role of the guardian is to ensure that the court is fully informed of facts relevant to determining the best interests of the child. She also seeks to ensure that the court is made fully aware of the child's feelings and wishes. Guardians are provided by the Children and Family Courts Advisory and Support Service (CAFCASS), established in 2001 by the Criminal Justice and Court Services Act 2000. In defined cases, the guardian is also required to appoint a solicitor to act for the child, to ensure proper legal representation.

In private law cases, a somewhat analogous role is played by the Childrens and Family Reporter, also appointed by CAFCASS.

---

[5] They may be transferred to a county court where this would minimize delay, or would enable proceedings to be consolidated with other proceedings, or where the matter is exceptionally grave, complex or important.

The County Court

County courts are divided into five distinct categories:

- Non-divorce county courts, with no power to deal with any family law matters;
- Divorce county courts, which can issue all private law family proceedings but from which, if a matter is contested, it is referred to a family hearing centre for trial;
- Family hearing centres which can issue and hear all private law family cases whether or not they are contested;
- Care centres, with full powers to deal with all private law and public law matters;
- Specialized adoption centres, which have power to issue, hear and process adoption applications under guidance issued by the President of the Family Division.[6]

The circuit judges and district judges who deal with matters relating to children under the Children Act 1989 have to be specially 'nominated'[7] for family work by the Lord Chancellor, and will not be so nominated without receiving special training and guidance. They are formally known as 'nominated care judges'.[8] Those circuit judges who are so nominated have full powers to deal with all public and private law matters. District judges who have been nominated as care judges can hear uncontested public law cases, and contested private law cases. In addition to the nominated care judges there is also a group of 'circuit family judges' who can deal with private law matters, but not public law matters.

County courts also have a large case load. In 2001 they received over 86,000 private law applications, plus nearly 10,000 public law cases.

The High Court

Although there are no formal training requirements for those High Court judges who do family work, nonetheless they sit in a separate division of the High Court known as the Family Division. There are seventeen such judges, plus a President, specially appointed to give appropriate leadership to the work of this specialist group of judiciary. The smallness of their number enables them to operate in a collegiate style with a fair degree of common purpose and approach.

The High Court has power to hear all cases relating to children. It has exclusive power to decide matters relating to wardship, whereby the court assumes responsibility for the child, taking over from the parents. It also hears appeals from family proceedings courts. The work-load of the High Court is numerically trivial by

---

[6] *Adoption Proceedings—A New Approach* (London, Lord Chancellor's Department, 2001).

[7] One exception is that circuit judges who are not 'nominated' can still hear cases involving requests for injunctions arising from allegations of domestic violence and some other matrimonial work.

[8] There are also 'designated family judges' who, besides undertaking normal judicial duties as nominated care judges, also chair local Family Court Business Committees and Family Court Forums—both mechanisms for improving working relationships between the courts and their users.

comparison with those of the other two courts—just 140 public law and 332 private law applications in 2001. But its more important decisions will be reported and thus develop the jurisprudence of the family justice system.

Orders

The Children Act 1989 provides for a wide range of orders which can be made by the courts. They include:

- Care/supervision orders;
- Emergency protection orders;
- Exclusion requirements;
- 'Section 8' orders.

Care/supervision orders

These are made on application by either a local authority or the NSPCC.[9] Before an order may be made, the court must be satisfied either that a child is suffering or is likely to suffer significant harm, and that the harm or likelihood of harm is attributable to:

(1) the care given to the child; or

(2) the likelihood of the care not being what it would be reasonable to expect a parent to give a child;

or that the child is beyond parental control.

If the court is so satisfied, it may make an order:

(1) placing the child in the care of a designated local authority; or

(2) putting the child under the supervision of a designated local authority or probation officer.

Such orders cannot be made in relation to a child who has reached the age of 17 (16 if the child is married).

The effect of a *care order* is to impose a duty on the local authority to keep the child in care, to exercise parental responsibility over the child, and determine the extent to which a parent or guardian may meet his or her parental responsibility towards the child.[10]

The effect of a *supervision order* is to impose a duty on the supervisor to advise, assist and befriend the child, and to take the necessary action to give effect to the order, including whether or not to apply to vary or discharge it.

---

[9] The National Society for the Prevention of Cruelty to Children. It is the only 'authorized person' under the terms of the Children Act able to bring such proceedings.

[10] The impact of placing children in care, particularly in care homes run by the authority, can be extremely severe; see Tribunal of Inquiry into Child Abuse, *Lost in Care* (HC 201, 1999–2000) (London, The Stationery Office, 2000).

Emergency protection orders

These may be made where the court is satisfied that there is reasonable cause to believe that a child is suffering, or is likely to suffer, significant harm if not removed to accommodation provided by the applicant, or that the child should not remain in the place where she is currently living. Emergency protection orders may be sought where anyone, including a local authority, believes that access to a child is being unreasonably refused.

Exclusion requirements

From October 1997, the courts have had power to order the exclusion of a suspected abuser from a child's home, where ill-treatment of the child is alleged, and either an interim care order or an emergency protection order has been made. A power of arrest can be added to the exclusion requirement, so that anyone in breach may be instantly arrested. Before an exclusion requirement can be ordered, the court must be satisfied that there will still be a person remaining in the premises with the child, and that that person has agreed to care for the child and has consented to the exclusion requirement.

'Section 8' orders

Orders made under section 8 of the Children Act include:

- *residence* orders, determining where the child should live;
- *contact* orders, deciding whom the child may see;
- *prohibited steps* orders, to prevent a defined action(s) taking place; and
- *specific issue* orders, dealing with particular aspects of a child's upbringing.

Nearly 95,000 private law applications resulted in the making of section 8 orders, as compared with just over 3,000 arising from public law applications. The vast bulk of section 8 orders relate to residence and contact.

A Children's Commissioner?

One institutional development that has taken place, at present only in Wales, is the appointment of a Children's Commissioner to champion the cause of children. This is a new development, but one that has attracted a great deal of interest. It raises the obvious question whether such a post is needed in England. The Government is not yet persuaded that this would be a good idea, but, particularly if the post operates effectively in Wales, there will be pressure for a similar appointment to be made in England.

Adoption

The other main activity of the courts in relation to children concerns adoption, a process whereby the rights, duties and obligations of a child's natural parents are legally extinguished and are vested, by order of the court, in the adoptive parents. It is essential that the court is satisfied that the adoptive parents are suitable and have consented to the adoption. Where possible it is also necessary to obtain the consent of the parents (including, since 1991, any guardian with parental responsibility), though this may be dispensed with if there is evidence that the natural parent has persistently ill-treated the child or that consent is being unreasonably withheld.

Once again, the primary objective of the courts is to safeguard and promote the welfare of the child. This includes taking the views of the child into account. In 2001 some 5,000 applications for adoption orders were made. Just over 4,400 orders were actually made, 30 per cent being in favour of the child's step-parents.

After a long period of gestation, major changes to the law of adoption have recently been made.[11] The intention is, while continuing to protect children, to make it easier for those wishing to adopt children to do so, thereby increasing the number of adoptions currently sanctioned by the legal process. The Government is particularly anxious that more children, currently in the care of local authorities, should be adopted. It is too early to determine whether this objective will be achieved.

Matrimonial matters

The other principal work of the courts in the context of the family relates to the dissolution of marriages. For these purposes the courts are the county courts, save those designated as *non-divorce county courts*. Family proceedings courts do not deal with the dissolution of marriage.

There are two ways in which a marriage may be dissolved: divorce and nullity. *Divorce* is the much more frequently used procedure. To obtain a divorce, the petitioner must prove that the marriage has broken down irretrievably. This can be demonstrated by proof of: adultery; behaviour which the petitioner cannot reasonably be expected to live with; desertion for at least two years; two years' separation where the respondent consents; five years' separation where there is no such consent.

---

[11] The Adoption and Children Act 2002. The history of this measure can be traced back at least 10 years. See Department of Health and Welsh Office, *Review of Adoption Law* (London, HMSO, 1992); *Adoption: The Future* (Cm 2288) (London, Department of Health, Welsh Office, Home Office and Lord Chancellor's Department, 1993); *Adoption—A Service for Children: Adoption Bill—A Consultative Document* (London, Department of Health and Welsh Office, 1996); Prime Minister's Review, *Adoption* (London, Performance and Innovation Unit, July 2000); White Paper, *Adoption—a New Approach* (Cm 5017) (London, The Stationery Office, 2000).

Most applications for divorce are dealt with in the county court.[12] Evidence of irretrievable breakdown is usually considered by a district judge. If proved to the satisfaction of the judge, a provisional measure, the *decree nisi*, will be made. The divorce becomes final only after a final decision, the *decree absolute*. The existence of this two-stage process is to provide an opportunity, albeit infrequently used, for second thoughts. Most cases are disposed of on the basis of paper evidence without the need for a hearing.

Where children are involved, the court must also be satisfied with the arrangements for their welfare. These must be written down and, if possible, agreed between the parents. If agreement is not possible, the judge may order the parents to come to court so that the issues may be resolved. If the issues are uncontested at this point, the judge may issue a *section 8 order* (see above).

The divorce caseload is enormous.[13] In 2001, over 161,000 petitions for divorce were filed; nearly 147,000 decrees nisi were made, and over 137,000 decrees absolute were made.

Nullity is the other mode of dissolving a marriage. However this can be used only where there is proof that the marriage either was void in the first place (e.g. because one of the parties was under the age of 16 or was already married), or was voidable (e.g. because one of the parties was pregnant by someone else at the time of the marriage or the marriage was not consummated due to incapacity or wilful refusal). To obtain a decree of nullity, a two-stage process, similar to the divorce process, must be gone through. By contrast with divorce, this mode of dissolution is very infrequently used: 657 petitions were filed in 2001; 297 decrees nisi and 241 decrees absolute were made.

Judicial separation is an alternative procedure for those who do not wish to or who for some reason cannot get divorced. It does not terminate the marriage, but legally absolves the parties to a marriage from the obligation to live together. Just 535 petitions were filed in 2001; 925 decrees were granted.[14]

Ancillary relief

Ancillary relief is the term given to the powers of the court to make orders related to divorce or other matrimonial proceedings. These relate to maintenance (periodical payments to an ex-spouse) and to lump sum payments or property orders (usually dealing with the matrimonial home). As with divorce, the courts for these purposes are the county courts.

---

[12] Except for the 'non divorce county courts'—see above p. 173.

[13] Numbers of divorces have grown enormously over the last 50 years, reflecting both changes in social attitudes and changes in the law. Even in 1968 only 54,000 petitions were filed. The peak was in 1990, when 191,615 petitions were filed.

[14] A reducing caseload enabled the courts to clear a backlog of pending cases.

The power of the courts to deal with maintenance orders relating to the children of the marriage have largely been taken over by the child support system (see below). Since April 1993, most new applications for maintenance have been dealt with by the Child Support Agency. Initially there was a plan to transfer then existing court orders to the Agency by a process that was due to start in April 1996. However the controversies and operational chaos that have surrounded the Agency have led to an indefinite deferment of this plan. Thus the county courts still have to make a large number of orders relating to the maintenance of children. In 2001, nearly 11,000 such orders were made.

In addition, the court's jurisdiction to make maintenance orders for spouses has remained in place, with around 10,000 such orders being made in 2001.

In 2001, the courts also made over 26,000 orders relating to the payment of a lump sum or the transfer of property and approved another 54,000 ancillary relief orders which were made with the consent of the parties.

Enforcement

One of the problems with the maintenance system was that people just did not pay. Enforcement procedures are available. For example, where the relevant ex-spouse is in work, the other former spouse may ask the county court for an *attachment of earnings order* which requires the employer to pay a proportion of salary or wages to that former spouse. In 2001, 614 applications for such an order were made, but only 150 were granted.

In addition it is possible to register the maintenance order in the magistrates' courts which are then made responsible for collecting the maintenance. 926 registration orders were made in 2001. Failure to pay is a contempt of court, the ultimate sanction for which may be an order committing the person in contempt to prison. This is a threat that on occasion can be used to stimulate the payments due. However the reality is that enforcement of periodical maintenance payments against an ex-spouse who is not willing to make such payments is not easily achieved.

Reform

Detailed reform of procedures relating to ancillary relief was introduced in June 2000. It is based on a pilot scheme whereby, from October 1996, twenty-nine courts were involved in a pilot scheme which used new procedures designed to promote early settlement between the parties, to eliminate unnecessary delay and to keep costs down.[15] As with the broader reforms to the civil justice system (see Chapter 8), the key is active judicial case management, combined with the need for proportionality— ensuring that the costs of the proceedings are proportionate to the assets in dispute.

---

[15] An extreme example of costs not being proportionate to the resources available is found in *Piglowska v. Piglowska* [1999] 2 FLR 763 (HL).

Both sides are required to make the other party aware of how costs are mounting up, particularly if there is unnecessary delay in reaching a conclusion. A further innovation is that the parties are required to undergo a financial dispute resolution appointment in which, with the assistance of a judge, the attempt is made to get the parties to agree the outcome, rather than have a solution imposed on them by the judge.

Child support

One of the most controversial recent structural changes made to the family justice system has been the creation of the child support system, operated by the Child Support Agency. It runs its own collection and enforcement service for child maintenance assessments.

The principle behind its establishment in 1993[16] was straightforward. Far too many single parents, mostly women, found it impossible either to obtain a court order for the maintenance of their children or, if they did obtain an order, were unable to enforce it. A consequence of this was that lone parents were heavily dependent on the provision of social security benefits for the financial resources to bring up their children, rather than being supported by the child's natural but absent parent. Indeed during the preceding decade, while the number of children living in lone-parent families increased substantially, the proportion of children receiving maintenance fell. In 1989, 23 per cent of lone parents claiming income support were receiving maintenance, compared to around 50 per cent in 1979. The child support system was intended to reverse this decline, by providing consistent rules for assessing maintenance liability and a readily accessible means for collecting and enforcing payment that was due. A system for getting absent parents to pay for their children had been introduced in Australia in the 1980s, apparently with great success. Thus, it was argued, a similar scheme could be introduced in the United Kingdom.

Criticism of the scheme

From the outset the child support legislation and its implementation have been dogged by controversy. One crucial difference between the British and Australian models was that, in the former, for every pound paid by the absent parent a pound of social security benefit was lost; in Australia, for every dollar of maintenance paid by the absent parent, the parent with care lost only 85 cents of her social security payments. Although the Australian model was less advantageous from a purely public expenditure point of view, it had the supreme psychological advantage that the absent parent felt that (usually) he was, by making the payments, actually improving the quality of

---

[16] Child Support Act 1991.

life for his child(ren). In the United Kingdom, by contrast, there was no such positive incentive.

The force of these criticisms was to a limited degree acknowledged by the previous government in the Child Support Act 1995. This introduced:

- the *Child Maintenance Bonus*, intended as an incentive to encourage parents with care into work, and

- the *departures* scheme which allowed for the normal rules for the assessment of child support liability to be departed from in order to take account of exceptional circumstances not recognized in the formula-based assessment.

However, these changes did not go far enough. The outcome has been legislation that has never fully worked as it was intended to do. Indeed, there is evidence that, notwithstanding the efforts in other parts of the family justice system to reduce tensions between former partners, the child support system has actually exacerbated the problems existing between them.

The system has also been severely criticized for damaging the new relationships that the absent parent may be trying to establish. The reason for this is that the formula for determining the amount to be paid to the parent with the care of the child resulted in not insubstantial sums having to be paid, with the result that the level of resource available for the new family was thereby reduced.

There is a substantial literature on the child support scheme.[17] The underlying principle, on the face of it, seems reasonable. Certainly it seems to be accepted and defended by the main political parties. However, its implementation in practice has been a disaster—the antithesis of 'justice'. This is not a part of the English legal system that is currently fit for the task it should be seeking to perform.

New reform proposals

Given these difficulties, the present Labour Government passed legislation to enable further reform of the child support system to be put in place.[18] The Government defined the principal problems thus:

- while the Child Support Agency (CSA) has almost 1.5 million children on its books, only around 300,000 gain financially from child support payments. Of these 300,000, only around 100,000 see the benefit of all the maintenance that is due.

- the complexity of the current formula led to long delays in assessing liability.

---

[17] See, e.g., Davis, G., Wikeley, N., and Young, R., *et al.*, *Child Support in Action* (Oxford, Hart Publishing, 1998).

[18] The Child Support, Pensions and Social Security Act 2000. Proposals were first published in July 1998 in the consultation document *Children First: a New Approach to Child Support* (Cm 3992) (London, The Stationery Office, 1998). This led to the White Paper, *A New Contract for Welfare: Children's Rights and Parents' Responsibilities* (Cm 4349) (London, The Stationery Office, 1999).

This in turn made it difficult to ensure that child support was paid regularly. Because the assessment process is complex, the CSA had less time to help parents understand what they should pay or chase up non-payment.

- families living on income support do not gain from the payment of maintenance as their benefit is reduced by an amount equal to the maintenance paid.

The key changes provided for in the legislation include:

- the existing formula for assessing child support is replaced with a simpler system of rates;
- the processes for applying for child support and the way in which child support liability will be decided are simplified;
- there are clear penalties for parents who deliberately misrepresent their circumstances to the CSA—and for those who refuse to provide the information needed to calculate liability and collect maintenance;
- there is the possibility of the variation of the normal rate of maintenance liability to recognize certain exceptional costs and sources of income;
- there are rights to appeal decisions on child support liability and the processes by which liability will be kept up to date;
- the formation of a complete and comprehensive collection scheme with financial and other penalties for late and non-payment;
- improvements to the provisions for establishing paternity.

Given the history of the scheme, there was bound to be scepticism whether the problems that have attracted so much criticism will in fact be addressed, particularly given the reluctance of absent parents in particular to co-operate with the working of the scheme. A more reasonable scheme might make it easier for the Government to gain the public support it needs to take effective steps against those who still refuse to co-operate. Whatever these theoretical problems, the new scheme was delayed. The Government was advised not to introduce it until the supporting information technology was in place. The minister announced on 20 March 2002 that the IT was not ready, and this led to a postponement of the reformed scheme. Recently it was announced that the scheme would start, for new cases, in March 2003.

Domestic violence

Another way in which the family justice system has been transformed over the last twenty-five years has been the recognition of the problem of domestic violence and the need for the law and legal procedures to deal with cases swiftly and effectively. There are now two principal items of legislation relevant in this context:

- Family Law Act 1996, Part IV;
- Protection from Harassment Act 1997.

Family Law Act 1996, Part IV

This Act provides for a single body of remedies in cases of domestic violence which can be sought either in the county court or the magistrates' court or (rarely) in the High Court. Two types of order may be made:

- a *non-molestation order*, which is an order to prohibit a person from behaving in a particular way towards another or which may seek to prohibit molestation in general; and

- an *occupation order* which can define or regulate the rights of a person to occupy a home (irrespective of his ownership rights in that home).

This body of law is available not only to married couples, but much more widely to cohabiting couples, others who live or have lived in the same household as the person seeking the order (though not tenants, boarders or lodgers), certain relatives (such as parents, or brothers or sisters) and those who have agreed to marry.

If the court thinks that the respondent has used or has threatened violence against either the applicant or any child of the applicant, then the court must attach a power of arrest to the order, unless satisfied that the applicant or child will be adequately protected without such a power being attached.

In addition, the court may at the same time add an *exclusion requirement* to an *emergency protection order* or *interim care order* made under the Children Act 1989 (see above, p. 175), so that the suspected abuser (rather than the abused child) may be removed from the dwelling.

There is a substantial caseload arising from these provisions. In 2001, over 17,500 applications for non-molestation orders were made, and over 10,500 applications for occupation orders—all but a handful in the county court. In the same year nearly 21,000 non-molestation orders were made, of which nearly 17,500 had the power of arrest attached. Around 9,700 occupation orders were made, with the power of arrest attached to just over 7,800 of them. There were a further 4,245 cases in which the court did not make a formal order, but instead accepted undertakings as to behaviour from the respondent. In the same year, just over 140 arrest warrants were issued.

Protection from Harassment Act 1997

This Act was initially introduced to combat the problem of stalking, but it applies more generally to the victims of harassment. Section 3 allows civil proceedings to be taken against anyone pursuing a course of harassment. The remedies available are an injunction—an order to prevent such behaviour in the future—and/or damages. Since September 1998, the courts have had power to make breach of an injunction enforceable by warrant of arrest. To date no information is available on the use of these new provisions.

The practitioners

Lawyers

Given the fact that so many aspects of family life are regulated by law, in particular the issues noted above relating to children, relationship breakdown and other financial matters, it is inevitable that legal practitioners should be deeply involved in family law issues. This is indeed a very considerable area for legal specialism, with large numbers of lawyers offering family law services. A considerable part of the legal aid budget (now the Community Legal Services Fund) is devoted to family law issues.

Practitioners have given considerable thought to the proper role of lawyers in assisting the resolution of family disputes. For example, should they engage in heavily adversarial forms of litigation process designed to advance their clients' interests, irrespective of the interests of the other party to the marriage or relationship and the children? Or should they adopt a more conciliatory approach?

The perception that lawyers often added to the problems of separating couples rather than helping their resolution led, some years ago, to the formation of the Solicitors' Family Law Association. (There is an equivalent for barristers—the Family Law Bar Association.) It set itself the aim of bringing a less hostile atmosphere to the resolution of family disputes.

Recent research suggests that, in general, solicitors have been rather successful at not exacerbating the conflicts between couples. This is not to say that lawyers are above criticism in the area of family disputes. They are criticized for, for example:

- a desultory approach to negotiation;
- large caseloads but with little activity on each individual case;
- high costs;
- high levels of pressure to reach final settlements, as cases approach court.

Nevertheless client demand for legal services to assist in the resolution of family disputes has remained high. Surveys of clients' responses to the legal services provided have, in general, been positive.

One of the ways in which practitioners have sought to develop the nature of their work with clients in the family law area has been through schemes of specialist training. For a number of years, the Law Society has run a *Childrens' Panel*, aimed particularly at solicitors who act for children in public law cases. Admission to the panel involves the lawyers demonstrating appropriate levels of qualifications and experience.

In addition the Law Society, during 1999, announced that it would establish a Family Law Panel. The Solicitors' Family Law Association has also established its own Family Law Panel and, in 1999, it launched its own scheme for the accreditation of those lawyers who sought to join the panel.

Those who practise family law have recognized the particular character of the work they have to undertake, dealing not only with the very considerable complexities of the law but also the strong emotional context within which such work has to be carried out. As the need for special training of the judiciary has been accepted, the importance of special training for practitioners has also been acknowledged.

Mediation and mediators

Notwithstanding the efforts of professional lawyers to shape the nature of family law practice to the needs of clients, the view of government has been that there need to be further changes in the ways in which family disputes are resolved, particularly those which are funded by the state. This has led to the view that a preferable way of resolving family disputes should be through *mediation* outside the courts, rather than *litigation* in the courts.

Mediation is in effect a form of negotiation. However, instead of the process taking place just between the parties to the dispute and/or their representatives, mediation involves the intervention of an impartial third party, the mediator. The mediator's function is to attempt to assist the parties to a dispute to reach an agreement accept-able to both sides. The mediator cannot impose any solution on the parties; never-theless the presence of the mediator can contribute to the pressure to settle disputes.

Family mediation services are provided, broadly, by two distinct groups:

- a 'not-for-profit' largely volunteer sector of people who have received special training in the mediation process and are affiliated to specialist organizations that provide mediation services; and

- a 'for-profit' sector, principally lawyers who have received specialist training and who want to add mediation (and other forms of ADR) to the range of profes-sional services that they are able to offer to clients.

Mediation to resolve family disputes has been used for many years. Experience suggests that it is often successful in bringing the parties to an agreement. There is also evidence that it is liked by those who have gone through the process. Nevertheless, despite the enthusiasm of those who offer mediation services, there is also clear evidence that only a small number of parties to family disputes actually ask for their disputes to be the subject of mediation.

Notwithstanding this relative lack of consumer demand, the previous Government decided that it would encourage the use of mediation in the context of family dis-putes. At least one of the reasons in the Government's mind at the time was that use of mediation might well save costs, particularly for those who were using legal aid funding to obtain a divorce or obtain other remedies from a court.

Part III of the Family Law Act 1996 amended the Legal Aid Act 1988 by providing that legal aid money could be used to pay for mediation services. These provisions were to apply in the context of all 'family matters',[19] not just divorce proceedings. The key test in the legislation was whether or not mediation might be suitable in any particular case. Those engaged in mediation were to operate under a code of practice which provided, for example, that mediation would clearly not be suitable if there was any fear of violence; nor, more generally, if either of the parties was not willing to use mediation. The teeth in the new provisions were found in section 29, which provided that, before legal aid for representation of a party before a court could be granted, the party to a family dispute who was seeking legal aid (usually the woman) had to attend a mediation meeting to determine whether or not mediation would be suitable. These provisions were introduced in September 1998, in six pilot areas.

The impact of these provisions on costs and outcomes was researched on behalf of the Legal Aid Board. The researchers found that the number of cases deemed not suitable for mediation rose substantially, doubtless because prior to the introduction of section 29 only volunteers sought to use mediation services. Further, relatively few cases got beyond the intake appointment stage. In addition, the researchers have found that the bulk of the work is provided by not-for-profit, rather than by for-profit providers. The challenge which the researchers identified was that the statutory goal of establishing a national network of specialist mediation services provided by the not-for-profit sector was unlikely to be achievable cost effectively, at least while levels of the use of mediation remained so low.

A number of more specific problems were also identified:

- Solicitors remained reluctant to use mediation, and were critical of the delays inherent in the process, particularly in cases where mediation would clearly not be suitable;

- Very little could be done at present to engage the second party, if he would not attend the intake appointment. Even a case deemed suitable for mediation cannot go to mediation if the second party was not willing to contemplate mediation;

- A lot of resource was being expended on the intake appointment where no actual mediation resulted.

Notwithstanding all these difficulties, the new funding code for the provision of the Community Legal Service (see further below) has retained the principles set out in the Family Law Act, Part III, which are carried into the new funding regime. The present Government has accepted that family mediation should remain an important form of dispute resolution for family disputes.

---

[19] Defined in s. 26(1). Broadly this covers most of the issues considered in this chapter.

Couple counselling: the work of Relate[20]

Relate is a national charity—formerly known as the Marriage Guidance Council. It offers counselling services either to couples or to individuals whose relationships are in difficulty. Counsellors undergo a lengthy period of training. The primary object of their work is not so much to save marriages (or other long-term relationships) as to assist partners understand better the nature of the difficulties that have arisen in the relationship. This may, of course, have the effect of enabling couples to rethink their relationship and may lead to the relationship continuing. Equally it may help couples to realize that the relationship is unlikely to succeed, but by assisting understanding of the reasons for the relationship failure, this may lead to less friction after the relationship has ended. This may be of particular benefit in helping the children of a relationship to adjust to the consequences of the relationship failure. Relate is not the only agency offering such services, but is perhaps the best known.

At present the provision of counselling services, whether through Relate or otherwise, is patchy; thus the ability of people to take advantage of the service will depend on whether or not a service is available in any given location. In many areas long-established services are having to close for lack of resources. Furthermore, the fees payable for the service vary considerably. Many Relate centres have to charge quite high fees just to cover their overhead costs. This has the effect of preventing the less well off from using the service. Finally the service will be used only by those who wish to take advantage of it. Many of those who might benefit most from the service will not do so, as they will not see themselves as the sorts of people for whom counselling will be of assistance.

The Government has been considering the extent to which the provision of such services should form part of its family policy. (*See Box 7.3.*) It cannot be said that the response (*see Box 7.4*) so far has been particularly generous. There is still a considerable way to go before the perfectly sensible objectives of the Government's strategy will be achieved. Short-term grant funding is no substitute for the regular income that can allow counselling services to become securely established. But the fact that this issue is now accepted as a responsibility of government is an important step forward. In this respect, this service may be seen as part of the family justice system, in the broad sense adopted in this book.

Funding family law cases

Family law matters were subject to special rules under the former Legal Aid scheme. Under the Access to Justice Act 1999, special rules relating to the provision of funded legal services in family law matters continue to apply. Under the Community Legal

---

[20] Relate is not the only body offering counselling services; in London such services are provided by London Marriage Guidance. The websites of both organizations offer links to other counselling bodies.

Box 7.3 The funding of marriage support

A report by Sir Graham Hart[21] noted that marital breakdown and divorce not only cause much damage to couples and their children, but also impose very substantial costs on the taxpayer—estimated at around £5 billion a year.

Sir Graham was asked to consider the extent to which support for marriage might be developed and funded. He defined marriage support to include not only support when relationships were going wrong, but also the provision of help and support for people to enable them to enter and maintain long-term and stable relationships. Where marriage support can help to save marriages, there is a direct saving to the taxpayer.

Current provision is through voluntary sector organizations, such as *Relate* and *Marriage Care*. But the availability of services throughout the country is patchy, and many of those seeking divorce never use their services. Those who do often do so very late in the day when difficulties are extreme and the marriage is close to breakdown.

While Sir Graham saw the development of marriage support as the responsibility of the voluntary sector, in partnership with local authorities, relevant statutory bodies and the universities, he thought this would only occur with increased investment by government in the funding of this provision. In addition, he felt that the Lord Chancellor's Department, as the department with a prime responsibility for family policy, should take a positive role in the promotion of these developments.

Sir Graham argued that it was important to develop service provision by assisting with the costs of running nationally provided services. He also suggested it was necessary to invest in relevant research and development projects. Although initially large sums of public money were not thought necessary (an increase of only £1 million for each of the next three years), this would form the platform for further expansion thereafter.

Service's *Funding Code*[22] family proceedings are defined to apply to all proceedings which arise out of family relationships, including cases in which the welfare of children is determined.

A new level of service, *Approved Family Help*, has been created. It takes one of two forms:

- either *help with mediation*, for clients who need legal advice in support of the mediation process;

- or *general family help* to obtain disclosure from the other party to enable negotiations to take place, leading to early settlement of cases where this is possible.

The approach to the funding of mediation in family disputes and the possibility that a client who refuses to use mediation services may be denied further legal aid funding (discussed above) are carried forward into the new *Funding Code*. The

---

[21] *The Funding of Marriage Support* (London, Lord Chancellor's Department, 1999).
[22] Discussed in more detail, below in Chapter 10.

Box 7.4 A new strategy for marriage and relationship support

The Lord Chancellor's Department has developed a new strategy for marriage and relationship support. It says it is important because:

- Stable relationships and families are key to a healthy society;

- When relationships break down there can be adverse effects on couples, children, society and the taxpayer.

There are various life stages where changes in relationships may impose challenges or difficulties, e.g. birth of a first child, children starting school. In addition, challenges that may cause distress and problems can arise at any time in a relationship—for example, serious ill-health, unemployment, financial problems. Supporting couples at these times may give them resources to cope more successfully.

Family life is undergoing unprecedented change. Marriage and partnerships are more fragile than they were even a generation ago. The focus of current counselling provision is on the later stages of relationship breakdown, when crisis point is reached. In the majority of cases, counselling does not save the relationship, as it comes too late. In any event, the majority of couples in difficulties do not use counselling. There is a lack of public awareness about how to improve relationships. For many, there is antipathy, embarrassment or stigma attached to seeking help. Many do not know where to go for help if they have problems. Services are not always readily accessible. Support has concentrated almost exclusively on adults, but children's needs and concerns must also be met. Best practice, where identified, is insufficiently publicized.

New aims, criteria and outcomes for marriage and relationship support should be:

- to invest in the couple;

- to enable adults and children to have access to the information, advice and help they need at the time they need it; and

- to make available effective and appropriate support at the key life stages, and at times of particular challenge or crisis, which may be associated with the start of (or an increase in) relationship difficulties.

It should meet the criteria of being accessible, affordable, timely, appropriate and effective.

And its outcomes should be:

- to increase public knowledge of relationship issues, services, rights and responsibilities and family law;

- to raise the importance of the couple as the cornerstone of the family;

- to improve the quality of relationships and relationship skills and to improve resilience in couples and families;

- to reduce acrimony, blame and distress within relationships;

- to help save saveable marriages and relationships;

- to improve the lives of children by reducing damaging unresolved conflict in families;

- to help couples to part with the minimum of acrimony when relationships do break down and promote a continuing relationship between them and any children that is as good as possible.

Ways of delivering the new strategy include:

- a new LCD Grant Programme allocating the £5 million available annually, in accordance with the strategy, in 2002–3 and beyond;

- increased partnership working within government, between government and others, and between organizations in both the voluntary and statutory sectors; and

- increased resources to allow for successful delivery and development of the new strategy.

Source: Adapted from Advisory Group on Marriage and Relationship Support, Moving Forward Together: A Proposed Strategy for Marriage and Relationship Support for 2002 and Beyond (London, Lord Chancellor's Department, 2002)

requirement to mediate does not, however, apply in domestic violence cases, nor in public law children cases.

General family help is an alternative form of approved family help for those cases which either do not have to be referred to a mediator or are unsuitable for a mediator, or where a mediation has broken down. This is designed to cover investigation, disclosure and negotiation to resolve a dispute as quickly as possible, without recourse to substantive court action.

Children Act proceedings

Funding remains automatically available for a child in respect of whom an application for a care or supervision order, a child assessment order, an emergency protection order or the extension or discharge of an emergency protection order has been made. In addition funding will be available for any parent of or person with parental responsibility for such a child. A child against whom a secure accommodation order might be made restricting the child's liberty will also obtain legal services funding. This applies only to first instance proceedings. However, funding for any appeal will be subject to a merits test—assessing the merits of the case. A limited merits test will also operate in the case of adoption proceedings.

In the case of private law children disputes, legal representation may be refused unless reasonable attempts to resolve the dispute through negotiation or in other ways without recourse to proceedings have been made. A similar principle applies in cases relating to financial provision and other proceedings, such as contested divorce proceedings or nullity proceedings. Special rules apply to child abduction cases.

Total expenditure by the Legal Services Commission on family cases is substantial, over half the total expenditure in the Community Legal Service. In the year 2001–2, nearly 141,000 legal aid bills were paid, at a total cost of over £406 million. Nevertheless practitioners report that achieving profitability in legal aid practice is increasingly difficult; there are signs that the Legal Services Commission is beginning to share that concern.[23]

Conclusion

Family law disputes involve extremely difficult decisions which have to be handled with particular care—especially where children are involved. The evidence suggests that this is an area both of substantive law and of legal practice which has evolved considerably in recent years, and will continue to do so. It is also an area in which the impact of research on the development of law and practice has been significant.

Looking to the future, many of the issues likely to come onto the agenda for the reform of family law will be very controversial, particularly if there are significant moves away from thinking of the heterosexual, married family as the primary focus of law and policy. Pressure is mounting for the recognition of other long-term relationships, both heterosexual and homosexual. The Government will face difficult issues about the educational message the adoption of a more liberal legal regime might send to the public at large. Although governments may claim that they are happy for individuals to make their own choices about how they should structure their lives and relationships, a desire to get 'back to basics' is one that successive Prime Ministers seem to find hard to resist.

Questions for discussion

1. How far should the state seek to regulate family relationships?

2. Should there be a separate Family Court?

3. How far can family disputes be mediated?

4. What contribution should counselling make to the resolution of family issues?

[23] See *Annual Report of the Legal Services Commission for 2001–2002* (HC 949) (London, The Stationery Office, 2002).

Further reading

BRIDGE, C., *The Legal Regulation of Family Relations* (Manchester, University of Manchester, Faculty of Law, 1992)

BROPHY, J., and SMART, C., *Women-in-law: Explorations in Law, Family and Sexuality* (London, Routledge & Kegan Paul, 1985)

CRETNEY, S.M., MASSON, J.M., and Bailey-Harris, R., *Principles of Family Law* (7th edn., London, Sweet & Maxwell, 2002)

CRETNEY, S., *Law, Law Reform and the Family* (Oxford, Clarendon Press, 1998)

DAVIES, G., *Partisans and Mediators: The Resolution of Divorce Disputes* (Oxford, Clarendon Press, 1998)

——, CRETNEY, S., and COLLINS, J., *Simple Quarrels: Negotiations and Adjudication in Divorce* (Oxford, Clarendon Press, 1994)

DEWAR, J., *Law and the Family* (2nd edn., London, Butterworths, 1992)

DINGWELL, R., and EEKELAAR, J., *Divorce Mediation and the Legal Process* (Oxford, Clarendon Press, 1988)

EEKELAAR, J., *Family Law and Social Policy* (London, Weidenfeld & Nicholson, 1984)

—— and MACLEAN, M. (eds.), *Family Law* (Oxford, Oxford University Press, 1994)

FISHER, T., *National Family Mediation Guide to Separation and Divorce: The Complete Handbook for Managing a Fair and Amicable Divorce* (London, Vermilion, 1997)

FREEMAN, M.D.A. (ed.), *The State, the Law, and the Family: Critical Perspectives* (London, Tavistock Publications, 1984)

HAYES, M., and WILLIAMS, C., *Family Law: Principles, Policy and Practice* (2nd edn) (London, Butterworths, 1999)

LAW COMMISSION, *Family Law: The Ground for Divorce* (London, HMSO, 1990)

MACLEAN, S., *Legal Aid and the Family Justice System: Report of the Case Profiling Study* (London, Legal Aid Board Research Unit, 1998)

MURCH, M., and HOOPER, D., *The Family Justice System* (Bristol, Family Law, 1992)

O'DONOVAN, K., *Family Law Matters* (London, Pluto, 1993)

PARKINSON, L., *Family Mediation* (London, Sweet & Maxwell, 1997)

ROBERTS, M., *Mediation in Family Disputes: Principles of Practice* (2nd edn., Aldershot, Ashgate Publishing, 1997)

Websites

www.lcd.gov.uk/family/famfr.htm *(General LCD site on family law matters)*

www.homeoffice.gov.uk/cpg/fpu2.htm *(Family Policy Unit, Home Office)*

www.nfpi.org/ *(National Family and Parenting Institute)*

www.cafcass.gov.uk/ *(Children and Family Court Advisory and Support Service)*

www.lcd.gov.uk/family/domviol.htm *(LCD page on domestic violence)*

www.homeoffice.gov.uk/domesticviolence/index.htm *(Home Office site on domestic violence)*

www.homeoffice.gov.uk/cpd/cpsu/domviol98.htm *(Official review of government policy on domestic violence, 2001)*

www.cjsonline.org/news/2002/november/consultation_domestic_violence.html
(Announcement of new consultation on domestic violence for spring 2003)

www.childcom.org.uk/ *(Children's Commissioner for Wales)*

www.csa.gov.uk/ *(Child Support Agency)*

www.lcd.gov.uk/family/abflmfr.htm *(Advisory Board on Family Law)*

www.sfla.co.uk/ *(Solicitors' Family Law Association)*

www.lawsociety.org.uk/ *(Law Society—follow the links to the family law panel and children panel)*

www.barcouncil.org.uk/document.asp?documentid=436&languageid=1&highlight=family%20law *(Family Law Bar Association)*

www.legalservices.gov.uk/fains/index.htm *(Legal Services Commission, Family Advice and Information Networks Pilot Project (FAINs))*

www.ukcfm.com/index.htm *(UK College of Family Mediators)*

www.nfm.u-net.com/ *(National Family Mediation)*

www.relate.org.uk/ *(Relate counselling site)*

www.londonmarriageguidance.org.uk/

8

The civil and commercial justice system

Introduction

In this chapter, mechanisms for the resolution of all those disputes that fall outside the criminal, family and administrative justice systems are considered. The scope of the civil and commercial justice system is very extensive, embracing a wide range of issues relating to legal obligations and entitlements. It is in the context of the civil and commercial justice system that many of the relationships between law and society considered in Chapter 2 are seen to operate—particularly those relating to law and economic order. This is the part of the English legal system where protection of property and other rights may be asserted, and where questions of the ownership of title to land, or to intellectual property, or to other forms of personal property are determined. So too are the consequences of breaches of contract and acts of negligence.

Much of the conceptual framework of the civil law has been shaped by the common law. The fundamental principles of contract, negligence, trusts and property, and the principles of the law of equity have all been created by the courts. In many respects, and in response to considerable social pressures, common law principles are either supplemented or even replaced by legislation—measures designed to protect the weaker party.[1] A great deal of the work of the courts is taken up with the application of fundamental common law principles, as moderated by modern protective legislation.

There are constant pressures to add to the scope of civil justice. For example:

- As commercial interests become ever more complex as the economy becomes more global, new needs for the protection of those interests arise.

- New forms of financial instruments have been created to take advantage of the internationalization of banks and other players in the capital markets, which

[1] Honoré, T., *The Quest for Security: Employees, Tenants, Wives* (London, Stevens and Sons, 1982); Anderman, S., *et al.* (eds.), *Law and the Weaker Party: An Anglo-Swedish Comparative Study* (Abingdon, Professional Books, 1981).

need protection not only within English domestic law but taking European and other legal regimes into account as well.

• New technologies present major challenges. There is much current debate about the legal implications of the use of the internet for commercial activity on the fundamental principles of the law of contract. How are consumers and suppliers of goods and services through the internet to be protected?

• The legal implications of newly emerging bio-technologies must be addressed. What can be patented? Which legal system should provide protection of the intellectual and other property rights involved? What are the legal implications of the human genome project?

While these issues may not routinely trouble the minds of the district judges dealing with a list of possession cases, they emphasize the point that the civil and commercial branches of the English legal system cannot be divorced from their social and economic context. The legal system will always need to change in response to external social and economic pressures. Apart from any other consideration, if the English legal system does not respond, other legal systems will. The globalization of economic activity implies increased globalization of legal activity. If those who seek the law's protection cannot find it in England, they will take their work elsewhere.

Notwithstanding these broader considerations, the bulk of the work of the courts is devoted to more mundane matters: dealing with the consequences of people getting into debt (breach of contract) or being the victims of personal injuries (negligence). There are also more specialist areas of activity—for example relating to bankruptcy and the winding up of companies.

The civil and commercial justice system plays a significant role, both in economic life and in the regulation of other social relationships, by seeking to ensure that bargains are kept, other entitlements are protected, and that compensation for the adverse consequences of legally unacceptable behaviour may be awarded to those who have been affected.[2]

Litigation and society

One complaint that is often heard is that modern society has become too litigious.[3] It is asserted that people are too willing to rush to court when something has gone wrong. This needs thinking about carefully.

It could be argued that, with better education, more people are now able to take advantage of those procedures and facilities that in the past were open only to the rich and powerful. Thus, rather than being a bad thing, an increase in the use of litigation

---

[2] The importance of these propositions is reinforced when one considers what happens in those countries where the rule of law to regulate social and economic behaviour is not accepted. It is extremely hard to attract investment into a country where there can be no guarantee that contracts will be enforced or property rights upheld.

[3] For current statistical trends in civil litigation see below, p. 207.

may indicate that ordinary people are no longer willing to accept things without question, as they might have done in the past. On that basis an increase in litigation may not only be expected, but welcomed.

There may come a point where the level of litigation suggests something rather different—a desire to complain and to put the blame on others in situations where one should be taking responsibility oneself. This in turn may lead to unacceptable levels of resource—both cash and manpower—being expended on taking or defending cases in court which could be better spent in more socially productive activity.[4] But the view that *any* rise in levels of litigation is automatically a symptom of a society ill at ease with itself, as is sometimes suggested, should not be accepted uncritically.

Indeed there is empirical evidence that one of the key problems which continues to confront the civil justice system is that too many people still do not know how to assert their legal entitlements through the legal system, either through ignorance or through fear of the costs that may be involved.[5]

The provision of a civil justice system

One question that does get raised is the fundamental one whether the state should provide a system of civil justice at all. Since the disputes arising in this context are, by and large, private disputes between private parties, why should they not make arrangements for resolving those disputes themselves? There are many answers to this provocative question, which go back to the important constitutional role of the legal system in the overall system of government.[6] Among them are:

(1) As discussed in Chapter 3, the common law system requires a mechanism for the development of the principles of the common law. Fundamental legal concepts could not develop without the existence of the courts and the authority that our constitutional arrangements give to them and the judges that sit in them. Although the law-making functions of Parliament and other institutions are now far more predominant than they were 100 years ago, modern statute law is still set in the common law context which has been developed by the senior courts.

(2) The very fact that statute law is now a much more significant source of law means that there is a constitutional need for a body—the court system—to provide independent interpretations of the meaning of statutory provisions. All legislation has social and political objectives. Much modern legislation is designed to reduce imbalances in power, for example between landlords and tenants or employers and employees or manufacturers and consumers. If the

---

[4] E.g., something seems to be wrong if, as was the case in the state of Massachusetts a few years ago, one third of all professionally qualified obstetricians were engaged full-time in giving expert testimony in litigation being brought against their professional colleagues.

[5] See Genn, H., *Paths to Justice* (Oxford, Hart, 1999).

[6] See above, Chapter 2.

courts did not exist, much of this protective legislation—designed to achieve a wide range of policy objectives, including altering the nature of the relationships between parties—would be rendered even less effective than is often the case in any event.

(3) A third reason is more legalistic. Article 6 of the European Convention on Human Rights, incorporated into English law by the Human Rights Act 1998, provides that people should have a right to a fair trial for the determination of civil as well as criminal matters. The provision of a court system is therefore necessary to satisfy this international obligation.

(4) A fourth reason for the continued existence of a civil justice system is that there would be a danger that resort to private dispute resolution procedures would, in practice, be likely to benefit more those who could afford to establish them and take advantage of them than those who could not afford them. At least the rhetoric and ambition of the courts is that all those who appear before them should be treated equally, even if this does not always happen in practice.

Problems with the civil justice system

There has in recent years been a wide recognition that the civil justice system has not been operating effectively. The main criticisms were that:

- it cost too much to bring cases to court;
- the system was too slow;
- court procedures were unnecessarily complex; and
- even if an issue was decided by a court, it might be impossible to enforce the decision.

These were not new problems. Over the last 100 years, there had been numerous reviews of and attempts to change the civil justice system. (Indeed these problems are not unique to England; they can be found in most other countries with well-developed economies and justice systems.) The latest attempts at reform culminated in the introduction, on 26 April 1999, of a new set of principles as well as new rules for the operation of the civil justice system.

Access to Justice: reform of the civil justice system

The process began in 1994 when Lord Woolf was asked to undertake a review of the civil justice system. He produced first an interim and then, in 1996, a final report under the title 'Access to Justice'. He had a vision that those who wanted to bring cases to court should be able to do so efficiently, and at a cost proportionate to the amount in dispute. At the same time, the court should be the forum of last resort; every encouragement should be given to parties to settle their own disputes. At its most ambitious, Lord Woolf sought to change the culture of litigation by creating a framework within which both professional lawyers and those who wished to take their own cases to court (litigants in person) could do so with their eyes focused on the issues which needed determination by a judge and setting aside those matters which were not essential to the determination of the issue. Following a further review of the potential impact of Lord Woolf's proposals by Sir Peter Middleton, the Government accepted that a programme of change to the civil justice system should be introduced. This led to the enactment of the Civil Procedure Act 1997.

Track allocation and case management

There are two essential features to the reformed civil justice system. First potential cases are allocated to a 'track', the allocation depending on the size and complexity of the case:

- 'small claims track' for the simpler, low value cases up to £5,000;
- 'fast track' for moderately valued cases (usually between £5,000 and £15,000[7]); and
- 'multi-track' for the most complex.

Once the track allocation has been made, the progress of the case is to be determined by judges managing the timetable for the case, rather than, as used to happen, the parties (or more usually their lawyers) being largely in control of progress. Both these principles—track allocation and case management—are directed to tackling delay, and to ensuring that costs do not get out of proportion to the value of what is in dispute.

Civil Procedure Rules

Before 1999, procedure in civil litigation was subject to two distinct codes of practice:

- the *Rules of the Supreme Court* for cases dealt with in the High Court; and
- the *County Court Rules* for cases heard in the County Court.

These two bodies of procedural law had broadly the same purpose, but there were myriad differences between them that added to the complexity of proceedings. These two codes have been replaced by a single code of procedural law, the *Civil Procedure Rules 1999*, made by the Civil Procedure Rule Committee. (*See Box 8.1.*)

Practice directions

In order to keep the structure of the new procedural rules relatively straightforward, a feature of the new scheme is that much of the detailed implementation of the rules is

---

[7] The limit is £1,000 for personal injury cases and housing cases.

Box 8.1 Civil Procedure Rules and the Rule Committee

The Civil Procedure Rules are made under the authority of section 1 of the Civil Procedure Act 1997. In addition, section 5 of the Act provides for the making of practice
directions. The rules and practice directions are made by the Rule Committee, which is
given its legal authority by section 2 of the same Act. The Rule Committee is chaired by
the Head of Civil Justice, currently Lord Justice May.

Once approved by the Lord Chancellor, they are published as statutory instruments.
They are also issued in loose-leaf format, on CD, and can be downloaded from
www.lcd.gov.uk/civil/procrules_fin/index.htm.

Unlike their predecessors, the rules have been consciously drafted in a more 'plain
English' style than had previously been adopted. They also incorporate at the outset a
statement of the overriding objectives of the new rules, against which arguments about
the meaning of specific rules must be set.

found in supplementary *practice directions*. These have been used before, but not to
the same extent as under the new scheme. This has a very practical consequence that
both practitioners and other potential users of the civil justice system must be as
aware of the directions and the requirements they impose as of the rules themselves.
The mix of rules and practice directions, and the frequency with which they were
being amended following commencement of the new scheme, led to fears that it
might result in the re-introduction of some of the complexity it was hoped the new
system might eliminate. However, the pace of change has slackened and, in general,
the new rules and directions have been welcomed.

Pre-action protocols

One of the most significant innovations of the post-Woolf era is that of the *pre-action
protocols*. These are in effect guides to good litigation practice, setting standards and
timetables for the conduct of cases before court proceedings are started. They are
negotiated and agreed by experienced practitioners, and approved by the Head of
Civil Justice. They are designed to ensure more exchange of information and fuller
investigation of claims at an earlier stage so that potential litigants may be able better
to assess the merits of a case and to ensure that proper steps are taken to resolve as
many of the issues in dispute as possible, prior to the parties getting anywhere near a
courtroom. The protocols relate to defined classes of case: currently, personal injury,
clinical negligence, construction and engineering disputes, defamation and professional negligence. Others are in contemplation. A proposal for a general protocol to
cover all civil procedures has been abandoned. It was felt that protocols were more
effective if they related to specific types of action. The protocols that have been agreed
are also set out in the *Civil Procedure Rules*.[8]

---

[8] A protocol relating to judicial review cases was introduced on 4 March 2002: Practice Statement
(Administrative Court) [2002] 1 All ER 633.

Other reforms

Many other related reforms were introduced, including:

Legal language. The language of the rules has been changed to make it more easily understandable. For example, those who bring cases to court are now referred to as 'claimants' rather than 'plaintiffs'; they swear or affirm 'statements of truth' instead of 'affidavits'; the claimant may seek 'specified damages' instead of 'liquidated damages' or 'unspecified damages' instead of 'unliquidated damages'. The essential features of the case are set out in a 'statement of case' instead of 'pleadings'. There are numerous other examples. In short, the new rules seek to eliminate the Latin phrases and other old terminology which were thought to make legal proceedings more complex than they really needed to be.[9]

Forms. A related development, which continues a process begun some years ago, is that the Lord Chancellor's Department has done a great deal to devise forms which can be used to start and progress potential cases. Again this is designed to make it easier for the ordinary individual to use the courts, and to reduce professional costs by ensuring that particular documents do not always have to be specially drafted by professional advisers—they simply download the relevant document and fill it in.[10]

Use of experts. Another change introduced by the rules relates to the use of experts. Lord Woolf had wanted to limit the use of experts to one; this was felt to be too draconian a step to take. Nevertheless the *Civil Procedure Rules* provide that experts have a duty to help the court on matters within their expertise, and this duty overrides any obligation to the person by whom they have been instructed or by whom they are paid. Experts will give evidence only if the court gives permission. Instructions to experts are no longer privileged, and thus their substance must be disclosed in their report.

The purpose of the civil justice system: the forum of last resort

It might be thought that the primary purpose of the civil justice system was the resolution of disputes by a judge. While it would be overstating it to say that nothing could be further from the truth, the situation is much more complicated than that. The courts have long been used very much as a last resort in situations where the parties to a dispute cannot themselves resolve their differences without a court hearing. Even before the Woolf reforms were introduced, the 'typical' dispute was resolved by negotiation and settlement, not by any trial in court. The Woolf reforms have made

---

[9] Of course, the law student will still have to be aware of the former terms, as an understanding of reported decisions made before the changes came into effect will depend on that knowledge. But for the future, things should be clearer.

[10] The forms are available on the Court Service website: **www.courtservice.gov.uk.**

it explicit that the courts must be the forum of last resort for the resolution of disputes.

Latest figures show that in 2001 over 1.7 million claims were issued in the county court, but there were only around 12,700 trials plus around 58,000 small claims hearings. The typical civil proceeding was thus resolved outside the courtroom, not in it. The civil justice system was much more frequently used *indirectly* as part of the process of resolution, rather than *directly* with a case being tried before a judge.

There are many incentives on parties to settle:

- *Costs.* The costs of litigation increase dramatically as the parties get closer to the courtroom door. It is at this point that the numbers of lawyers involved in a case tend to increase and, where barristers are used, their fees are significantly higher when they appear in court than when they are sitting in chambers providing written advice to clients.

- *The indemnity principle.* This provides that, in the usual case, the loser of the case pays a large proportion of the costs of the winner. Given that clear-cut cases should not be coming to court at all, and that therefore there is always some uncertainty about the outcome of a trial,[11] this rule also helps to concentrate the minds of litigants.[12]

Payments into court and offers to settle. The Civil Procedure Rules (CPR) also provide that a defendant to proceedings may offer to settle a case or pay a sum of money into court. The formalities for making an offer or payment are set out in Part 36 of the CPR. If the offer or payment is not accepted, and the claimant fails to do better at the end of any trial than the offer or payment in, then the claimant will be ordered to pay any costs incurred by the defendant after the latest date on which such offer or payment could have been accepted without needing the permission of the court. The court has a discretion to depart from this principle where application of the rule would, in its view, be unjust. This is another rule which creates a very powerful incentive to settle a claim without the case coming to trial.

The pre-Woolf system did little to prevent delay. Although there were incentives to settle, they did not really bite until a trial date was getting near. The speed at which a trial date approached was on the whole determined by the parties to the dispute and their advisers. There was considerable scope for delay. By giving the judges clear powers of case management to set the timetable for the litigation process,[13] the Woolf reforms are intended to ensure that settlements are reached much more speedily than before.

---

[11] The trial process has been described as a forensic lottery; see the book of that name written by Ison, T., *The Forensic Lottery: A Critique of Tort Liability as a System of Personal Injury Compensation* (London, Staples Press, 1967).

[12] The indemnity principle is now under severe attack and may well be restricted. See further Chapter 10.

[13] Each court circuit now has a special *designated judge* who acts with the authority of the Vice-Chancellor, the Head of Civil Justice, to ensure that judges are actively managing the case timetables.

Alternative dispute resolution (ADR)

The Woolf reforms embraced another development that has occurred over recent years—*alternative dispute resolution* (*see Box 8.2*) or, as it is perhaps better labelled, Appropriate Dispute Resolution. This is an umbrella term describing a range of practices designed to assist parties achieve a resolution of their dispute without the necessity of going to court for a full trial in a courtroom. Many of these techniques have been developed in the USA where they are widely used. Their use in England has been less marked,[15] but seems likely to grow, though such growth is currently very slow.

Box 8.2 Forms of ADR

ADR comes in a variety of forms.[14] The principal ones are:

- arbitration,

- mediation, and

- early neutral evaluation.

Arbitration is a process whereby the parties to a dispute choose an arbitrator to determine their dispute. It is a private process. The arbitrator is often an expert in the matter which is the subject of the dispute, say a building contract. The parties are usually bound, contractually, to accept the decision of the arbitrator. It is thus like a court decision, an imposed decision, though, unlike with the court, the whole process takes place in private, out of sight of the general public. Indeed confidentiality is one of arbitration's perceived advantages for many disputants.

Mediation is a technique whereby a third party—mediator—who is neutral so far as the parties to the dispute are concerned, attempts to explore the possibilities for the parties reaching an outcome which satisfies both of them. This is sometimes known as 'win-win', to contrast it with a court process which may be characterized as 'win-lose'. This outcome will not necessarily be one which a court would have reached (or would have had power to reach), for example because the particular remedy—e.g. saying sorry—is not a remedy available in court. It has the advantage that the decision will be one at which the parties have themselves arrived, albeit with the advice and assistance of the mediator.

Early neutral evaluation is a process where someone with legal or other relevant expertise is given a preliminary view of the case and is asked to provide a frank appraisal of the likely outcome, should the case go as far as court. This may be used as a stage in attempting to reach a settlement by negotiation, rather than going to a full trial in court.

---

[15] For the use of mediation in the family justice system see Chapter 7, p. 184.

[14] For a helpful review see Genn, H., *Mediation in Action: Resolving Court Disputes without Trial* (London, Calouste Gulbenkian Foundation, 1999).

In the case of small claims, the court system itself has long used a form of ADR, as the district judges who determine these cases do so not in a formal trial but by an informal procedure, with only the parties to the dispute present and—usually— lawyers excluded. They used to be called small claims arbitrations, although, since the introduction of the small claims track, such cases are now known as small claims hearings. Nevertheless the same procedural informality will apply.

An ADR scheme has been available in the Commercial Court (see below) since 1993. An ADR scheme is also available in the Court of Appeal. The largest-scale experiment in the use of court-centred ADR has been in the Central London County Court, started in May 1996. This was the subject of detailed evaluation by Professor Genn.[16] Experiments in the use of ADR are currently in progress in a number of other courts around the country.

The common feature of all these experiments is that, to date, their use has been very modest. There is evidence that those who take advantage of ADR in general find it a helpful way of resolving their disputes. But the use of ADR has not become as wide-spread as in other countries, particularly the USA, and certainly not as widespread as those who provide ADR services would like.

The importance of ADR to the success of the Woolf reforms is also not yet clear. Some argued that the procedural changes, combined with changes in the rules on the funding of litigation (see Chapter 10), would result in a substantial increase in the potential use of the courts. This would lead to a need to divert cases from the courts, and thus ADR would become an important means of achieving such diversion. However, levels of civil litigation commenced in courts have fallen in recent years. Thus these particular pressures may not materialize.

A different set of arguments suggests that a consequence of the new procedural rules will be to change litigation culture; that as the nature of litigation changes so both clients and their professional advisers will want to move away from the adversarial procedures of the litigation process towards the less confrontational forms of ADR to resolve disputes. However, it is far too early to predict whether this will actually happen. No doubt much will depend on the extent to which lawyers and other ADR providers become entitled to receive payments for this form of dispute resolution, particularly from the Community Legal Services Fund (see below, Chapter 10).

The post-Woolf civil justice system does give power to the judge, as part of the case management strategy, to stay a case for up to twenty-eight days to give the parties a chance to use ADR where this seems to be appropriate. It does not appear that these powers are widely used. However, the Court of Appeal has in a number of recent cases[17] been stressing the importance of parties using ADR

---

[16] Genn, H., *Central London County Court Pilot Mediation Scheme: Evaluation Report, Research Series 4/98* (London, Lord Chancellor's Department, 1998).

[17] See *Cowl v. Plymouth City Council* [2001] EWCA Civ 1935, [2001] All ER (D) 206 and *Dunnett v. Railtrack* [2002] EWCA Civ 303, [2002] 2 All ER 850.

where they can, and that failure to do so may result in adverse rulings on the recovery of costs.

The Lord Chancellor is anxious to promote the use of ADR where possible. In 2001, he sponsored a 'pledge' which committed government departments to exploring the possibility of using ADR where possible. The LCD has also published a discussion paper inviting comments on the potential use of ADR and the part that government should (or should not) play in its development and an analysis of responses.

There are a number of difficult issues relating to the development of ADR which are currently unresolved. Among these issues are:

- *Compulsion.* At present no court can *require* the use of ADR.[18] Experience in the USA suggests that use of ADR does not take off until at least an element of compulsion is introduced. But is it right for the courts to require parties to a dispute to pay for something that may not resolve the matter but only add to costs and delay?

- *Standards.* If ADR is to become in some sense compulsory, how are proper standards for those who offer ADR services to be achieved? At present there are many different groups offering ADR services. But there is no common training programme nor any mechanism for complaint where things go wrong (if things go wrong). Those providing ADR services are moving towards the setting of common standards, but agreements on these have not at present been finalized. It is difficult to see how ADR could be made compulsory without the resolution of these issues.

- *Costs.* Another question relates to the costs of ADR. There is at present no intention on the part of the Government to include ADR services within the framework of the Court Service. Nor, save for measures in the Community Legal Service (see Chapter 10), are there any other proposals for the government funding of ADR. But ADR services have to be paid for. If the costs are too high and nevertheless parties are required by the courts to use a process of ADR, may this not add to the cost of dispute resolution—something the Woolf reforms were attempting to reduce?

- *Outcome.* Will the fact that the parties may well be happier at the end of the ADR process than they might have been at the end of a trial compensate them for the expense of using ADR? It may well do. One of the most powerful claims for ADR is *not* that it is cheaper, but that it enables parties to disputes to retain control of the dispute resolution process, which may in turn enable them to move on with their lives more amicably than they might be able to do after a court hearing. But this will not always be the case. Indeed there will always be those who, on principle, will want to litigate and refuse to use any form of ADR.

---

[18] For the position in the family justice system see above, Chapter 7, p. 179.

The court structure: preliminary issues

Having considered the context within which the civil and commercial justice system has developed in recent years and noted the very considerable changes that have occurred, the structure of the courts will now be considered. Four preliminary issues will be mentioned.

Generalist v. specialist

One of the claims made for the courts in the civil justice system is that they are, and should be, generalist rather than specialist in nature. Certainly, any type of case that does not fall into any other of the jurisdictional categories considered in this book must be disposed of in the civil courts. While the claim that the courts are generalist in nature is still to a large extent true, it is a claim that should be treated with caution. There is now an increasing number of specialist courts that have been created, primarily because of the technicalities of the law and issues to be determined by those courts. This raises the obvious further question whether there should be more specialist courts. In recent years arguments have been made, for example, for the creation of a specialist housing court and for a specialist environment court.

There are many arguments in favour of greater specialization. The judges dealing with the issues should be better informed about the relevant law; thus the quality and consistency of decision-making might be enhanced. Procedures could be better adapted to suit the users of the specialist courts and the types of issues to be dealt with in those courts. For example, special facilities might be available to deal with the particular types of emergency cases that might arise out of ordinary court hours. The practitioners who specialize in the areas of law concerned might be able to operate more efficiently by concentrating their resources in more specialized courts. Against, it is argued that judges might become too narrowly focused. As a consequence judges might become bored with the tasks they were required to perform. Judicial manpower in specialist courts could not be used efficiently if the caseloads in those courts were insufficient to keep the relevant judges busy. Given recent trends, however, it seems likely that there will be more rather than less specialization in the years ahead.

Court fees

A second preliminary issue that needs to be borne in mind is the decision by government that the civil justice system should be—broadly—self-financing.[19] A consequence of this policy decision is that the Court Service sets court fees which claimants have to pay before they can get their cases started and allocated to the appropriate

---

[19] This has recently been the subject of sharp criticism by the Civil Justice Council: see www.civiljusticecouncil.gov.uk/files/Full_Costs_Recovery_v1.3_Draft_to_CJC.pdf.

track. This has led to considerable controversy. One of the principal objections now heard is that when this policy was introduced, in the early 1990s, it was done so without any Parliamentary announcement or debate.

There are those who argue that, on principle, 'justice' should be regarded as a 'free good', which should not be subject to the principle of self-financing at all. Access to the courts for the determination of legal rights and entitlements is a constitutional right to which there should be no barriers—certainly not financial ones. Against that, others argue that the well-heeled, who may be fighting over financial matters worth thousands, if not millions, of pounds, should make—through the payment of fees—a relatively modest contribution towards the running of the civil justice system.

There was a chorus of complaints from judges, lawyers and consumer groups that the combination of the fee for issuing the claim together with the fee that had to be paid when a case was allocated to a particular track was having a disproportionately adverse impact on those bringing small claims. This was deterring access to justice rather than improving it. The government therefore decided to abolish the £80 allocation fee for defended civil actions worth £1,000 or less.[20] However, it seems unlikely that there will be any other relaxation in the civil justice fees regime; indeed other court fees have been adjusted upwards to cover the cost of this concession. Proposals for further changes to the fees structure are currently under consideration. This is a significant subject of conflict between the judiciary and the government.

Enforcement of judgments

A third issue with which the civil justice system needs to be seen to be grappling is the problem of enforcement of judgments. There can be nothing more frustrating than taking a case to court, winning it, but then finding that it is well-nigh impossible to obtain satisfaction of the judgment. In situations where the loser has the backing of an insurance company, or (either private individual or company or other legal body) is extremely resource-rich, this will not usually be a problem. But where the person against whom proceedings are brought is herself of moderate means or is a company without extensive resources, enforcement may be a great problem.

The Government has recognized this and, as part of the continuing programme of reform of the civil justice system, is undertaking a new review of the procedures available to the courts for the enforcement of judgments. This is, in fact, an exceptionally difficult issue. There would be considerable political opposition to a return to the Dickensian days of throwing debtors into jail.[21] Yet there is no doubt that the inability of the civil justice system to force those against whom judgments are made, in particular awards of damages, to pay up is seen by users of the system as a serious weakness.

---

[20] This decision was effective from April 2000. New fees were introduced in April 2003.

[21] Even under present law, failure to pay certain taxes—a particular form of debt—can result in the imposition of a prison sentence.

Delivering the Court Service: local initiatives and centralized justice

The courts are managed by the Court Service, an executive agency set up in April 1995. The day-to-day running of the courts is carried out on a regional basis through six *circuits*.[22] Supervision of the judicial work of each circuit is the responsibility of the *presiding judges*. These are judges of the High Court appointed—two for each circuit—by the Lord Chief Justice. They operate under a Senior Presiding Judge.

One of the issues which Lord Woolf highlighted when he was preparing his Access to Justice report was that many courts had developed their own particular procedures for dealing with specific types of matter. This did not imply that the outcomes of cases would differ, but the ways in which the courts worked certainly did. Lord Woolf felt that it was important that someone appearing for trial in one town should be dealt with in essentially the same way as in any other. One of his hopes for the reform of the Civil Procedure Rules was that this would encourage greater uniformity of process. Given the not inconsiderable discretion that is given to judges to manage cases it may well be that Lord Woolf's hopes in this respect will not be fully realized.

Indeed there is an argument that a degree of procedural experiment should be encouraged to see whether the work of the courts can be made more efficient. However this should be as part of a controlled programme of pilot projects which can be properly evaluated by the Court Service, rather than the result of individual courts going their own way. It is also important that when new procedures are tested and found helpful, the results of good practice should be spread throughout the court system as a whole, not kept as a 'private custom' in a particular court or circuit. This will happen only if innovations are managed by the Court Service.

The County Court

The court which deals with the largest numbers of civil cases is the county court. Founded in 1846 it was designed to provide a forum for the resolution of what would these days be regarded as relatively modest consumer complaints. Over the years, its jurisdiction has expanded. Today all civil actions can be started in the county court, save for a small number of cases where there are special statutory rules which require proceedings to be started in the High Court (see below). There are around 220 county courts throughout England and Wales.

County courts deal with all contract and tort cases, and all proceedings for the recovery of land, irrespective of value. They deal with certain equity and contested probate actions (e.g. arising from alleged breaches of trust obligations or questions

---

[22] Midland and Oxford, run from Birmingham; North Eastern from Leeds; Northern from Manchester; South Eastern from London; Wales and Chester from Cardiff; and Western from Bristol.

about the administration of a will) where the value of the trust fund or the estate does not exceed £30,000, plus any case which the parties agree can be heard in the county court.

Each court is assigned at least one circuit judge[23] and one district judge. Although circuit judges are full-time appointments, most do not spend all their time on civil matters, but also sit as trial judges in criminal cases in the Crown Court. The district judges, however, work full-time on civil issues (including some family justice matters).[24] There are about 605 circuit judges in England and Wales, compared with around 420 district judges. The former sit for a total of around 15,000 days a year on civil matters; the latter for over 72,000 days. District judges thus carry out the bulk of the work in the county court.

According to the latest edition of *Judicial Statistics*,[25] there is a downward trend in the activity levels of the county court—which challenges the claim that we are becoming an increasingly litigious society. The reasons for this decline are not clear. In part, economic prosperity has led to a 12 per cent reduction in mortgage possession work; set against this there has been a 9 per cent increase in bankruptcy petitions. It may be that the new Civil Procedure Rules have encouraged parties to settle their differences before contemplating legal proceedings. It may be that people are increasingly deterred by fears of costs from starting legal proceedings. In those (rare) cases which actually go to trial, the average waiting time between the issue of the claim and the start of the trial is seventy-three weeks.

The High Court

The High Court consists of three divisions. The Family Division has been considered in Chapter 7. The other two divisions are:

- The Queen's Bench Division; and
- The Chancery Division.

These two divisions handle different types of civil and commercial work.

The courts in these divisions handle cases both arising at first instance (i.e. cases being determined for the first time) and on appeal from courts lower in the hierarchical structure—the county court and a number of administrative tribunals. When sitting as an appeal court and when dealing with analogous matters such as judicial review, the High Court is known as the *Divisional Court*. Each division has a divisional court.

---

[23] They are assisted by over 1,300 part-time recorders who are in effect potential judges in training.
[24] They may be assisted by deputy district judges who are also judges in training who sit part-time.
[25] For 2001 (Cm 5551) (London, The Stationery Office, 2001).

The Queen's Bench Division

The Queen's Bench Division is headed by the Lord Chief Justice,[26] who is supported by seventy-two full-time High Court judges.[27] It deals primarily with common law business—actions relating to contract[28] and tort. Torts (civil wrongs) embrace not only negligence and nuisance, but also other wrongs against the person, such as libel, or wrongs against property, such as trespass. Contract cases involve, for example, failure to pay for goods or services, or other alleged breaches of contract. Some fact situations give rise to actions both in tort and contract.

It is central to the philosophy of the post-Woolf era that only the most important cases should be dealt with in the High Court. As a result only personal injury claims with a value of £50,000 or more may be started there. In other cases the claim must be for £15,000 or more. In addition, three specialist jurisdictions come within the scope of the Queen's Bench Division:

- the Admiralty Court,
- the Commercial Court, and
- the Technology and Construction Court (see further below).

Cases to be tried in these courts are required to be started in the High Court, irrespective of financial amount (though in practice they will usually be substantial). There are also a number of other types of proceedings which, by statute, must be started in the High Court.

Jury trial

There is a right to trial by jury in civil proceedings for fraud, libel, slander, malicious prosecution or false imprisonment. In other cases, a judge may in her discretion allow trial by jury; but this rarely happens. Where there is a jury, the jury will decide not only liability (e.g., were the words used libellous or not) but also the amount of any damages.

Workload

In 2001, only 21,613 claims and originating summonses were issued in the Queen's Bench Division. About a quarter were issued in London, the rest in High Court District Registries around the country. In 2001, 2,383 actions were set down for trial; of these only 460 resulted in a full trial. As in other parts of the legal system, the full trial remains the exceptional, not the ordinary, mode of disposal. The average waiting time for a case to come to trial was 173 weeks (an increase of 5 per cent over the previous year). The average time taken for a full hearing was just under eight hours.

---

[26] Currently Lord Woolf.

[27] They are assisted by part-time deputy High Court judges, and circuit judges sitting as High Court judges. These part-time judges deal with nearly 50% of all trials.

[28] Some questions of contract are referred to the Chancery Division.

In those cases where damages were sought, awards in excess of £15,000 were made in nearly all cases where the claimant won; most personal injury cases resulted in awards in excess of £50,000.

Divisional Court

When sitting as a Divisional Court, the Queen's Bench Division deals with judicial review cases,[29] appeals by way of 'case stated',[30] habeas corpus,[31] committal for contempts of court committed in an inferior court, or appeals and applications under a variety of statutory provisions.[32] The bulk of the work is judicial review. Over 4,700 applications for permission to bring judicial review proceedings were made in 2001, of which only 1,400 were granted. The largest single group of cases—over half the total—relates to matters arising out of decisions relating to immigration law.[33] This area of the High Court's work has been subject to rapid increase. When dealing with judicial review, the court is known as the Administrative Court.

The Chancery Division

The Chancery Division of the High Court comprises the Lord Chancellor (who rarely sits as a Chancery judge in practice), the Vice-Chancellor (the effective Head of the Chancery Division), supported by seventeen other High Court judges.[34]

The principal categories of business dealt with by the division relate to corporate and personal insolvency disputes; disputes relating to business, trade and industry; the enforcement of mortgages; intellectual property matters including copyright and patents; disputes relating to trust property; and disputes arising from wills and the administration of deceased people's estates (probate matters). (For uncontested probate matters, see Box 8.3.) The bulk of the work is handled in the Royal Courts of Justice in London, together with eight provincial centres which have High Court Chancery jurisdiction.[35]

In 2001 a total of just over 37,000 proceedings were started in the Chancery Division; but only 522 cases were disposed of following a trial. The Divisional Court of the Chancery Division also disposed of seventy-one appeals in 2001, over half being appeals on bankruptcy matters.

---

[29] Powers of judicial review are exercisable both over inferior courts and tribunals—e.g. where it is alleged that there has been a breach of proper fair procedure or an incorrect interpretation of the law—and against public bodies or government ministers or others carrying out public acts or duties. Judicial review is considered further in Chapter 6 on administrative justice.

[30] A process used, for example, by the Crown Court or a magistrates' court to obtain a ruling on a particular provision of criminal law.

[31] Where unlawful detention is alleged.

[32] E.g., under the town and country planning legislation.

[33] See Bridges, L., et al., Judicial Review in Perspective (London, Cavendish, 1995).

[34] They are assisted, as needed, by deputy High Court judges, who are either practitioners approved to act as such by the Lord Chancellor, or retired High Court or circuit judges. The extent of their use depends on the level of business before the courts.

[35] Birmingham, Bristol, Cardiff, Leeds, Liverpool, Manchester, Newcastle upon Tyne and Preston.

Box 8.3 Uncontested probate matters: the Family Division

Although the Chancery Division deals with contested probate matters, uncontested matters are dealt with in the Principal Registry of the *Family* Division of the High Court or any of the eleven district probate registries that exist in England and Wales. Grants of probate are made in cases where there was a will; grants of administration where there was not. There is a heavy workload involved. Over 260,000 grants were issued in 2001, of which nearly 75 per cent were grants of probate, the remainder grants of administration.

In addition to the general work of the Chancery Division, there are two specialist jurisdictions: the Companies Court and the Patent Court, considered further below. As with other parts of the civil justice system, the court is very much the place of last resort for the resolution of disputes.

The commercial justice system

Notwithstanding the reluctance, noted above, of the judiciary to specialize, the fact is that within both the High Court and the county court systems, there now exists a range of specialist courts, established to deal with a range of (primarily) commercial and company law matters. These developments reflect the position of London in the global economy, and the need for the courts to provide appropriate levels of expertise in specialist areas. They have spread to provincial centres where there is also significant commercial activity. The specialist courts may be listed as follows:

The Companies Court

This court is part of the Chancery Division of the High Court. It deals primarily with the compulsory liquidation of companies and other matters arising under the Insolvency Act 1986 and the Companies Acts. For example, a registered company which seeks to reduce its capital may do so only with the approval of the court. The bulk of this work is done in London, but the eight provincial district registries have the same powers.[36] Nearly 20,500 originating proceedings were started in these courts in 2001.

The Patents Court

This is another specialist part of the Chancery Division, dealing not only with patents, but other forms of intellectual property, including registered designs. It also hears appeals against decisions of the Comptroller General of Patents.

[36] See above n. 35.

Cases suitable for determination by a county court are heard in a specially designated county court—the Central London County Court. The workload of this court
is not high—only twenty actions were heard in 2001.

The Admiralty Court

This is part of the Queen's Bench Division of the High Court, dealing—as the name
suggests—with shipping matters, principally the consequences of collisions at sea and
damage to cargos. As with patents, most cases are dealt with in London, but there is
power to refer suitable cases to specially designated county courts. 281 actions were
started in 2001; only seven trials were actually heard in the court.

The Commercial Court

This is also part of the Queen's Bench Division of the High Court. This deals with a
wide range of commercial matters, for example, banking, international credit and the
purchase and sale of commodities. It also deals with shipping matters not handled by
the Admiralty Court—contracts relating to ships, carriage of cargo, insurance, as well
as the construction and performance of mercantile contracts more generally. The
Commercial Court also deals with the practice of arbitration and questions which
may arise from arbitrations.

The Technology and Construction Court

This is the name given in 1998 to the former Official Referees' Court. This is another
section of the High Court which sits in London with seven full-time *circuit* judges,
presided over by a High Court judge. Hearings are also possible outside London
before specially designated or nominated judges. The court deals primarily with
building and engineering disputes and also computer litigation. It can also deal with
other matters such as valuation disputes and landlord and tenant matters involving
dilapidations. And it handles questions arising from arbitrations in building and
engineering disputes. During 2001, about 450 proceedings were started; only sixty-
one trials were held in London. (Figures for cases dealt with outside London are not
available.)

Other courts and offices

In addition to the courts so far identified, there are also a number of other offices
which form part of the Supreme Court. These include:

- *The Office of the Official Solicitor and Public Trustee.* The Official Solicitor operates under the authority of section 90 of the Supreme Court Act 1981. His primary duties are to protect the interests of children and mental patients, i.e. those who do not have full legal capacity to look after their own affairs. His department has a fairly substantial work-load, dealing with around 2,700 cases in 2001. Among his responsibilities are child abduction cases. In 2001, the Official Solicitor took over responsibility for the *Public Trust Office.* The Public Trustee acts as executor or administrator of deceased persons' estates or trustees of wills or settlements where he has been named and has accepted the nomination.

- *The Court of Protection.* This is an office of the Supreme Court which exercises judicial functions in respect of the property and financial affairs of persons incapable, by reason of mental disorder, of running their own affairs. The principal legislation conferring power on the court is the Mental Health Act 1983 and the Enduring Powers of Attorney Act 1985. It shares accommodation with its Executive Agency, the Public Guardianship Office, established in 2001.

Appeals and the appeal courts

We have already noted in passing that many of the courts listed above have power to hear appeals in defined circumstances. Many appeals are satisfactorily disposed of in that context.

However, there is also a number of courts that deal exclusively with appeals. They are particularly important in the English legal system, not just because they have greater authority within the hierarchical court structure, but also because it is through the reported judgments delivered in those courts that the primary source of authority for the development of the common law and the interpretation of statutes is to be found. (See above, Chapter 3.) It can be argued that these appeal courts are the only truly generalist courts, in that they have the responsibility for dealing with whatever is presented to them by way of appeal.

Policy issues

In recent years, it has been suggested that there may be too many avenues of appeal; and that the level of court at which an appeal is determined may not always be the right one. To deal with this, important changes of principle were introduced into the law on appeals by the Access to Justice Act 1999.

Permission to appeal

It was always the case that, in order to bring an appeal in the Court of Appeal, it was necessary for the appellant to seek the permission (or—as it used to be called—the leave) of the court to bring the appeal. Under section 54 of the Access to Justice Act

1999 rules of court have been made that require permission to appeal to be obtained for all appeals to the county courts, the High Court or the Court of Appeal (Civil Division). There are limited exceptions, for example appeals relating to court orders which affect the liberty of the individual. There is no appeal against a decision either to give or refuse permission. Where permission is refused, there remains the possibility of making a further application for permission, either in the same or another court.

Second appeals

Once a county court or the High Court has decided a matter on appeal, section 55 of the Access to Justice Act provides that there will be no possibility of a further appeal unless either the appeal would raise an important point of principle or practice, or there is some other compelling reason for the appeal to be heard. All applications for permission to bring a further appeal are dealt with by the Court of Appeal, irrespective of the court which determined the first appeal. If permission is granted, the Court of Appeal hears the appeal as well.

Destination of appeals

Section 56 of the Access to Justice Act gave the Lord Chancellor power to vary, by order, the avenues of appeal to and within the county court, the High Court and the Court of Appeal. Thus:

(1) For fast track cases heard by a district judge appeals lie to a circuit judge;

(2) For fast track cases heard by a circuit judge appeals lie to a High Court judge;

(3) In multi-track cases, appeals against interlocutory decisions by a district judge are to a circuit judge; by a master[37] or circuit judge to a High Court judge; and by a High Court judge to the Court of Appeal.

(4) In multi-track cases, appeals against final orders will be direct to the Court of Appeal, irrespective of the court making the initial decision.

Reform of the highest courts?

The question whether the House of Lords and the Judicial Committee of the Privy Council should be retained or be replaced by a new top court is an issue that is currently receiving a good deal of attention. (*See Box 8.4.*) The present government is not intending to pursue the idea, notwithstanding its commitment to modernization. Nonetheless, it is an issue that is likely to remain controversial.

The particular courts of appeal to be considered here are:

• The Judicial Committee of the Privy Council;

• The House of Lords;

• The Court of Appeal.

---

[37] Masters are judicial officers of the High Court who determine interlocutory matters.

Box 8.4 The future of the United Kingdom's top courts

One issue that is attracting a lot of attention in legal circles, and notably amongst the judiciary, is whether the present place of the House of Lords and the Judicial Committee of the Privy Council as the United Kingdom's highest courts should be retained. The arguments, together with analysis of what happens in other countries, were brought together in a report published in 2001 by the Constitution Unit at University College London. *The Future of the United Kingdom's Highest Courts* by Professor Andrew Le Sueur (University of Birmingham) and Richard Cornes (University of Essex) considers:

- whether the UK's two top-level national courts—the Appellate Committee of the House of Lords and the Judicial Committee of the Privy Council—are in need of reform;

- and, if so, why, when, how and in what form change might occur.

The report draws attention to the changed contexts within which the House of Lords and Judicial Committee of the Privy Council now have to function. These include:

- unease about the ambiguous position of the Lord Chancellor, as a member of the court as well as a member of the Executive and the Legislature;

- the potential tasks which may fall to the court arising from the new constitutional arrangements following devolution;

- the role of the court under the Human Rights Act 1998 and its functions in relation to declaring legislation incompatible with the European Convention on Human Rights.

The report identifies options which might be pursued in the future. They include:

- maintaining the status quo,

- creating a supreme court for the UK,

- creating a constitutional court,

- creating a UK court of justice.

The Judicial Committee of the Privy Council

This remains the final court of appeal for twenty-four British Commonwealth Territories[38] and six independent republics within the Commonwealth.[39] It also acts as a constitutional Supreme Court determining constitutional issues arising from those

---

[38] This group includes both independent territories that retained this right of appeal when they achieved independence—e.g., New Zealand and Jamaica; and UK overseas territories that remain dependent on the UK, e.g., Gibraltar and the Cayman Islands.

[39] This group includes Mauritius and The Gambia.

independent territories that have a written constitution. The Judicial Committee also has jurisdiction over a number of domestic matters[40] and 'pastoral' matters (which relate to the Church of England). The statutory powers of the Committee derive from the Judicial Committee Act of 1833, though the history of the Committee can be traced back to mediaeval times. The judges who sit in the Judicial Committee are (broadly) the same as those who sit in the House of Lords (below), though they are on occasion joined by a senior member of the judiciary from the country whence the appeal has come.

Many find the jurisdiction of the Judicial Committee highly anachronistic—a throw-back to a British imperial past that is long gone. Nevertheless the Judicial Committee has a steady stream of work. Eight-five appeals and fifty-eight petitions for special leave to appeal[41] were lodged in 2001; and the Committee sat on 123 days. The issues it deals with are, by definition, of very considerable legal and social importance, not just for the country in question but in the common law world in general.

The House of Lords

This is the supreme court of appeal in Great Britain and Northern Ireland, although it cannot hear appeals in Scottish criminal cases. The House of Lords can, with leave, hear appeals from any orders or judgments of the Court of Appeal in England, the Court of Session in Scotland or the Court of Appeal in Northern Ireland.[42] In addition, appeals may be taken, with leave, from the High Court when it has been sitting as a Divisional Court (i.e. as a court of appeal or when dealing with cases such as judicial review). In limited circumstances, an appeal may be brought direct from the High Court or the High Court in Northern Ireland, when sitting as a trial court.[43]

Permission may be granted either by the relevant Court of Appeal or, if that is not forthcoming, by the Appeal Committee of the House of Lords. (If a lower court grants permission, the House of Lords cannot overturn that decision.) In practice, permission is granted by the lower courts rather infrequently.[44] In 2001 the Appeal Committee dealt with 274 petitions for leave to appeal; only seventy-three were allowed. The right of the citizen to 'take her case to the highest court in the land' is in reality a highly contingent one, subject to considerable procedural constraint. The House of Lords is a judicial resource that is sparingly used.

---

[40] Hearing appeals from a number of professional bodies, in particular under the Medical Act 1983 and the Dentists Act 1984. The Judicial Committee has recently been given power to deal with 'devolution issues' arising out of the passing of the Wales Act and the Scotland Act 1998.

[41] These special petitions relate to appeals in criminal cases where the Judicial Committee will not hear an appeal unless satisfied that the case raises a matters of great general importance or where there appears to be the danger of a grave miscarriage of justice.

[42] Save, in the case of Northern Ireland or Scotland, where this is prevented by statute.

[43] This is known as 'leapfrogging' and can occur where is it clear that the law in question needs clarification at the highest level, perhaps because there are inconsistent decisions from the Court of Appeal.

[44] It is not uncommon for the Criminal Division of the Court of Appeal to certify that a point of law of general public importance is involved in a case, but still to refuse leave to appeal to the House of Lords.

Appeals themselves are heard by an Appellate Committee of the House of Lords, consisting usually of five Lords of Appeal in Ordinary. Hearings are tightly time-controlled, lasting usually only two to three days. In 2001 eighty-four appeals were determined, fifty-three of which came from the Civil Division of the Court of Appeal and related to a wide variety of quite different issues.

The Court of Appeal

The Court of Appeal is divided into two divisions: the criminal and the civil. The two senior judges are the Lord Chief Justice, who heads the Criminal Division, and the Master of the Rolls, who heads the Civil Division. They are assisted by, currently, thirty-five Lords Justice of Appeal.[45] Both the President of the Family Division and the Vice-Chancellor of the Chancery Division sit in the Court of Appeal for part of their time. By contrast with the House of Lords and the Privy Council the Court of Appeal has a substantial caseload.

The Criminal Division

As with the House of Lords appeals either against sentence or conviction can be made only with the permission of the court. In 2001, 7,440 applications were made, of which 1,943 were against conviction. Around 2,000 applications for permission were granted by a single judge. Of the 4,500 or so applications for permission which were refused by a single judge, 1,181 were taken to the Full Court for determination, of which about a quarter (390) were allowed.

Of the actual appeals heard during 2001, 30 per cent of those against conviction were allowed; and 66 per cent against sentence were allowed. Fifty-eight retrials were also ordered.

The Civil Division

The number of appeals coming to the Civil Division rose steadily during the early 1990s. They began to fall in 1996, and are now holding steady. During 2001, 1,071 final appeals were filed, and a similar number were disposed of, of which about 800 went to a hearing before the court. 338 appeals were allowed. During the same period about 280 interlocutory appeals—on matters that are related to the proceedings, but not finally determinative of the issues in question—were filed, and a similar number were disposed of. About 40 per cent of the interlocutory appeals were allowed.

---

[45] Other High Court judges assist, as required and as available, in the Criminal Division.

Commentary

(1) While the popular rhetoric may suggest that it is the right of every English person to have his or her day in court, in practice access to the courts is surrounded by barriers. There are substantial procedural and financial pressures on litigants to settle their difference outside the courts; and appealing the decision of a court is even more problematic.

(2) Judicial manpower is an expensive resource to be used sparingly. There is a notable tendency for much of the simpler case work to be dealt with by part-time judges. There are also many contexts in which judges sit in a level of court to which they have not been appointed—circuit judges in the High Court; High Court judges in the Court of Appeal, for example. There is thus considerable flexibility in how the available resource is used, though this begs the question—given the policy on court fees[46]—whether the public is actually getting the judicial service it thinks it is paying for.

(3) Delay and cost were the principal issues identified as in need of reform by Lord Woolf. Preliminary research suggests that the new Civil Procedure Rules are working well, though there are still complaints about the cost of taking proceedings.[47] There is also considerable frustration at the slow pace of investment in information technology in the civil justice system, that was promised at the time the Woolf reforms were introduced but which has not yet been fully achieved.

Questions for discussion

1. Has England become over-litigious?

2. Should courts be more/less specialized?

3. How should the civil justice system be funded? What level of state funding is justifiable?

4. Should there be so many avenues of appeal? Are there sufficient avenues of appeal?

5. Should there be a Supreme Court to replace the House of Lords?

---

[46] See above p. 204.
[47] See Goriely, T., Moorhead, R., and Abrams, P., *More Civil Justice? The Impact of the Woolf Reforms on Pre-action Behaviour* (Research Study 43) (London, The Law Society and Civil Justice Council, 2002).

Further reading

ABEL, R.L., *The Politics of Informal Justice* (London/New York, Academic Press, 1982), 2 vols

BALDWIN, J., *Small Claims in the County Court* (Oxford, Clarendon Press, 1996)

—— *Lay and Judicial Perspectives on the Expansion of the Small Claims Regime* (LCD Research Paper 8/2002) (London, Lord Chancellor's Department, 2002)

BLOM-COOPER, L., and DREWRY, G., *Final Appeal: a Study of the House of Lords in its Judicial Capacity* (Oxford, Clarendon Press, 1972)

BROWN, H., and MARRIOTT, A., *ADR: Principles and Practice* (2nd edn., London, Sweet and Maxwell, 1999)

BULLE, L., and NESIC, M., *Mediation: Principles, Process, Practice* (London, Butterworths, 2001)

GENN, H., *Mediation in Action—Resolving Court Disputes Without Trial* (London, Caloute Gulbenkian Foundation, 1999)

—— *Court-based ADR Initiatives For Non-Family Civil Disputes: The Commercial Court and The Court of Appeal* (LCD Research Paper 1/2002) (London, Lord Chancellor's Department, 2002)

JACOB, SIR JACK, *The Fabric of English Civil Justice* (London, Stevens, 1987)

JACOB, J., *Civil Litigation: Practice and Procedure in a Shifting Culture* (Welwyn Garden City, Emis Prefessional Publishing, 2001)

NATIONAL CONSUMER COUNCIL, *Ordinary Justice: Legal Services and the Courts in England and Wales* (London, HMSO, 1989)

PALMER, M., and ROBERTS, S., *Dispute Processes: ADR and the Primary Forms of Decision-Making* (London, Butterworths, 1998)

POLDEN, P., *A History of the County Court, 1846–1971* (Cambridge, Cambridge University Press, 1999)

SHAPLAND, J., SORSBY, A., and HIBBERT, J., *A Civil Justice Audit* (LCD Research Paper 2/2002) (London, Lord Chancellor's Department, 2002)

WOOLF, LORD, *Access to Justice: Final Report to the Lord Chancellor on the Civil Justice System in England and Wales* (London, The Stationery Office, 1996)

Websites

www.lcd.gov.uk/civil/cjustfr.htm *(General LCD website with links to material on the civil justice system)*

www.courtservice.gov.uk/index.htm

www.courtservice.gov.uk/info/reps/reports.htm *(List of links to court service reports)*

www.courtservice.gov.uk/notices/mcc consultation_paper.pdf *(Consultation paper on modernizing the civil courts, 2001)*

www.courtservice.gov.uk/info/reps/mcc_report.pdf *(Analysis of response to the consultation paper on modernizing the civil courts, 2002)*

www.lcd.gov.uk/civil/procrules_fin/index.htm *(Civil Procedure Rules)*

www.lcd.gov.uk/civil/adr/index.htm *(LCD website on alternative dispute resolution)*

www.academy-experts.org/defaultin.htm *(The professional body for expert witnesses)*

www.arbitrators.org/ *(Chartered Institute of Arbitrators)*

www.arbitrators-society.org/ *(Society of Construction Arbitrators)*

www.cedr.co.uk/ *(Centre for Effective Dispute Resolution)*

www.adrgroup.co.uk/ *(ADR group)*

www.adrchambers.co.uk *(ADR chambers UK and Europe site)*

www.northernmediators.co.uk/ *(regional group of mediation providers)*

www.civiljusticecouncil.gov.uk/

www.lcd.gov.uk/enforcement/indexfr.htm *(Web site on the enforcement review)*

www.lcd.gov.uk/cj2000/cj2000fr.htm *(A vision of civil justice in the information age)*

www.ucl.ac.uk/constitution-unit/reports/courts.htm#76 *(Constitutional Unit report on reform of top courts)*

www.offsol.demon.co.uk/ *(Official Solicitor and Public Trustee)*

www.guardianship.gov.uk/ *(Public Guardianship Office)*

PART III

THE DELIVERY AND FUNDING OF LEGAL SERVICES

This Part consists of two chapters. Chapter 9 looks at those who deliver legal services, including both professionally qualified lawyers and others providing legal services; it also includes consideration of the judges and legal scholars who should also be seen as groups responsible for developing and delivering the law. Chapter 10 looks at the funding of legal services, and analyses in particular the profound changes that have occurred to the funding of civil litigation following the restructuring of the legal aid scheme.

9

Delivering legal services: Practitioners, adjudicators and legal scholars

Introduction

Discussions about the delivery of legal services tend to focus on the role of the legal profession and its two branches: *solicitors* and *barristers*. Here a broader approach is adopted. In the same way that we have argued that the institutional framework of the English legal system can only be understood by referring to a wide range of institutions, not simply the courts, so too thinking about the full range of those who deliver services about legal rights and entitlements involves consideration of a much greater range of actors. The purpose of this chapter is to provide an introductory account of the principal groups that provide legal services. It considers not only the professionally qualified, but also those who provide legal services without necessarily having legal professional qualifications.

The bulk of the chapter focuses on those who deliver legal services directly or indirectly to clients. The chapter also includes consideration of those who provide legal services by adjudicating disputes, whether as judges or other types of dispute resolver. Finally the role of the legal scholar is considered. The teaching and writing of the scholars helps (or should help) to shape both the law and those who deliver legal services to the public.

The practitioners

Three groups are considered in this part of the chapter:

- those professionally qualified as lawyers;
- those in professional groups allied to law; and
- lay legal advisers.

Professionally qualified lawyers: solicitors and barristers

There are currently over 90,000 practising solicitors in England and Wales, plus another 10,000 or so barristers. The majority of these are in private practice, though a substantial minority are employed lawyers working 'in-house' for a wide variety of companies, government departments and agencies. Both these totals have increased very rapidly over the last quarter of a century. They reflect increased demands for legal services resulting from economic growth, structural changes affecting the commercial world such as globalization and involvement in Europe, and numerous other social changes with greater emphasis on citizens' rights.

These global figures mask two important developments. First, there is a significantly improved gender balance of those entering the legal profession than there was twenty-five years ago. For a number of years now, more women than men have become solicitors. Secondly, the ethnic balance of entrants, though far from satisfactory, has improved. While the legal profession may still be a predominantly middle-class one, it is significantly less white and male than it used to be.[1]

What lawyers do

It is impossible to summarize the enormous variety of work that lawyers undertake. A long list could be presented, but would not be particularly enlightening. Much of the work of the large city firms relates to the commercial activities of their clients, for example the headline-grabbing financial deals or take-over bids that shape economic and commercial life. Others offer services focused on the individual client, for example defending people accused of crime, dealing with the consequences of personal injuries particularly arising from road traffic accidents, buying and selling property, handling divorces or winding up estates after death.

The focus of this chapter is on lawyers who work in private practice. However, the work of other significant groups of qualified lawyers should also be noted. Three specific examples may be given:

Lawyers in industry. Considerable numbers of lawyers work for industry, not indirectly through the services provided for companies by those in private practice, but directly through their employment by the firms concerned. Most major companies have legal departments, staffed by professionally qualified lawyers, able to advise them on those legal issues which directly affect the company and its operations, for example matters relating to employment law, or health and safety legislation.

Lawyers in the Civil Service and local government. There are—broadly—two ways in which those professionally qualified as lawyers may be employed in central govern-

---

[1] These changes are not yet reflected in the number of women and members of ethnic minority groups who have reached the highest positions in the law, e.g. judicial appointments, QCs or partners in solicitors' firms.

ment. First they may be specifically employed for their technical legal expertise: to draft legislation (Parliamentary Counsel), or to deal with the wide range of legal issues that arise in departments (the Government Legal Service). In addition, there are those with law degrees and other legal qualifications who are not employed as lawyers, but who form part of the general civil service complement of government.

In local government, lawyers often play a very important role in ensuring that local authorities act within the scope of the powers given to them by Act of Parliament.

Lawyers in court administration. Lawyers play a very important part in the work of those courts and other dispute resolution bodies which do not use legally qualified adjudicators, for example Justices' Clerks in the magistrates' courts.

One of the great attractions of the law is the enormous range of employment opportunities that the law provides for those who wish to practise or work in the legal system. There are also increasing opportunities to work in international agencies of various kinds, particularly in Europe.

Preliminary issues

When thinking about what lawyers do, two preliminary distinctions should be drawn: (1) between litigious and non-litigious matters; and (2) between lawyers' services and legal services.

Litigious and non-litigious matters. It is essential to bear in mind from the outset the fundamental distinction between litigious and non-litigious matters. A great deal of the work of lawyers is directed to non-litigious work—work designed to prevent litigation. This includes, for example, the provision of advice or the drafting of documents designed to ensure that the affairs of people run smoothly without the need to litigate in a courtroom or any other forum. By contrast, litigious work arises where things have gone wrong, where there are disputes that need to be resolved either between individuals or companies or between the citizen and the state. The right to be heard in a court and the right to conduct litigation are subject to particular statutory rules.

Legal services and lawyers' services. A second distinction worth drawing is between *lawyers' services*, services which must be provided only by professionally qualified lawyers, and *legal services*, which may, though do not have to, be provided by professional lawyers. One of the features of the English legal system is that many people, other than those professionally qualified as lawyers, provide legal services, which are required by members of the public, and which deal with legal issues, e.g. advice about legal entitlements or the completion of legal transactions. The role of para-legal staff and lay advisers is discussed later in this chapter. (Some examples are given in *Box 9.1.*)

Professional organization

The organization of the practising legal profession in England and Wales is very different from that in many other countries. There is still an important distinction in

Box 9.1 Legal services and lawyers' services

Some examples of the distinction in practice are:

- the first source of legal advice for many people faced with problems about their employment ('have I been unfairly dismissed by my employer?') will be a *Citizens' Advice Bureau* or a *Trade Union*. The person they see will be trained to give the appropriate advice; the adviser may indeed recommend that the person should see a qualified lawyer. But the initial *legal service* will not usually come from a lawyer, but from a trained lay adviser.

- Similar points may be made in relation to advice sought by a tenant in a dispute with her landlord.

- Many people anxious to obtain advice regarding their legal entitlements to social security benefits are more likely to turn to the services of a *welfare rights officer*— again a lay person, albeit specially trained, rather than to professionally qualified lawyers.

- Those who buy or sell houses may use the services of a *licensed conveyancer* rather than a solicitor to complete their transaction.

Some legal services, in the sense set out above, are provided by other professional groups. The most obvious example is that the bulk of matters relating to individuals' legal liability to pay tax are dealt with, not by lawyers, but by *accountants*. *Legal services* are not provided exclusively by qualified lawyers.

Lawyers' services may be seen as a special sub-set of the total provision of legal services: they are services which either *have* to be provided by those qualified as lawyers (such as the provision of advocacy services in court—which are restricted to those who have achieved particular professional qualifications) or which, as a matter of practice, are provided by those qualified as lawyers. For example, it is inconceivable that large corporations would turn to lay advisers—however well trained—for advice on questions relating to a corporate take-over. Such clients want the expertise that professional lawyers hold themselves out as offering, and, should anything go wrong, the comfort of the insurance protection that is a part of professional responsibility.

This distinction, between legal services and lawyers' services, should be borne in mind when reading this chapter.

professional identity between *solicitors*, who are professionally regulated by the Law Society, and *barristers*, who are regulated by the General Council of the Bar (the Bar Council).

Solicitors in private practice usually come together to form partnerships, though a substantial minority practise on their own as 'sole practitioners'. Barristers in private practice come together in 'chambers' but they are all self-employed within those chambers. Barristers are not currently permitted to form partnerships.[2]

Independence

One of the key attributes claimed for the legal profession is that it should be independent. This is, constitutionally, an extremely important claim, as it involves lawyers asserting their right to give advice independently of the views of the government of the day. It also involves a professional obligation to take on cases which may be widely regarded as disagreeable or distasteful. The proposition that a person is innocent until proved guilty depends on lawyers being willing to develop and advance arguments on behalf of their clients no matter how unpleasant those clients may be. The 'cab-rank' principle which applies to the Bar, whereby barristers are professionally obliged to take on whatever case comes to them next, is perhaps the clearest example of the operation of this principle.

The assertion of independence also implies that the professions should be left free to regulate themselves in accordance with their own rules of professional conduct, and without interference from government. As will be seen, there has been significant erosion of the freedom from government intervention in the legal profession over recent years. The abolition of restrictive practices, the changes to legal aid and modes of dealing with complaints about the quality of work will all be noted as examples of government intervention. Each example of government involvement may be justified, particularly in contexts where the legal profession has not been willing to reform itself in ways which the public interest might seem to demand. However, the question where the boundaries should be drawn in the involvement of government in the legal profession is one that needs constant attention, if the role of the legal profession in assisting the individual, often against agencies of the state or other powerful bodies, is not to be compromised.

Trends in legal practice

In the same way that the institutional framework of the legal system has undergone profound change in recent years, so too has the legal profession. A number of trends affecting the profession are noted here.

The blurring of the distinction between solicitors and barristers

First, though the line between 'solicitor' and 'barrister' can still be drawn as a matter of professional identity, the practical implications of the distinction are much fewer today than they were twenty years ago. Many of the services which used to be the exclusive preserve of one branch of the profession are now open to all. (*See Boxes 9.1 and 9.2.*)

---

[2] The ability of the Bar to sustain the notion that barristers are all self-employed and are not permitted to enter into partnerships is coming under attack. The commercial pressures arising from the increased overheads which chambers must absorb suggest that the case for a more commercial approach to the organization of chambers will need addressing in the near future.

Box 9.2 Lawyers' services: rights of audience and rights to conduct litigation

Two of the most important rights asserted by professionally qualified lawyers are to undertake advocacy in the courts and to prepare cases for court. Before 1990, these were regulated by the professional rules of conduct of the Bar Council and the Law Society. Under the provisions of the Courts and Legal Services Act 1990, the Government began to put these rights on a statutory footing. Instead of the professional bodies simply prescribing rules relating to advocacy and litigation, as they had done in the past, the Act now permitted 'authorized bodies' (the Bar Council, the Law Society and the Institute of Legal Executives) to set the rules. The Act also provided a statutory process of approval for the adoption of new or altered rules. This turned out to be extremely cumbersome; some applications for approval took years to complete the prescribed procedures.

Under the Access to Justice Act 1999, the Government has intervened further. The Act makes the following provisions:

- All barristers and solicitors are to have the right of audience before every court in all proceedings;[3]

- Crown prosecutors and other employed advocates (whether solicitors or barristers) will have the same rights of audience as if they were in private practice;[4]

- Advocates and litigators employed by the Legal Services Commission or by bodies established by the Legal Services Commission will be enabled to provide services directly to the public, without the need to receive instructions through a solicitor or other person acting for the client;[5]

- Where a person has been granted the right of audience by one professional body (e.g. the Bar Council), she is entitled to retain that right if she becomes a solicitor, and thus a member of the Law Society;[6]

- Barristers employed by firms of solicitors are also enabled to act on the same basis as solicitors;[7]

- The General Council of the Bar and the Institute of Legal Executives are given power to grant their members the right to conduct litigation;[8]

---

[3] S. 36; these are not unqualified rights, those wishing to exercise them must obey the rules of conduct of the professional bodies and meet prescribed training requirements.

[4] S. 37. The campaign fought by the CPS to obtain rights of advocacy under the Act of 1990 was a source of very great frustration.

[5] S. 38.

[6] S. 39.

[7] S. 44; the Bar Council rules that treat barristers employed by solicitors as 'non-practising' and thus able to offer only a limited range of services are disapplied.

[8] S. 40; they are under no obligation to do so.

- Procedures for authorizing (and in extreme cases revoking authorizations to) new bodies to grant rights of audience and rights to conduct litigation, and for approving alterations to or the adoption of new regulations or rules of conduct have been streamlined;[9] and

- The overriding duties of advocates and litigators to the court to act with independence in the interests of justice and to comply with their professional bodies' rules of conduct is put on a statutory footing.[10] All authorized advocates and litigators must refuse to do anything required, either by a client or an employer, that is not in the interests of justice (e.g. the suppression of evidence).

The implications of these changes for the regulation of the legal profession are clear; while it would be going too far to assert that the legal profession is now being directly regulated by government, it is quite clear that the government is—whether the legal professions like it or not—acting in 'partnership' with the professional bodies.

The blurring of the distinction is largely the result of a sustained attack on the restrictive practices of lawyers which has lasted for over thirty years. (*See Box 9.3.*) But there has also been a concern that there should be no unnecessary restrictions on the tasks which people may perform within the legal system. The most important change in this context has been the adoption by statute of the principle that the highest judicial offices should be open to solicitors just as much as to barristers (who formerly had the monopoly in these appointments).[15]

Some of the changes have resulted from the professional bodies deciding to change their rules. Others, particularly in the last decade, have been the result of intervention by government.

Fusion? The obvious question that all these developments pose is whether the time is not approaching when the two branches of the legal profession should now fuse into a single profession, as happens in most other countries in the world. Should the long-standing distinction between solicitors and barristers continue to be defended? This is an issue that has been debated on many occasions, though surprisingly not

[9] S. 41 and Sched. 5. There are other professional groups, e.g. Patents Agents, who might wish to achieve 'authorized body' status.

[10] S. 42. This was thought to be necessary to guarantee the ability of the individual lawyer to act independently.

[15] The appointment of Mr Laurence Collins, QC, a very distinguished commercial solicitor, to the High Court was the first such appointment, made in 1999. The possibility of distinguished legal scholars being appointed to the highest levels of the judiciary just on the strength of their academic record has not been formally accepted. However, the appointment of Dame Brenda Hale (who prior to her appointment as a Law Commissioner had had a distinguished academic career at the University of Manchester) first to the High Court bench and then to the Court of Appeal is, perhaps, the start of a development in the direction of acknowledging the contribution legal scholars might make to the judiciary. The more recent appointment of Professor Jack Beatson, QC from the University of Cambridge to the High Court is another example. This certainly happens in the European Courts and the USA. Academics have long been appointed judges to the International Court of Justice.

Box 9.3 The attack on restrictive practices

The attack on the restrictive practices of the legal profession began with a study by the Monopolies Commission, which was published in 1968. In his evidence to the Commission, Michael Zander provided a devastating critique of various professional practices, which he argued were not in the public interest.[11] Many others joined the attack. For example, during the early 1970s, Austen Mitchell, MP, led a sustained attack on the conveyancing monopoly then enjoyed by solicitors.[12]

A Royal Commission on Legal Services, under the chairmanship of Lord Benson was established in 1976 and reported in 1979.[13] It came to the conclusion that, while a large number of detailed changes to professional practice needed to be made, many of the practices of the legal professions were in the public interest.

Further pressure to change developed, however, when the Thatcher Government came to power in 1980. Mrs Thatcher was determined to make the British economy generally much more competitive. The legal profession became caught up in a general attack on monopolistic power.[14]

The first, and probably the most symbolically significant, alteration in the restrictive practices which had been adopted by the legal profession occurred in 1987, when the conveyancing monopoly was broken. Until that date, only solicitors were entitled to charge for the work required to convey the title in real estate from a vendor to a purchaser. Following enactment of the Administration of Justice Act 1985, Part II, a system of licensed conveyancers, regulated by the Council for Licensed Conveyancers, was established. The first licences under the scheme were granted in 1987. In addition, the practice of using fixed-scale fees for conveyancing was stopped. There is no doubt that many solicitors had benefited very substantially from the original arrangements, though there is also evidence that there was at least some indirect social benefit, in that many solicitors used the profit from their conveyancing work to subsidize other less profitable activity in their practices.

The loss of the conveyancing monopoly was not the only change to hit the solicitors' branch of the profession. There were many other significant changes. In particular rules on advertising were significantly relaxed so that, within the boundaries set by the Law Society's *Guide to Professional Behaviour*, firms of solicitors were entitled to advertise their services. While advertising in the UK may not have the flamboyance of lawyers' advertisements in the USA, nevertheless this development was a significant break with past tradition. All significant legal practices, both solicitors' and barristers', now engage in a wide range of promotional 'practice development' activity.

---

[11] Zander, M., *Lawyers and the Public Interest* (London, Weidenfeld and Nicolson, 1968).

[12] An attack joined by at least some members of the profession themselves: see Joseph, M., *The Conveyancing Fraud* (Harmondsworth, Penguin, 1975).

[13] (Cmnd 7648) (London, HMSO, 1979).

[14] There is a tendency for each professional grouping to feel that it is being 'picked on' and is being uniquely subjected to pressure to change. In fact nearly all professional groups have been subject to these pressures.

seriously in the last few years, despite the developments which have occurred and which are sketched out above. The arguments asserted by the Bar for its independence, in delivering both advocacy and other forms of legal advice, are actually very powerful, more powerful than some of the advocates for fusion allow. But in other countries with fused professions, the independence of the advocate is still strongly asserted. Other ways could be found to protect professional independence without the retention of a divided profession. It seems inconceivable that at some point in the not too distant future this issue should not again become the subject of public debate.

Growth and globalization

A second trend to be noted is the growth in the size of law firms and the increasingly global scope of their practices. These have resulted from the context within which lawyers practise, which cannot be divorced from other changes in the economy at large. The last twenty years have seen a major shift from an economy based on manufacturing to one based on services. Increased globalization of the world economy has led to a growth in the need for lawyers able to advise corporations about all the national contexts within which they are required to operate. Globalization in the provision of legal services has accompanied the globalization of the economy.[16] British lawyers have responded in a variety of ways:

- Many of the large law firms in the City of London have gone through substantial programmes of merger and expansion;[17]

- Significant groupings of leading firms in provincial commercial centres—e.g. Leeds, Birmingham, Bristol—have also developed, either through mergers and takeovers or the creation of 'networks' of legal practices;

- Many of these firms have established presences in other key centres of economic activity, in Europe, the Middle East, the Far East and the Americas;

- Mergers of English law firms with firms in other countries in Europe and the USA have resulted in the creation of new forms of international partnership;

- There has been a significant increase in the presence of overseas law firms, in particular US law firms, in London, which has added to the competitive pressures on British-based firms;

- There have been moves towards the creation of professional groupings that cut across traditional disciplinary boundaries—in particular, lawyers and accountants. The issue of the establishment of multi-disciplinary partnerships—which have been around for many years—has fast risen up the policy agendas of the professional bodies.

[16] Halliday, T. C., and Karpik, L., *Lawyers and the Rise of Political Liberalism* (Oxford, Clarendon Press, 1997); Dezelay, Y., and Garth, B., *Dealing in Virtue: International Commercial Arbitration and the Construction of Transnational Legal Order* (Chicago, University of Chicago Press, 1996).

[17] Galanter, M., and Pulay, T., *Tournament of Lawyers: The Transformation of the Big Law Firm* (Chicago, Chicago University Press, 1991).

There is every likelihood of further developments of these kinds in the years ahead.

Specialization and niche practices

A third trend to be noted has been the increasing development of specialist/niche practices. In part this is a response to the trend towards 'mega-lawyering' noted in the previous section. Increasingly, small firms of solicitors and sets of barristers' chambers have come to specialize in particular areas—family law, criminal law, employment law, housing law, to give some examples. These developments have been supported in part by the legal professional bodies themselves. For example, the Law Society has established a number of specialist panels which practitioners may join, including the Childrens' Panel, the Mental Health Panel and the Medical Negligence Panel.

In addition, members of the profession themselves have taken the lead in establishing an increasing number of specialist groups, many of which cross over traditional solicitor/barrister boundaries. There are now well over forty such groups. They act in a variety of ways:

- They may be able to act collaboratively (within the competitive market) to promote the specialist services that they offer (thereby seeking to exclude non-specialists from their work).

- Some, such as the Solicitors' Family Law Association, have promoted new modes of legal practice, designed to provide a different form of lawyering for their clients—in the context of family law, a less confrontational approach designed to assist those whose relationships have broken down.[18]

- Others, such as the Patent Lawyers' Association, have developed specialist programmes of advanced legal education and training designed to give their members special expertise and, thus, it is hoped, a competitive edge in the legal services market place.

- The specialist lawyer groups have also developed a very important influence in government. They are able to offer advice on how particular areas of legal practice may be affected by proposed policy changes, in ways in which the general professional bodies such as the Law Society or Bar Council may be unable to achieve.

Legal services to the poor

A fourth noteworthy trend in the shape of the legal profession has been a complete transformation in the operation of the legal aid scheme. The details of the new scheme are considered in Chapter 10. Here the principal point to note is that, whereas ten years ago in effect any firm of solicitors who wished to do legal aid work could do so, now only those firms with a contract to provide services from the Legal Aid Commission are able to undertake publicly funded legal aid work. Many practitioners

---

[18] See above, Chapter 7.

who used to do modest amounts of legal aid work as part of a portfolio of general legal services provided to mainly private clients are affected by these changes.

High street practice

A consequence of these last two developments is that the general 'high street prac- tices', found in the high streets of towns, suburban areas and other locations, which have in the past provided a general service to private clients have come under increas- ing commercial pressure and face considerable uncertainty. The ability to make a living from a mixed practice of some criminal work, some property transactions (such as conveyancing or probate), a little bit of family and divorce work and some personal injuries work, which even ten years ago was quite common, is now increasingly

---

Box 9.4 Competition and the public interest

Notwithstanding all the pressures for change set out in these pages, the desire of government to keep up pressure on professional bodies not to behave in an anti- competitive fashion has led to yet another review of aspects of the ways in which lawyers organize themselves. In March 2001, the Director General of Fair Trading published a report entitled 'Competition in Professions'. It was accompanied by a spe- cialist consultants' report. In July 2002 a consultation paper by the Lord Chancellor's Department 'In the Public Interest?' was published which raised for wider consultation a number of issues discussed by the DGFT.

These included:

- Further liberalization of the conveyancing practice market.

- Opening the market for probate services to new providers.

- The provision of legal services by solicitors in multi-disciplinary practices.

- The extension of legal professional privilege to non-lawyers providing legal advice.

- Changes to the system of appointing Queen's Counsel.

The Government has also been concerned at the level of efficiency the legal pro- fessional bodies demonstrate in dealing with complaints from the public about the quality of professional services. While the consultation paper does not deal with these matters directly, a new review of the regulatory framework for legal services has been announced.

The outcome of the present exercise cannot at present be predicted. The Govern- ment has accepted that where a restrictive practice can be demonstrated to operate in the public interest it should remain. It is also committed to ensuring that its policies take account of the particular needs of rural communities. Given these two constraints, it is not clear how far the current consultation paper will lead to further change. However it is an issue that should become clearer during the lifetime of this book's new edition.

difficult. Many of the remaining sole practitioners and small firms fall into this category. The future of the 'generalist' high street practice is under considerable threat,
unless those who remain in this sector of the legal services market are prepared to
rethink their commercial strategies. (*See above Box 9.4.*)

Other trends

A graduate profession. A significant change over the last quarter of a century is that the
legal profession has become a largely graduate one. The old days when professional
qualifications could be obtained simply by apprenticeship in a solicitor's office or a
barrister's chambers (and the passing of some not very demanding professional
exams) are now long gone. Despite this, many of the graduates who enter the legal
profession come with degrees other than in law. They obtain their legal qualifications
through conversion courses undertaken following the obtaining of a first degree
in another discipline. This has been the subject of fierce argument between the
legal professional bodies and the legal academics, the latter asserting that only the
grounding of a good law degree gives potential entrants to the legal profession a
real understanding of how law is made and fundamental legal principles.

Information technology. Secondly, and in common with everyone else, the legal
professions have been increasingly affected by the development of new information
technologies.[19] To date this has not perhaps delivered all the reductions in the use of
paper that might have been anticipated, though it has undoubtedly transformed
practice management. But as legal information from government and the legal publishers and other sources becomes increasingly available in electronic form, and as
court procedures become increasingly technology driven, the impact of IT on legal
practice will intensify.[20] Legal practice will change enormously in the next decade,
reflecting these technological changes.[21]

Pay and conditions. Thirdly, the expectations of those entering the profession about
the pay and conditions they should receive have also changed considerably in the last
quarter of a century. A real problem in this context is that the financial rewards for
those in some parts of legal practice, particularly the corporate sector, are hugely
different from those in many specialist or niche areas, particularly those offering
services to the less well-off groups in society. Much of the problem is the result
of a type of 'macho' legal journalism which has developed over the last ten to
fifteen years, but which arguably is not wholly in the interest of the legal profession.
(*See Box 9.5.*)

---

[19] See Susskind, R., *Transforming the Law: Essays on Technology, Justice and the Legal Marketplace* (Oxford,
Oxford University Press, 2000).

[20] See, e.g., the LCD consultation paper, *Civil Justice: Resolving and Avoiding Disputes in the Information
Age* (London, Lord Chancellor Department, 1998).

[21] One of the biggest changes is likely to arise from the introduction of electronic conveyancing, to which
the Land Registry is strongly committed. This should greatly speed up the process of buying and selling
land.

Box 9.5 Legal journalism

One consequence of this changed context of legal practice, particular the relaxation of restrictions on advertising, is that a significant branch of journalism has developed, devoted to the telling of stories about individuals and firms in the law and their doings. All the main broadsheet newspapers have a weekly law section, much of which is concerned with what is in effect legal gossip. In addition there are specialist papers for the profession which focus in particular on the activities of law firms and sets of chambers. The 'free' paper, the *Lawyer*—which appears weekly—is supplemented by the expensive and glossy *Legal Business* which focuses in particular on firms operating in the city and overseas.

One consequence of this new journalism is that public information about lawyers is to a large extent dominated by the stories which the PR departments of the large firms are able to place in this press. Stories about the impact and importance of the small high street firms find little place beside dramatic tales of take-overs, mergers and other commercial/corporate activity. This creates at least three distortions:

- those thinking of entering the law as a profession are denied the opportunity to consider the full range of legal careers open to them;

- they come to assume that the only type of lawyering worth undertaking is that which pays enormous salaries; and

- the public assume that all lawyers act—and most significantly are paid—in ways suggested by the stories that appear in this press.

Much of the public hostility towards lawyers is, it may be surmised, the result of assumptions that legal services are very expensive and thus affordable only by the very rich. A more balanced picture would indicate that there are still many lawyers providing valuable services to the public for extremely modest fees.

Regulation of the profession: complaints and ethical standards

Another of the major developments that has taken place over the last fifteen years has been the enormous change in the way in which the legal profession is regulated. There is a wide range of issues that might be discussed under this head. Two specific issues— dealing with complaints and setting ethical standards—will be addressed here.

Handling complaints and ensuring quality control

Until the 1980s the hallmark of any 'profession' was that those who made up the profession were regarded as the best qualified to run the profession, to set standards of practice and to remove miscreants from their ranks. One of the challenges that has confronted the legal professions over the last fifteen to twenty years is how they should respond to the pressures to deliver a standard of service demanded by an increasingly critical client base. The professional bodies have taken steps designed to ensure that lawyers keep up to date with developments in law and in practice management. For example, both the Law Society and, more recently, the Bar Council have introduced rules requiring practitioners to undergo regular amounts of *continuing professional development*. This might seem to be the least that could be expected of a 'learned profession'.

In addition, in the specific context of legal aid, great attention to quality issues[22] has been paid by the Legal Services Commission—arguably doing work that the professional bodies had failed to do.

In relation to the handling of complaints, both the Law Society (for solicitors) and the Bar Council (for barristers) still to a degree retain the ability to run their professional affairs. But, in common with other professional groups, the former position has been replaced by much greater public and political scepticism. There is now a widespread feeling that professional bodies cannot, despite their protestations to the contrary, be fully trusted to run their affairs in the public interest. The legal profession has not been immune from this change in attitude. The arguments of the professional bodies have been regarded by politicians and others outside the law as 'trade union' arguments, designed to advance the private interests of the members of the profession, rather than the broader public interest. Unfair though that charge is in part, it was undeniably the case that too often in the past the legal professional bodies were seen to be defending the frankly indefensible.

The arrival of the Thatcher Government, with a commitment to do away with restrictive practices that would undermine the competitive economy, led to a series of changes some of which have been considered above, the effects of which are still being worked through. But the argument has not come only from the political right. A Fabian Society paper suggested that '[s]elf-regulation is [now] an out-dated concept and has no place in modern Britain'.[23]

At the same time, there has been a considerable increase in the influence of consumer groups, arguing that the services provided to consumers (which include the provision of legal services to clients) must be to a standard expected by the consumers, not as determined by the providers.

The situation before 1990 was—very broadly—that while the courts were able to deal with the most serious cases of professional negligence, and while the professional bodies were able to control other forms of *gross* misconduct, the more mundane complaints—rudeness, slowness in responding to letters, general inefficiency—were not being dealt with seriously. Yet these were precisely the sorts of issues which the ordinary client, who felt she was not getting good value for the money she was being

---

[22] See further Chapter 10.
[23] Arora, A., and Andrew, F., *The Rule of Lawyers* (London, Fabian Society, 1998).

asked to pay, wanted to complain about. Both the Law Society and the Bar Council took steps to try to address these concerns.

The Law Society started the process in the mid-1980s following the long-drawn-out and very unsatisfactory handling of a complaint against one of its Council members, Mr Glanville Davies. In 1985, the Society commissioned Coopers and Lybrand to review the Society's disciplinary procedures. The consultants recommended that all these procedures be transferred to a new independent agency. The Law Society did not accept this recommendation, but it did, in 1986, establish the Solicitors' Complaints Bureau (SCB), relaunched[24] as the Office for the Supervision of Solicitors (OSS) in 1996. The Society's disciplinary powers were delegated to the SCB/OSS. Although established by the Law Society, the SCB/OSS is physically quite separate from the other activities of the Law Society, with premises in Leamington Spa.

In 1991, the Law Society also made a number of changes to its Practice Rules, most notably the introduction of Practice Rule 15, requiring all solicitors to operate a complaints-handling procedure designed to ensure that clients know who to approach in the event of a problem with the service with which they have been provided. Part of the reason for the introduction of this rule was to encourage firms to resolve complaints internally, and thus, it was hoped, reduce the pressure on the SCB.

The Bar was slower off the mark. A proposal in 1994 from its Standards Review Body[25] to set up a Barristers Complaints Bureau did not meet the approval of the membership of the Bar. Instead the post of lay Complaints Commissioner was agreed.[26] In addition, the Bar Council in 1995 developed new practice management standards,[27] which are not mandatory but rather guidelines to good practice, and to which the Bar's Code of Conduct requires barristers to have regard. These practice management standards stated that barristers' chambers should have a written code of procedure for dealing with complaints. In 1997, changes were made to the Bar's Code of Conduct. Among other things, the code recognized for the first time the concept of 'inadequate professional service',[28] against which the Complaints Commissioner can determine complaints from barristers' clients. This goes at least some way to addressing the gap between what clients typically wanted to complain about and the rather narrow concepts of 'negligence' and 'gross misconduct' mentioned above.

Recent research into these developments,[29] and in particular into the rules relating to the local office/chambers resolution of disputes, suggests that the response from

---

[24] Following considerable criticism from both within the profession and outside. See, e.g., National Consumer Council, *The Solicitors Complaints Bureau: A Consumer View* (London, National Consumer Council, 1994).

[25] Chaired by Lord Alexander of Weedon, QC, former Chairman of the Bar.

[26] The first holder of this post was Sir Michael Scott, appointed in 1997.

[27] One way in which chambers can attest that they fall within the principles implied by the Practice Management Standards is by acquisition of the 'Barmark', a British Standards Institute accreditation.

[28] 'Conduct . . . or performance of professional services . . . which falls significantly short of that which is to be expected of a barrister in all the circumstances.'

[29] Christensen, C., *Report of an Investigation into the Operation of Complaint-handling Mechanisms Operated by Barristers' Chambers* (Bristol, University of the West of England, 2000).

practitioners still remains somewhat underwhelming. Heads of chambers, for example, still assert that the 'market' will deal with the incompetent—they will not get briefed and thus go to the wall. They are not convinced that taking complaints seriously is either professionally important or commercially desirable.[30] There remains considerable pressure for the creation of a more 'independent' complaints-handling procedure.[31]

Statutory developments: Courts and Legal Services Act 1990 and Access to Justice Act 1999

The changes by the professional bodies have been accompanied by significant statutory developments. The Courts and Legal Services Act 1990 established the office of Legal Services Ombudsman and the Advisory Committee on Legal Education and Conduct. The Access to Justice Act 1999 has extended the power of the Ombudsman; abolished the Advisory Committee and replaced it with a consultative panel, and made provision for the appointment of a Legal Services Complaints Commissioner.

Legal Services Ombudsman. The office of Legal Services Ombudsman (LSO) was established by section 21 of the Courts and Legal Services Act 1990. The post-holder cannot be qualified as a lawyer and is independent of the legal profession. She oversees the handling of complaints against solicitors, barristers and licensed conveyancers. However, complainants cannot come direct to her. They must first utilize the procedures of the Law Society's OSS, the General Council of the Bar or the Council for Licensed Conveyancers. Because of this filtering process, the numbers of complaints reaching the LSO is relatively modest—around 1,500 a year compared with over 27,000 cases taken to the professional complaints' bodies. The LSO does, however, use her annual report not just to comment on individual cases, but to advise the professions more generally on their complaints-handling procedures. One of the pressures on the professions is undoubtedly the LSO, who has over the years made trenchant criticisms of the profession's procedures.

In particular, the LSO has argued that the professions' procedures must deliver results without undue delay; must be credible to complainants; and must provide effective redress where this is appropriate. Given that, in the case of the Law Society, there is one complaint to the OSS for every three solicitors,[32] the challenge to the professions is clearly significant.

The Access to Justice Act 1999 has extended the powers of the Legal Services

---

[30] In the case of the Bar, which is still in theory based on the principle of the barrister being self-employed, there may be some difficulties in taking a 'corporate' approach to complaints handling. Senior clerks, however, seem much more aware of the commercial importance of chambers presenting a corporate image and learning corporate lessons from individual lapses in standards than barristers themselves.

[31] The Government's power to establish a *Legal Services Complaints Commissioner* is considered below, p. 239.

[32] This does not, of course, mean that a third of all solicitors are complained against; there are many solicitors with more than one complaint against them. But it demonstrates the size of the task facing both the OSS and the Law Society to improve public confidence in the performance of solicitors.

Ombudsman, to enable her to make binding orders that a professional body or individual practitioner pay compensation or costs to a complainant. Until then, she could only make recommendations.

Legal Services Consultative Panel (replacing the Advisory Committee on Legal Education and Conduct). The Advisory Committee gave the Lord Chancellor advice on applications from groups that did not have rights to conduct litigation or rights of audience to have such rights (as was envisaged by the Courts and Legal Services Act 1990). In addition it was to give general advice on the training and education needed for modern legal practice. The procedures of the Advisory Committee turned out to be very slow in practice, causing frustration both to the legal profession and to those who wished to see new groups authorized to have rights of audience and rights to conduct litigation.

Under the Access to Justice Act, the rules on these rights were changed. (*See above Box 9.2.*) At the same time, the Advisory Committee was abolished and replaced by a new Legal Services Consultative Panel. Members of the panel also attend the Standing Conference on Legal Education. The Consultative Panel works on issues referred to it by the Lord Chancellor, and on other matters.[33]

Legal Services Complaints Commissioner. The Act of 1999 gave the Lord Chancellor the power to establish a Legal Services Complaints Commissioner, to take over the handling of complaints against the legal profession, if the systems in place within the legal profession continue to operate as unsatisfactorily as they currently appear to do. The present intention of government is not to put these provisions into effect; but this restraint is contingent upon the professions being able to demonstrate that they have put their own houses in order. (*See above Box 9.4.*)

The promotion of ethical standards

The second issue to be considered is the role of the legal professions in the promotion of ethical standards amongst practitioners. This is an issue that has received considerable attention in recent years, not only in relation to the work of lawyers, but in all areas of professional activity. Here is not the place to enter a detailed consideration of the need for the legal profession to adopt an ethical approach to its work, nor to the role of the professional bodies in promoting that work. It may be suggested, however, that much contemporary hostility towards lawyers is fuelled by the feeling that in general lawyers are a rather amoral group.[34]

It is perhaps the case that, until relatively recently, the provision of legal services by lawyers was seen by members of the legal profession themselves as a public service to which, in some rather mysterious way, commercial pressures somehow did not apply. The adoption of an ethical approach was, on this view, inherent in the provision of the service.

Whether there was ever any real justification for this belief, there can be no doubt

---

[33] The current programme is at www.lcd.gov.uk/atoj/lscp/lscp_workprog03.htm.
[34] Anti-lawyers jokes certainly reflect this.

that in the modern world the provision of legal services is quite clearly a business. If lawyers cannot make a profit at the end of the year, they go bust. Legal practice must be subject to the disciplines of financial control, quality control and efficiency that characterize all business activity. The concern with ethical standards may have arisen from a perception that concentrating exclusively on the financial and commercial imperatives of legal practice may encourage lawyers to forget the ethical principles which should also underpin their work.

The professional bodies seek to provide guidance on professional conduct which is designed to provide some ethical framework for professional activity. Understanding these principles is a key feature of professional legal education, not least because failure to follow the guidance can result in the worst cases in loss of the right to practice as a barrister or solicitor.

The question whether the codes of practice go far enough to incorporate an ethical dimension to legal practice is beyond the scope of this work, though the works cited in the suggestions for further reading take the issue further.

There are, perhaps, two particular respects in which the legal profession is able at least in part to demonstrate its ethical commitment: pro bono work; and test case litigation.

For free (pro bono) work. There has long been a tradition that lawyers offer free legal services to the poor; before there was any legal aid, there was a history of such provision in London and other major conurbations. In recent years, there has been a renewed emphasis on pro bono work. Because the large commercial firms in the City of London and other commercial centres have been so obviously financially successful, there has been a renewed interest in the provision of free legal services by their staff in citizens' advice bureaux and other agencies. This may seem to many as little more than a token gesture. But, given the precarious funding position that many such agencies are in, it is likely that this activity does make a significant contribution to local legal service delivery.

Test case litigation. Test case litigation, or as it is sometimes called 'cause lawyering', is also often associated with lawyers being willing to take up broad general issues, particularly on behalf of more disadvantaged groups in the community. Historically, test case litigation in the UK has not had the same impact as, for example, in the USA, where legal provisions or policies were able to be tested for their constitutionality against the provisions of the US Constitution. However, with ever greater involvement in Europe, both through the European Union and, in relation to human rights, through the Council of Europe, many challenges to English law have been mounted, in some cases with dramatic success. The Human Rights Act has generated an additional amount of test case legislation, as provisions of English law are tested for their compatibility with the European Convention.

Professional groups allied to the legal profession

Following the lengthy discussion of the legal profession, consideration of the professional groups allied to the legal profession will be briefer. There are two groups which will be considered here: legal executives; and other specialist groups.

Legal executives

Many of the staff employed in solicitors' offices are not formally qualified as solicitors, but nonetheless provide a great deal of legal service to the public. These are known collectively as 'legal executives'. Many of these are members and fellows of their own professional representative body, the *Institute of Legal Executives* (ILEX). ILEX organizes its own training programmes and examinations which must be passed before a legal executive can call him- or herself a Fellow of the Institute. The Institute has its own Code of Professional Conduct, analogous to that of the Law Society.

Legal executives play a central role in many legal practices, often being more expert in their areas of expertise that their fully professionally qualified colleagues. Legal executives who are fellows of ILEX are able, by taking additional courses and sitting additional examinations, to qualify as solicitors, and a number do so each year.

Other specialist groups

In addition to the legal executives, there are also a number of other more specialist groups providing particular kinds of legal and law-related services whose existence may be noted. These include:

- Licensed conveyancers (noted in passing above) whose activities are regulated by the Council of Licensed Conveyancers;
- Patent agents;
- Insolvency practitioners; and
- Tax advisers. This last group is not subject to the same forms of regulation as the other groups mentioned.[35]

---

[35] Green, S., and Leacham, K., *Tax Advice in the UK: Why Things Go Wrong and the Implications for the Tax Adviser's Profession* (London, Chartered Institute of Taxation, 1997).

Lay advisers and other providers of legal services

Lay advisers/advocates

In addition to the formally qualified, there are substantial numbers of people who have not obtained legal qualifications, but who nevertheless deliver legal services, These include: the lay advisers who work in advice agencies, such as the Citizens' Advice Bureaux; welfare rights workers, often employed in local authority sponsored welfare rights offices; housing aid workers working in housing advice centres; and many other lay advice workers working in a vast range of social, environmental and other agencies.

Law centres

One particular context in which the professionally qualified lawyer and the lay adviser come together is the Law Centre. The Law Centre movement started in the 1970s with the specific objective of targeting legal services to those who lived in deprived areas, principally towns and cities. Historically they have had a somewhat hand-to-mouth existence. Some have been funded by local authorities; others by private charities; one or two by central government. The rules of the new Funding Code which underpins the Community Legal Service provide that those agencies that satisfy standards set by the Legal Services Commission will be able to obtain public funding for defined categories of work (see Chapter 10).

Membership services

A number of membership organizations also provide legal services to their members. These services may either be general or related to the matters which arise from membership. Examples at the more general end of provision are the legal services provided as the result of membership of trade unions or other professional groups (for example the Medical Defence Union); more specific legal services are provided to members of, e.g., the Automobile Association or the Royal Automobile Club.

Specialist agencies

In addition to the foregoing, a number of pressure groups also provide legal services. One motiviation for this is to find appropriate text cases that might be brought to test the boundaries of statutory provisions. Examples include the Citizens' Rights Office, which is attached to the Child Poverty Action Group; the Public Law Project; Liberty (formerly the National Council for Civil Liberties); and a number of environmental groups, such as Greenpeace. These agencies have been particularly successful in expanding the range of groups entitled to make representations to the courts in judicial review cases.

Adjudicators: the judiciary, ombudsmen and other dispute resolvers

Much has been written about judges in the English legal system. As with other topics in this book, however, most accounts have focused on a rather narrow body of the judiciary, namely those who sit in the High Court, Court of Appeal and the House of Lords. There can be no doubting the influence of the judges who sit in these higher courts in shaping English law. But the chances of any one individual member of the public appearing before one of these judges is remote in the extreme. Far more likely is an encounter with a district judge, a lay magistrate, a tribunal chairman, a circuit judge or one of the army of other 'dispute-resolvers'/complaints-handlers that now exist. It is these adjudicators who are, in practice, the 'face' of the judiciary, as seen by the public at large.

Definition

For the purposes of this book, adjudicators are all those who are empowered by law[36] to determine disputes that have been brought to them for adjudication. This definition includes all the senior judicial figures who sit in the High Court and other courts just mentioned, as well as:

(1) *Circuit judges* who determine civil cases in the county court, and criminal cases in the Crown Court;

(2) *District judges* who determine civil cases, including small claims hearings, in the county court;

(3) *Recorders*, who are, in effect, circuit judges in training;

(4) *Magistrates*, both lay and professionally qualified,[37] who determine the vast majority of criminal cases which are dealt with in magistrates' courts;

(5) *Arbitrators* who determine a wide range of disputes referred to them under specially agreed arbitration agreements. Arbitrators are particularly used to resolve commercial disputes, both national and international;

(6) *Tribunal members and chairmen* who deal with specific issues arising in defined legislative contexts: for example, disputes about entitlement to social security benefit, which go to Social Security Appeal Tribunals; or disputes about immigration status, which go to Immigration Adjudicators;

(7) *Ombudsmen*, as they appear in their various guises; and

---

[36] Thus this definition excludes those who determine disputes under purely private contractual arrangements, e.g., internal employment dispute resolution procedures or student disciplinary procedures.

[37] They are called *District Judges (Magistrates' Courts)*; see above Box 5.9.

(8) *Mediators, conciliators, complaints handlers* and others who offer alternative forms of appropriate dispute resolution (ADR).

Comment

These groups have all been encountered in different contexts earlier in the book. Here a number of general points about those who perform adjudicatory functions in the legal system may be made:

- They are not all professionally qualified as lawyers. Some have other professional qualifications, such as accountants, surveyors or doctors. But many have no specific professional qualification at all. In the same way that many legal services are provided by persons other than professionally qualified lawyers, so too many adjudication services are provided by those without legal qualifications.

- Many academic lawyers are embraced by this broader definition. The notion that somehow those with an academic background have no capacity to determine disputes in a fair and proper manner is simply not borne out by the evidence.

- Their total numbers are considerably larger than traditional definitions of the judiciary suggest.

- Many adjudicator appointments are full-time, but many more are part-time.

- Only the highest judiciary hold office 'on good behaviour'—a concept designed to enhance the fundamental independence of the judiciary by guaranteeing their right to remain a judge until the statutory retiring age, so long as they are of good behaviour. Most other groups, particularly the part-timers, hold office on terms which can result in their being required to step down before the official retirement age.

- Only a limited number are able to take advantage of the attractive (non-contributory) pensions that are provided by government to full-time members of the judiciary.

- Many judges sit in more than one jurisdiction. For example a full-time social security tribunal chairman may sit as a part-time circuit judge, thereby enabling him or her to acquire wider judicial experience.

- Many judges now start to sit in their early forties, some even in their thirties.

- There are many more women holding judicial office than is often appreciated, though the numbers at the highest levels are still too low. The numbers from the ethnic minorities are significantly less impressive.

- Most judicial appointees now receive at least some training for the job, though the amount of training decreases with the seniority of the post.[38]

---

[38] For the development of the work of the Judicial Studies Board see above, Chapter 4.

- There is still only a limited amount of monitoring of judicial performance. Such monitoring as does take place is limited to the performance by part-timers, and is often undertaken by those in full-time office. While too heavy monitoring could compromise judicial independence, certain factors, e.g. the ability to be civil to those appearing before them or to deliver written decisions within agreed timescales, would not seem impossible targets for assessment.

- Most appointments to adjudicatory positions are now filled only after open competition, following public advertisements in the press.[39]

- There is a huge variety of procedural variation as between each of the adjudicative systems. The formal courts operate within a very detailed procedural framework, with a large number of rules of practice supplemented by yet more practice directions and protocols. Many other bodies have only the barest procedural outline prescribed by law, and instead operate with considerable discretion as regards procedural matters.

- Not all tribunals operate on the basis that their 'typical' adjudication will involve a formal hearing of the parties. Many reach determinations on the basis of information presented in written form alone.

- While it is usual for tribunals that hold hearings to sit in public, in the sense that members of the public are entitled to attend hearings should they so wish, many do not, particularly where sensitive personal or financial information is being discussed.

- The dress of the judiciary is also much more varied than is often realized. The highly formalized process of the High Court, with impressive uniforms, oak panelling and advocates in wigs and gowns—the image of the television or film drama—is in fact a statistical rarity. The vast majority of adjudicative tribunals operate with none of these formal trappings.

- Adjudicators work in a wide variety of locations. Many sit in court buildings or other specially furnished accommodation. But there are many examples of adjudicative bodies sitting in local authority accommodation, or in hotel accommodation, or even on occasion in people's homes.

If one takes this broader view of the judiciary, it will be seen that there is considerably more variety and flexibility of approach to adjudication than is often realized. Different procedures and practices have been developed to meet the specific needs of particular bodies.

Numbers

It is actually not possible to give a complete picture of the total number of people holding various kinds of adjudicative office. The Lord Chancellor's Department now

---

[39] For further discussion about the procedures relating to judicial appointments and criticisms thereof see above, Chapter 4.

issues statistics of the numbers of judicial office-holders. In addition to the five chief judicial office holders—the Lord Chancellor, the Lord Chief Justice of England, the Master of the Rolls, the President of the Family Division and the Vice-Chancellor, the number of judicial office-holders at 1 October 2002 is set out in Table 9.1.

In addition there are some 24,500 lay magistrates.

Information about numbers of office-holders in other dispute resolution contexts is harder to establish as the figures are not always easily available, but it may be esti-mated that there are around 20,000 part-time tribunal chairmen and members.

The literature on the judiciary

With a few exceptions, books about the judiciary have, in many cases, not been in any strict sense socially scientific. Drawing inferences about how judges think and thus come to decisions simply from the skewed sample of their work represented by reported decisions in the law reports is a wholly inadequate basis for serious analysis of how judges approach the judicial task.[40] Further, it is all too easy to assume that because someone is white, male, middle-aged and probably public school and Oxbridge educated, he (occasionally she) brings attitudes to his (or her) judicial work which affect his (or her) decisions. Such links are not provable without the detailed empirical study that has only rarely been taken into the judiciary.[41]

There has, of course, been a problem, in that researchers who have sought access to the judiciary in order to conduct research into it have often found such access difficult

Table 9.1 Judicial appointments

Full-time	
Lords of Appeal (House of Lords)	11
Lords Justice of Appeal (Court of Appeal)	36
High Court judges	107
Circuit judges	620
District judges	427
District judges (criminal)	106
Total	1307
Part-time	
Recorders	1318
Recorders in training	110
Acting district judges (criminal)	152
Deputy district judges	802
Total	2382

[40] Griffith, J. A. G., *The Politics of the Judiciary* (5th edn., London, Fontana, 1997); cf Hodder-Williams, R., *Judges and Politics in the Contemporary Age* (London, Bowerdean, 1996).

[41] See Paterson, A., *The Law Lords* (London, Macmillan, 1982).

to obtain. The stereotype of judges as white, male, of middle to late age, and from the (upper) middle class may, broadly though by no means exclusively, apply to the higher judiciary. It is far less accurate as a descriptor of the totality of judges/adjudicators in the vast array of fora that determine the disputes brought to them by ordinary members of the public.

Judicial independence

The key claim made for adjudicators of all kinds is that they must not only be, but be seen to be, independent. Judicial independence relates centrally to the constitutional function of judges in interpreting and applying law outside the constraints of internal government departmental policies. Adjudicators not perceived as independent will be fatally compromised in the eyes of the public, particularly by those in relation to whom adjudicators are reaching a decision. One of the strong claims for adjudicators in the English legal system is that, with rare exceptions, they both appear to be independent and do act independently. This is not to say that they may not bring their own views of the world into play when reaching decisions or determining facts. But claims of corruption of those who hold judicial office—the worst case that could be imagined for compromising judicial independence—are not heard.

Slightly less dramatic attacks on judicial independence may be made in cases where it is suggested that there may be judicial bias, in the sense that a judge may have some direct personal interest in the outcome of a particular case. This issue was the subject of much public discussion following the revelation that Lord Hoffmann, one of the members of the House of Lords who sat in judgment in the case involving General Pinochet (the former dictator from Chile), was a member of Amnesty International, one of the parties in the proceedings involving the General. The issue having been raised, the House of Lords decided that the decision in which Lord Hoffmann had taken part could not be allowed to stand, and the matter was—in an unprecedented move—set aside for determination by another Appeal Committee from the House of Lords.[42]

Shortly thereafter a number of other cases were heard by the Court of Appeal which, though not as dramatic as that involving Pinochet, raised similar issues for consideration. In reviewing the position, the Court of Appeal laid down the following propositions:[43]

(1) In general, membership of professional, political or other organizations would not give grounds for an allegation of bias.

(2) Neither would racial or ethnic origin, class, extra-judicial activities, sexual orientation or previous judicial references to parties or witnesses, even if forthright.

---

[42] R v. Bow Street Metropolitan Magistrates, ex parte Pinochet Ungarte [1999] 2 WLR 272.
[43] See Locabail (UK) v. Bayfield [2000] 1 All ER 65.

(3) Personal acquaintance with or antagonism towards any individuals involved in a case, especially if their credibility might be an issue, would give rise to a real danger of bias.

(4) The independent status of barristers when sitting judicially absolved them from responsibility for the interests of other members of chambers.

(5) Solicitors maintained responsibility for acts of their partners and owed a duty to their firms' clients, even if they had not acted for them personally.

The legal scholars

Law claims to be a 'learned profession'. If that is so, then a third group, delivering a rather different kind of legal service and not usually given adequate recognition, should be noted, namely the law teachers and jurists. Law teachers in the university law departments and in other locations where legal education is provided have a variety of functions.

First, law teachers provide basic training in law and legal principles, which provides new generations of lawyers with the fundamental intellectual tools to enable them to become lawyers. The leading university law schools also offer, through their law degrees, a traditional liberal university education, giving students the capacity to think critically about law and its impact on society.

Secondly, law teachers deliver a wide range of professionally focused courses which transform the recent graduate from the preliminary academic stage to a person with the skills required to enter the world of practice. Some of these courses are offered within university law departments, but other providers including the College of Law,[44] and other private companies play a significant part in this market as well.

Thirdly, the law schools together with the private providers offer much of the further education and advanced training in new developments in the law which are needed by legal practitioners to enable them to keep abreast of developments in the law and to break into new areas of law.

Finally, those law teachers who work in the research universities assist in the development of law and the legal system through the research they undertake, the books and articles they write and the advice they give to governments and other agencies. The scope of legal scholarship has expanded enormously in recent years, again reflecting the growing complexity of the law, not only domestic law but also law coming from Europe and elsewhere. The impact of this legal scholarship on practitioners is hard to gauge. Certainly the old rule that only dead authors could be cited in court has long been abandoned. Advocates now often refer to academic articles in their submissions, and in many reported cases the judgments adopt (or reject) the analyses of legal

---

[44] An institution operated in close association with the Law Society.

scholars. But this is the tip of the iceberg. Many practitioners developing a legal argument, or simply struggling to understand a particular legal doctrine, will turn to the textbook writers for assistance. The importance of the work of the jurists in helping to shape legal argument should not be under-estimated. This work is also central to the work of the law reform agencies, particularly the Law Commission.

A number of areas of practice which have developed in recent years have been the result of a combination of the work of legal scholars who helped to shape the areas and the practitioners who took them into practice. Among examples that may be cited is the development of administrative law which has arisen from analysis of the principles of judicial review; many important developments in the area of family law are another; the law of restitution a third. A number of more specialist areas including private and public international law, housing law and social welfare law have similarly been shaped by important academic contributions.

Notwithstanding these observations, there has been a surprising reluctance by the jurists to get involved in the scholarly analysis of legal practice and procedure. Thus, while endless books and articles are published offering systematic expositions and analyses of substantive law, it has been left to a very small number of legal scholars to focus on the questions of practice and procedure which are in fact the lifeblood of most legal practice, an understanding of which is essential to understanding law and the legal system.

In addition, alongside what is sometimes described as 'black-letter' legal research, focusing on the detailed analysis of legal doctrine, there has emerged over the last twenty-five years an increasingly rich body of 'socio-legal' scholarship, in which the law is analysed in an interdisciplinary context, employing insights and methodologies from other social sciences, such as economics, social psychology, politics and sociology. Much of this research is empirical in nature, and much has involved research into the practice of law. A number of areas of government legal policy have been significantly influenced by the outcomes of socio-legal research.

The university law schools have played a very significant part in opening up access to the legal profession to people from a wider range of backgrounds (a trend noted at the outset of this chapter). Though the extent to which people from different *class* backgrounds have been able to take advantage of these developments may not be as dramatic as is sometimes thought, there is no doubting that the pattern of recruitment to universities in general and to law schools in particular has changed. This has been of particular benefit to women.

Further, the fact that the legal profession is now largely a graduate profession has greatly helped to change the nature of the relationship between the legal academic and the legal practitoner. The mutual disdain which all too often characterized the relationship twenty-five years ago has been replaced by much greater understanding and respect.

Questions for discussion

1. Should the legal profession become fused?

2. Can the legal profession be effectively self-regulating? What dangers arise from increased regulation by government?

3. What professional restrictive practices are justified in the public interest?

4. How can effective legal services to the poor be delivered?

5. Does legal journalism provide fair coverage of all the work of the legal profession?

6. How can ethical lawyering be encouraged?

Further reading

ABEL, R.L., *The Legal Profession in England and Wales* (Oxford, Basil Blackwell, 1988)

ABEL-SMITH, B., and STEVENS, R., with the assistance of Brooke, R., *Lawyers and the Courts: A Sociological Study of the English Legal System 1750–1965* (London, Heinemann, 1967)

——, ZANDER, M., and BROOKE, R., *Legal Problems and the Citizen: A Study in Three London Boroughs* (London, Heinemann Educational, 1973)

BALDWIN, R., *Regulating Legal Services* (London, Lord Chancellor's Department, 1997)

BLACKSELL, M., ECONOMIDES, K., and WATKINS, C., *Justice Outside the City: Access to Legal Services in Rural Britain* (Harlow, Longman Scientific and Technical, 1991)

COMMITTEE ON LEGAL EDUCATION, *Report* (Cmnd 4595) (London, HMSO, 1971)

DEVLIN, BARON P., *The Judge* (Oxford, Oxford University Press, 1979)

DWORKIN, R., *Political Judges and the Rule of Law* (Oxford, Oxford University Press, 1980)

ECONOMIDES, K. (ed.), *Ethical Challenges to Legal Education and Conduct* (Oxford, Hart, 1998)

GENN, H., *Hard Bargaining: Out of Court Settlement in Personal Injury Actions* (Oxford, Clarendon Press, 1987)

GRIFFITHS, J.A.G., *The Politics of the Judiciary* (5th edn., London, Fontana, 1997)

HODDER-WILLIAMS, R., *Judges and Politics in the Contemporary Age* (London, Bowerdean, 1996)

JUSTICE, *The Judiciary: The Report of a Justice Sub-committee* (Chairman of Sub-committee, Peter Webster) (London, Stevens, 1972)

—— *The Judiciary in England and Wales: A Report by Justice* (Chairman of Committee, Robert Stevens) (London, Justice, 1992)

LEE, S., *Judging Judges* (London, Faber, 1989)

LEWIS, P.S.C., *Assumptions about Lawyers in Policy Statements: A Survey of Relevant Research* (London, Lord Chancellor's Department, 2000)

NATIONAL CONSUMER COUNCIL, *Information and Advice Services in the United*

Kingdom: Report to the Minister of State for Consumer Affairs (London, National Consumer Council, 1983)

NICOLSON, D., and WEBB, J., *Professional Legal Ethics: Critical Interrogations* (Oxford, Oxford University Press, 1999)

PANNICK, D., *Judges* (Oxford, Oxford University Press, 1987)

PATERSON, A., *The Law Lords* (London, Macmillan, 1982)

SARAT, A., and SCHEINGOLD, S., *Cause Lawyering and Professional Responsibilities* (New York, Oxford University Press, 1998)

SHETREET, S., *Judges on Trial: A Study of the Appointment and Accountability of the English Judiciary* (Amsterdam/ Oxford, North-Holland, 1976)

STEVENS, R., *Law and Politics: The House of Lords as a Judicial Body, 1800–1976* (London, Weidenfeld & Nicolson, 1979)

—— *Law School: Legal Education in America from the 1850s to the 1980s* (Chapel Hill, NC, University of North Carolina Press, c1983)

TWINING, W., *Blackstone's Tower: The English Law School* (London, Stevens & Son/ Sweet & Maxwell, 1994)

WILSON, G.P. (ed.), *Frontiers of Legal Scholarship: Twenty-five Years of Warwick Law School* (Chichester/New York, Wiley, 1995)

ZANDER, M., *Lawyers and the Public Interest: A Study of Restrictive Practices* (London, published for the London School of Economics and Political Science by Weidenfeld & Nicolson, 1967)

Websites

www.barcouncil.org.uk/ *(Barristers)*

www.barcouncil.org.uk/document.asp?documentid= 15&languageid=1&textid=1215 *(Complaints Commissioner, Bar Council)*

www.lawsociety.org.uk/ *(Solicitors)*

www.oss.lawsociety.org.uk/ *(Office for the Supervision of Solicitors)*

www.olso.org/ *(Legal Services Ombudsman)*

www.gls.gov.uk/ *(Government Legal Service)*

www.clsa.co.uk/ *(Criminal Law Solicitors' Association)*

www.jc-society.co.uk/ *(Justices' Clerks' Society)*

www.ilex.org.uk/ *(Institute of Legal Executives)*

www.cipa.org.uk/home.html *(Chartered Institute of Patent Agents)*

www.itma.org.uk/intro/index.htm *(Institute of Trade Mark Attorneys)*

www.conveyancers.gov.uk/ *(Council for Licensed Conveyancers)*

www.insolvency.co.uk/ *(The UK bankruptcy and insolvency site)*

www.nacab.org.uk/ *(National Council of Citizens' Advice Bureaux)*

www.probonogroup.org.uk/ *(Solicitors' pro bono group)*

www.ncc.org.uk/about.htm *(National Consumer Council)*

www.lawcentres.org.uk/ *(Law Centres' Federation)*

www.fiac.org.uk/ *(Federation of Independent Advice Centres)*

www.covlaw.org.uk/ *(Coventry Law Centre)*

www.eoc.org.uk/ *(Equal Opportunities Commission)*

www.cre.gov.uk/ *(Commission for Racial Equality)*

www.drc-gb.org/drc/default.asp *(Disability Rights Commission)*

www.lag.org.uk/ *(Legal Action Group)*

www.childpoverty.org.uk/cro/CROHome.htm *(Citizens' Rights Office)*

www.liberty-human-rights.org.uk/ *(Liberty—civil liberties group)*

www.taxaid.org.uk/ *(Charity offering advice on tax matters)*

www.publiclawproject.org.uk/ *(Public law project)*

www.ukcle.ac.uk/SPTL/ *(Society of Legal Scholars)*

www.ukc.ac.uk/slsa/index.htm *(Socio-legal Studies Association)*

www.ukcle.ac.uk/ *(UK Centre for Legal Education)*

www.lawteacher.ac.uk/ *(Association of Law Teachers)*

www.legalease.co.uk/mags/jour_lb.htm *(Legal business)*

www.the-lawyer.co.uk/ *(The Lawyer)*

www.oft.gov.uk/default.htm *(Office of Fair Trading)*

www.lcd.gov.uk/consult/general/oftrept.htm *(LCD consultation on the OFT report)*

10

The funding of legal services

Introduction

The final issue considered in this book is how legal services provided to the public are to be paid for. It is essential for the overall effectiveness of the English legal system that services required by the public are actually available to it. This chapter will not devote attention to the funding of legal services for the corporate sector or for wealthy individuals. For present purposes it is assumed that they can afford the services they require. This chapter concentrates on the funding regimes for the delivery of legal services, in particular litigation, to the less well-off and the poor. The discussion is in two unequal sections: the first, and longer, looks at the changing shape of *publicly* funded legal services; the second considers new arrangements to assist the development of *private* funding for legal services.

Publicly funded legal services

The death of legal aid

When the Welfare State emerged in legislative form after the end of the Second World War, one of the measures introduced by the then Labour Government was the Legal Aid Act 1949. There are many accounts of the history of this fundamentally important development, so the story will not be repeated here. Initially the scope of the legal aid scheme was limited to *civil legal aid*—the provision of legal representation in proceedings taken in the civil courts. It subsequently developed to embrace:

- *criminal legal aid*—funding representation in criminal cases, and eventually including a scheme for the provision of legal advice in police stations;
- a *'green form scheme'* designed to permit the provision by lawyers of legal advice and assistance on any matter of English law; and
- *'assistance by way of representation'* (ABWOR) which permitted in a limited number of circumstances the lawyer to extend the assistance offered to the provision of some representation.

Despite these developments, policy on legal aid has been the subject of fierce debate and criticism over the last thirty years.

- Notwithstanding its potentially wide coverage, in practice civil legal aid was used primarily to fund litigation on matrimonial matters and on personal injuries/ accidents. Though important, other areas of social law, for example housing or social welfare provision, were in practice largely ignored by legal aid practitioners;

- The provision of legal aid was subject to means-testing—it went only to those falling below certain income and capital limits.[1] When the first Legal Aid Act was passed it was estimated that nearly 70 per cent of the population was potentially entitled to legal aid. However, as the costs of legal aid increased, one of the mechanisms used by government to restrain levels of public spending was to make the means tests meaner; thus the percentage of the population covered was severely reduced;

- New forms of legal service delivery—in particular through law centres, which began to develop in the late 1960s—were excluded from funding by the legal aid schemes, save where such centres took on individual cases which qualified for legal aid;

- There were many fora in which legal aid was just not available at all. In particular, there was no legal aid for proceedings before the majority of the tribunals established to deal with disputes between the citizen and the state arising out of the social provision of the welfare state;[2]

- From the government's point of view there seemed to be no way to control public expenditure, since it was a service that was 'demand-led'—the government was committed to paying for all those cases in which the individual established an entitlement to legal aid;

- There were also worries about the quality of some of the work undertaken. Any legal practice could offer to do legal aid work, irrespective of the level of expertise on the issue in question in the firm. This might have the perverse effect of driving legal aid expenditure up, as it could take longer for such a firm to deal with a matter than a firm that had expertise in the area.

Successive governments tried to reform the legal aid scheme in a way that would deliver a wider range of services to the public, without public expenditure on legal aid reaching unacceptable levels.[3]

---

[1] The criminal legal aid scheme was also the subject to means-testing, though the rules were not applied in practice with the rigour that applied in relation to civil law matters.

[2] See further Chapter 6. There were exceptions: e.g. legal aid was available for proceedings before the Lands Tribunal and (later) Mental Health Review Tribunals.

[3] Levels of public expenditure on legal aid rose from £1,093m in 1992–3 to £1,622m in 1998–9—a 48% increase in expenditure at a time when total inflation was only 16%.

The first change followed enactment of the Legal Aid Act 1988. Administration of the scheme was removed from the Law Society and transferred to a new government agency, the Legal Aid Board. The Board tried to address the problem of providing a quality service by establishing a scheme for 'franchising' legal aid services under which firms of solicitors could obtain a franchise only if they passed a special quality audit process. Under the scheme, solicitors were able to obtain a franchise in one or more of up to ten franchise categories.[4] Some 2,900 firms of solicitors obtained at least one of the available franchises. In addition, the Legal Aid Board began a series of pilot studies to test the viability of franchises being awarded to agencies other than solicitors' firms, such as advice agencies, which might provide legal advice and assistance to the same standards as solicitors' firms.

In 1997, the Legal Aid Board started to enter into contracts with franchised firms for the provision of defined categories of legal services. This had the advantage that firms with contracts were able to deliver legal services with reduced bureaucracy. Instead of having to submit claims for each item of legally aided work, they were able to deliver their services within the framework of the contract. A number of legal aid services had to be offered on the basis of a fixed fee, rather than the traditional method of charging by the hour.

However, these measures were felt still to be inadequate to address the paradox of ever rising costs, without any significant expansion in the range of services that were funded by the legal aid scheme.[5] The Access to Justice Act 1999, which came into effect in 2000, abolished the legal aid scheme and introduced in its place a new body—the Legal Services Commission—charged with running two new services: the *Community Legal Service* (CLS) and the *Criminal Defence Service* (CDS).

Community Legal Service

Introduction
Many people obtain advice on legal problems, not by going to see a solicitor in her office, but by visiting one of the over 1,500 citizens' advice bureaux, law centres and other independent advice agencies which it is estimated exist in England and Wales. These services often have lawyers or other professionally qualified staff attached to them. Around 6,000 people with a variety of qualifications work in these agencies, supported by nearly 30,000 unpaid volunteers. They deal with over ten million inquiries each year and receive around £250 million from a wide variety of sources of public funding, from both central and local government.

The services that these agencies offer have developed very haphazardly, often in response to specific local initiatives. Coverage throughout England and Wales is

---

[4] These include: criminal, family, personal injury, housing and social welfare. New franchise categories have been developed: e.g., a clinical negligence franchise was developed in February 1999.

[5] Although costs rose by 48% in a six-year period, the numbers of people assisted rose by only 7%. Indeed expenditure on civil and family legal aid rose by 42% while the numbers of people assisted fell by 30%.

therefore patchy. In some areas, there is no effective service at all. In others there may be a number of agencies offering very much the same service. Here there is over-provision and a consequent waste of scarce resources—both cash and manpower.

The *Legal Services Commission* is responsible for building on existing services to develop, in effect, a national legal service, funded by the Community Legal Service Fund, in partnership with other funders, such as local authorities and central government.

In undertaking its planning, the Legal Services Commission is aided by *Regional Legal Services Committees* (which were established prior to the creation of the Commission[6]) to assist in identifying current provision and to help shape the provision of new legal services to the community. In each local authority area there should be a *Community Legal Service Partnership*, which will provide a forum for the local authority, the Legal Services Commission and others jointly to plan and co-ordinate the funding of local advice and other legal services to try to ensure that service delivery matches local needs.[7] Funding for the Community Legal Service is under the terms of a *Funding Code*[8] which sets out the detailed framework within which legal services will be delivered.

A key feature of the Community Legal Service scheme is that legal services are delivered on the basis of contracts made between the Legal Services Commission and the suppliers of legal services. Building on the franchising and contracting initiatives launched by the Legal Aid Board, *only* suppliers with franchises can obtain contracts to provide publicly funded legal services.

Another key feature of the new scheme, and in many respects the most controversial, is that the funds available to the Legal Services Commission are cash-limited each year, rather than—as happened under the legal aid scheme—being 'demand-led'.

Priorities

In shaping the detail of the scheme, the Legal Services Commission is required to take into account certain priorities for funding legal services, which are set for it by the Lord Chancellor.[9] These priorities include:

- proceedings under the Children Act 1989 for which legal aid was formerly available without either a means or a merits test;[10]
- civil proceedings where the life or liberty of the client is at risk;[11]
- housing and other social welfare cases that enable people to avoid or to climb out of social exclusion;

---

[6] They were set up in October 1997 in each of the 13 Legal Aid Areas—administrative areas into which the country is divided for the purpose of running the legal aid schemes.

[7] Partnerships currently cover about 90% of England and Wales.

[8] See: www.legalservices.gov.uk/stat/fc3_cr2.pdf.

[9] Access to Justice Act 1999, s. 6(1).

[10] See below p. 259.

[11] This was the principle that led to the more recent extension of legal aid to hearings before the Immigration Appeal Tribunal.

- domestic violence cases;
- cases concerning the welfare of children;
- cases alleging serious wrongdoing, breaches of human rights or abuse of position or power by a public body or servant.

Exclusions

Only legal services for individuals may be funded under the scheme. Services for firms or other types of non-individual legal persona (e.g. partnerships or clubs) cannot be provided under the scheme. In addition, certain types of legal service are excluded from the scheme altogether. These include:

- services relating to allegations of *negligently*[12] caused injury or death, though not allegations of clinical negligence. (The reason for this is that it is assumed that such cases are suitable for conditional fee agreements (see below));
- cases relating to injuries caused by negligence, even where the legal claim is not cast in terms of the law of negligence (e.g. tripping cases, where the local authority is alleged to be in breach of a statutory duty to maintain the highway);
- other areas excluded because they have been judged not to have sufficient priority to justify public funding. These include allegations of negligent damage to property;[13] conveyancing; boundary disputes; matters of trust law or the making of wills; and matters arising from company or partnership law or the running of a business;[14]
- also excluded is representation in cases involving defamation and malicious falsehood.

Notwithstanding the general exclusions, help relating to making a will may be available to a person over 70, or a disabled person or a parent or guardian of such a person who wishes to provide for that person, and in certain cases involving those under the age of 16.

More generally funding of matters otherwise excluded may nonetheless be possible:

- where the matter is only incidental to an issue for which funding is permitted, or where the issue is brought into the proceedings by someone who is not being assisted by the scheme; or
- where there are two distinct claims, one of which is an excluded matter, but where is it impossible or impracticable to deal with them separately and the Commission thinks they cannot be funded by a conditional fee arrangement or in some other way;

---

[12] The exclusion does not extend to cases of injury arising from an alleged assault or deliberate abuse.

[13] Housing disrepair cases brought by a tenant against a landlord are not excluded, as the property is not owned by the claimant.

[14] The Government's view is that these risks should be covered by insurance.

- issues relating to boundaries, trusts or company or partnership law which arise in funded housing proceedings or funded family disputes or proceedings may be funded even though they are more than incidental to the principal proceedings;

- so too may conveyancing services where they arise in the course of other funded proceedings, or to give effect to a court order or agreement to settle;

- furthermore, and notwithstanding the general exclusion of personal injury negligence claims, both *investigative support* and *litigation support* (for definition of these terms see below) may be made available in such cases if the costs of the claim are exceptionally high (and thus likely to deter insurers or those offering conditional fee arrangements);

- cases which involve a wider public interest may also exceptionally be included even though they would otherwise fall in the excluded categories;

- the broad exclusion of funding services for representation before coroners' courts and tribunals is retained.[15] However, the Lord Chancellor has stated he might on occasion fund exceptional cases before tribunals or the coroner's court where strict criteria were met.

The Government has stated that as alternative funding sources develop, such as conditional fee arrangements and legal expenses insurance, then categories of work currently publicly funded may be removed from the scope of the Community Legal Service. Other work, such as some legal representation before tribunals, may then be brought within the scope of the scheme. The political difficulties of achieving this goal should not, however, be under-estimated.

Objectives of the Community Legal Service

Under the terms of the 1999 Act, the Community Legal Service has five broad objectives. These are the provision of:[16]

(1) general information about the law and legal system (e.g. the provision of leaflets in a supermarket or the creation of legal websites);

(2) help by giving advice about how the law applies in particular circumstances (e.g. the provision of initial advice at a Community Advice Centre or Citizens' Advice Bureau);

(3) help in preventing or settling or otherwise resolving disputes about legal rights and duties (e.g. the provision of more detailed assistance, such as telephone calls or letter writing or even some representation by a solicitor);

(4) help in enforcing decisions by which such disputes are resolved; and

(5) help in relation to legal proceedings not relating to disputes.

---

[15] Funded legal representation before the Lands Tribunal and the Commons Commissioners, which was possible under the legal aid scheme, was withdrawn by the 1999 Act.

[16] Access to Justice Act 1999, s. 4(2).

The scheme will fund the provision of services by lawyers (as did the former legal aid scheme) but will also extend to certain services provided by non-lawyers ('not-for-profit' providers). To ensure quality, service providers have to obtain a 'quality mark' relevant to the type and level of service they are offering.[17]

Service levels

There are seven service levels:[18]

- legal help (which replaces the former 'green form' advice and assistance scheme);
- help at court;
- approved family help (either general family help or help with mediation);[19]
- legal representation (either investigative help[20] or full representation);
- support funding (either investigative support or litigation support);[21]
- family mediation;
- such other services as are authorized by the Lord Chancellor.

Means test

As with legal aid, clients entitled to funded services have to demonstrate that they are financially eligible—in other words they are subject to a means test.[22] Where applicants fall below a lower threshold, they pay nothing. If they fall between a lower financial threshold and a higher one, the provision of a funded service will be subject to the funded client making a financial contribution towards the cost.[23] In addition, where the proceedings are designed to obtain an award of damages or other financial provision, any award of damages is subject to a 'charge' in favour of the Community Legal Service fund.

Merits test

The general approach to the funding of cases is that funding should be available where a reasonable private paying client would be prepared to fund the case. Thus account must be taken of whether the proceedings would be cost-effective;[24] and there must be

---

[17] See, for details, www.legalservices.gov.uk/qmark/index.htm. A new quality mark scheme for barristers was launched in September 2002. A quality mark standard for mediation in family law was launched in January 2003.

[18] The details are set out in the Funding Code: see www.legalservices.gov.uk/stat/fc3_cr2.pdf.

[19] This is considered in Chapter 7 on the family justice system.

[20] This will be available where the size of the claim is likely to exceed £5,000. This will be provided where the strength of a case needs to be assessed; it may lead to full representation.

[21] This is a new form of funding designed to allow a mix of private and public funding in personal injury cases.

[22] The provision of information and the provision of services to proceedings under the Children Act 1989 are outside this rule. For funding in family cases see above Chapter 7, p. 186.

[23] Legal Help, Help at Court and Family Mediation are not subject to the making of a contribution.

[24] In framing the Funding Code's provisions on these matters, the Legal Services Commission is required to take into account the *statutory factors* which are set out in s. 8(2) of the Act.

an assessment of the prospects of success.[25] Cost-benefit ratios are to be determined by relating the likely costs to the percentage prospect of success.[26] Funding will be refused in cases where a conditional fee agreement should be obtained. There are special rules for cases against public bodies that raise human rights issues. Where a court has given permission for a judicial review case to proceed to a hearing, there will be a presumption that legal services funding will be granted, so long as the client is within the financial threshold.

Very expensive cases

To prevent a large proportion of the Community Legal Services fund being expended on a relatively small number of very expensive cases, a Special Cases Unit will control the costs of such cases. Cases likely to exceed £25,000 in costs will be referred to the Unit. Special arrangements will also continue to be made in relation to multi-party actions, where a large number of claimants are claiming loss from a single event or cause.

Alternative dispute resolution

ADR may be funded where this may be more effective than court proceedings. Where complaints procedures or ombudsman schemes are available which might be appropriate to resolve the problem in question, funding will not be considered until these have been exhausted.

Comment

The basic concept of the Community Legal Service is not new. The case for the creation of a national legal service or a community legal service has been made by many pressure groups and other social activists on numerous occasions over many years. The importance of the latest developments is, first, that the Government acknowledges that the provision of legal services is an important component in the achievement of broader social goals, in their potential to empower the powerless and to enable them to take advantage of the protective provisions of social legislation. The new scheme indicates acceptance by the Government that the cost-effective provision of legal advice must be planned, so that it meets clear social needs, rather than just springing up in piecemeal fashion. It also makes clear that there will never be a truly national provision of legal services—particularly for the less well-off members of the community—provided exclusively by professionally qualified lawyers; other agencies must be involved as well.

---

[25] This criterion does not apply to many housing cases or cases with a wider public interest. The Legal Services Commission is advised on the public interest by a Public Interest Advisory Panel.

[26] E.g., where prospects of success are 80% or better, the likely damages must exceed the likely costs; where the prospects of success are 60%–80%, the likely damages must exceed likely costs by 2:1; where prospects of success are 50%–60%, likely damages must exceed likely costs by 4:1.

There are other very important features of the new scheme which should also be recognized. First, most of the research on legal services argues that the provision of good quality information and advice at an early stage can save costs later on. The emphasis in the new scheme on these early stages seems in principle to be correct. Secondly, the ability of the Community Legal Service to fund the provision of electronic[27] and telephone services[28]—not possible under legal aid—may alleviate problems of physical access, even though there are concerns that the primary client groups for the Community Legal Service may not have the same access to these facilities as other groups in the population.

Nevertheless, unlike the legal aid scheme which the Community Legal Service replaced, the new scheme is, as noted above, no longer to be 'demand-led' but is subject to cash limits. As with all public spending, there is a need for financial discipline. Further, the existence of cash limits does not *necessarily* mean that services needed by the public cannot be delivered. Much of the success or otherwise of the new scheme depends on the level at which those limits are set and the effectiveness of the use of available resources to deliver cost-effective legal services. It cannot be assumed *a priori* that the new scheme will not work.

In the financial year 2001–2, the Commission was allocated £1.2 billion;[29] in addition the Court Service paid out just over £474 million for legal representation of defendants in the higher criminal courts. Total expenditure on legal aid was, therefore, over £1.7 billion. This paid for over 2.8 million 'acts of assistance'. These may seem impressive figures. It is, however, clear that the Government is seeking to impose tight financial controls on the size of the Commission's budget. Thus the allocation for 2001–2 was the same as for 2000–1.

There are signs that this is beginning to have adverse consequences. In its latest Annual Report, the Commission reports its concern that a number of firms have already left the scheme,[30] and that a very significant number of other providers are seriously considering giving up doing work for the Community Legal Service. They say that the primary reason for this is the difficulty providers face in making legal aid work profitable. Indeed, official figures show that there has been a reduction in the overall number of contracts awarded to solicitors' offices. (*See Table 10.1.*) There has also been a significant rise in the average cost of each act of assistance, accompanied by a reduction in the number of acts of assistance.

There is a more general worry that the priority being given by the present Government to change in the criminal justice system will have the effect of starving the Community Legal Service of essential resources, given that the two schemes share a single budget.

---

[27] The *Just Ask!* website is an important source of information for the citizen. For address, see p. 272.

[28] Provision of a telephone Legal Advice Line is currently being piloted.

[29] This was the same figure as in the previous year; projected figures for future years following the latest Government Comprehensive Spending Review are not currently available.

[30] The Commission is particularly worried at the decline in the number of firms doing family work.

Table 10.1 Contracts awarded to solicitors' offices and not-for-profit organizations

Contract categories	March 2001	March 2002
Family	4,039	3,760
Non-family:		
Actions against the police etc.	60	71
Clinical negligence	251	300
Community care	38	49
Consumer	151	113
Debt	549	515
Education	44	52
Employment	373	316
Housing	788	707
Immigration	548	591
Mental health	355	352
Personal injury	1,888	1,494
Public law	26	28
Welfare benefits	636	588
Total	9,746	8,936

Source: *Legal Services Commission Annual Report 2001–2*

There have been a number of developments in response:

(1) There has been some relaxation in the means-testing rules which have resulted in a higher percentage of the population becoming potentially entitled to take advantage of the Community Legal Service.

(2) The Legal Services Commission has recently taken the decision to provide funding for a number of traineeships for those willing to undertake training contracts in legal services practices.

(3) The extension of legal services funding to not-for-profit agencies has brought additional diversity of provision into legal services.

But the argument, made by the Legal Services Commission, for a more general enhancement of levels of remuneration has not been acceded to by the Lord Chancellor.

The battle for an appropriate level of resources for the funding of legal services will become more intense in the coming years if the number of providers willing to offer publicly funded legal services continues to fall or there is inadequate provision of services in particular areas of legal activity (such as family law). Such a socially important service cannot depend simply on the public-spiritedness of individuals wanting to provide assistance to the ordinary citizen. As with all cash-limited public services there will always be argument about the extent to which further funding should or should not be made available. And there will never be public acknowledgement by those who provide the services that the service is adequately funded.

On balance, it can be argued that the Community Legal Service offers an imaginative framework for the delivery of legal services which goes a considerable way to addressing many of the criticisms that were raised over the previous twenty-five years in relation to legal aid. Whether this optimistic assessment will survive the experience of the Community Legal Service only time will tell.

Criminal Defence Service

The Criminal Defence Service is the other legal service introduced by the Access to Justice Act 1999. It has replaced the criminal legal aid scheme, which was also abolished by the Act. The Legal Services Commission has power to secure the provision of legal advice, assistance and representation for those suspected of committing a criminal offence and thus under investigations, or actually facing criminal proceedings[31] in court.

There are four principal components of the Criminal Defence Service:

(1) The provision of criminal defence services in police stations and magistrates' courts through contracts with private-practice solicitors' firms;

(2) the provision of a national network of police station and magistrates' court duty solicitor schemes;[32]

(3) the management of individual case contracts with defence teams for very high cost criminal cases; and

(4) the provision of services directly to the public through the Public Defender Service (PDS).[33]

A key difference from the Community Legal Service is that the Criminal Defence Service remains a 'demand-led', rather than a cash-limited, service.[34]

The bulk of legal services provided under the Criminal Defence Service are provided by solicitors in private practice. All such firms have to have a contract to provide such services with the Legal Services Commission. In April 2002 2,900 firms of solicitors held such contracts.

As with the Community Legal Service, the Commission is concerned about a downward drift in the numbers of firms with contracts; the 2002 figure was 500 down on 2001. In addition, the Commission notes that the average age of solicitors doing

---

[31] 'Criminal proceedings' are defined to include not only criminal trials, appeals and sentencing hearings, but also extradition hearings, binding-over proceedings, appeals on behalf of a convicted person who has died and proceedings for contempt in the face of any court: Access to Justice Act 1999, s. 12. The Lord Chancellor has power to add to this.

[32] In March 2002 the Legal Services Commission had 299 local schemes in operation and 5,465 duty solicitors working on them.

[33] The salaried providers employed in the PDS are subject to a Code of Conduct published by the Commission and approved by Parliament: Access to Justice Act 1999, s. 16.

[34] Access to Justice Act 1999, s. 18. It is this principle that leads those in the Community Legal Service to fear that they will be starved of resources if the costs of the Criminal Defence Service rise substantially.

criminal work is increasing, and that few young people are entering this sector of the legal profession. They anticipate that there may be significant problems of supply in small towns and rural areas.

During 2001–2, the Commission launched a new service, the Public Defender service. The aims of the service, as seen by the Commission, are to:

- provide independent, high quality, value-for-money criminal defence services to the public;

- provide examples of excellence in the provision of criminal defence services nationally and locally;

- provide the Commission with benchmarking information to be used to improve the performance of the contracting regime for private practice suppliers;

- raise the level of understanding within government, including the Lord Chancellor's Department and all levels and areas of the Commission, of the issues facing criminal defence lawyers in providing high quality services to the public;

- provide the Commission with an additional option for ensuring the provision of quality criminal defence services in geographical areas where existing provision is low or of a poor standard;

- recruit, train and develop people to provide high quality criminal defence services, in accordance with the PDS's own business needs, which will add to the body of such people available to provide criminal defence services generally; and

- share with private-practice suppliers best practice in terms of forms, systems, etc., developed within the PDS to assist in the overall improvement of Criminal Defence Service provision.

To date, six offices have been opened. They operate on the basis that the PDS must attract and retain clients as a result of the quality of service that it provides. Clients are not compelled to use the PDS in areas where it exists; they can choose between the PDS and solicitors with contracts from the Legal Services Commission. The initial development of the PDS will take place over the next four years; during that time, it will be the subject of a specially commissioned research report. The future of the PDS will be reviewed in the light of experience and the research findings at that time.

An important feature of the new arrangements is that the decision to fund representation in a criminal case is—unlike the position under the former criminal legal aid scheme—not subject to a means test. There were two problems with the mean-testing of criminal legal aid:

- First, it was wasteful of money. The means-testing process cost the Legal Aid Scheme almost as much as the money raised from individual defendants as a result of the means-testing exercise. Instead, under the Criminal Defence Service there will be a power for the judge, at the end of the trial, to order that a convicted person pay some or all of his costs. The Commission will have the power to investigate the means of individual defendants in order to assist the court in reaching that decision.

- Secondly, it added to delay, in that a trial could not proceed until the issue of representation had been sorted out.

This scheme was the subject of fierce debate in Parliament. Critics argued that:

(1) The new regime meant that the better off, who do not rely on publicly funded legal aid, still had complete freedom of choice over who should represent them. This would lead to an unacceptable distinction between what the better off and the less well off were able to receive by way of legal assistance. However, there was an opposing argument, that those providing legal services paid for out of public funds should be able to demonstrate basic levels of professional competence—which limiting provision to those with contracts is designed to achieve—so that there will be some guarantee that public money is not wasted on the incompetent or inexperienced.

(2) There is some evidence from the USA[35] that public defender schemes do not work as well at they should in defending the interests of the accused or suspect. There were therefore considerable worries that if the predominant form of provision in England were to become the public defender system, this would lead to a less competent mode of delivering criminal legal services. This could well become a problem were the publicly funded service to become the sole mode of delivering this form of legal service. However, this is certainly not going to be the situation in the short term. So long as there is competition with the private sector, this should ensure that adequate standards are maintained.

Certainly the new arrangements are more streamlined than the former, often highly fragmented, provision in which a person might get advice in the police station under one funding scheme, advice in the solicitor's office or in prison under another, and representation in court under yet a third. The new criminal law contracts provide for a single service from arrest until completion of the case.

Private funding mechanisms[36]

The changes to legal aid cannot be seen in isolation. Other means to promote the private funding of the cost of taking legal proceedings have also been introduced in recent years. The driving force behind these developments has been the desire to

---

[35] See McConville, M., and Mirsky, C. L., 'Criminal Defence of the Poor in New York City' (1986–7) 15 *New York University Review of Law and Social Change* 581–964.

[36] The emphasis in this section is on the funding of litigation, not the funding of non-contentious business, such as the drafting of wills, the administration of estates after a person has died or the buying or selling of property.

increase access to justice. The challenge has been to devise ways of enabling those who might want to litigate do so without incurring disproportionate costs.

Three developments are considered here:

- the new Civil Procedure Rules;
- conditional fee agreements;
- fixed fees.

The Civil Procedure Rules

As noted in Chapter 8, Lord Woolf saw reduction in the costs of taking a case to court as a key objective in the reforms that he was proposing. There were two principal ways in which he envisaged that this objective might be achieved.

Making costs proportionate. Before the Woolf reforms were introduced, the basic principle used to determine disputes about costs was that those charging the costs had to demonstrate that the costs they incurred were reasonable. Following the introduction of the CPR, this principle has been amended. The costs must be both reasonable *and* proportionate to the issue in dispute.[37] In cases where relatively small sums of money are involved, it might well be reasonable for a number of legal steps to be taken in preparing the case, but if the cost of taking those steps was substantial, the total costs, while reasonable, might still not be proportionate. A judge would therefore be required to disallow costs which, though reasonable, were not proportionate. The difficulty with this principle is the obvious one: what is reasonable? and what is proportionate?

Case management. The emphasis in the CPR on judicial case management was designed to ensure that cases were dealt with more quickly. By preventing proceedings from dragging on, it was thought that the cost of litigation could be reduced. The problem here is that this objective is, to a significant extent, in conflict with other changes introduced in the CPR. There is now an emphasis in the post-Woolf era on the need for parties to put their cards on the negotiating table earlier than they used to. This means that cases which, prior to the introduction of the Woolf reforms, would have settled well before any trial was likely to take place, now require more work to be done at an early stage. This leads to a 'front-loading' of expense, which increases the costs of such cases.

While there has been very broad support in general for the Woolf reforms, there is considerable anecdotal evidence and some harder empirical evidence that the goal of cost reduction has yet to be achieved.[38]

---

[37] The details are set out in CPR Part 44—general rules about costs.

[38] See Goriely, T., *et al.*, *More Civil Justice? The Impact of the Woolf Reforms on Pre-action Behaviour* (London, Law Society and Civil Justice Council, 2002).

Conditional fee agreements

The concept of the conditional fee agreement (CFAs) was introduced by the Con-servative Government in 1990 and expanded by the present Labour Government. CFA is defined in section 58 of the Courts and Legal Services Act 1990 as amended by section 27(1) of the Access to Justice Act 1999 as 'an agreement . . . which provides for . . . fees and expenses, or any part of them, to be payable only in specified cir-cumstances'. The importance of CFAs in the funding of litigation was significantly increased by the Access to Justice Act 1999, since it is now a principle that public funding of litigation through the Community Legal Service should not be provided in cases where alternative funding (including CFAs) is available.[39]

CFAs, also known as *'no win-no fee'* agreements, allow solicitors to agree to take a case on the understanding that, if the case is lost, they will not charge their clients for all or any of the work undertaken. The client also agrees that if the case is successful, the solicitor can charge a *success fee* on top of the normal fees, to compensate for the risk the solicitor has run of not being paid all or some of her fees. The success fee is calculated as a percentage of the normal fees and the level at which the success fee is set reflects the risk involved. Regulations provide that the 'uplift' of the success fee should be no more than 100 per cent of the normal fee. The Law Society has advised[40] solicitors that, in any event, the uplift should not exceed 25 per cent of any damages recovered, where that figure would be less than the figure agreed in the CFA.[41] (It is not actually a requirement of a CFA that a success fee must be charged, but it usually will be.)

The *no fee* element relates to the solicitor's fees alone and does not cover the ancillary expenses of the case, such as experts' reports, and may not cover counsel's fees. The solicitor may agree to fund these costs as part of the agreement; more usually, the solicitor will arrange insurance cover of these fees for his client. Alter-natively, a CFA can be entered into between a solicitor and counsel or, in very limited circumstances, between client and counsel.

After the event legal expense insurance (LEI) policies (*see Box 10.1*) are now also available which provide cover for the solicitor's fee and/or for the opponent's costs should the case be unsuccessful. The premiums paid for insurance cover are deter-mined by the provider and are dependent on a number of factors, including the strength of the case, the likely measure of damages involved in the case and the legal representative's experience of undertaking such cases. Premiums may range from relatively modest sums to many millions of pounds depending on the case insured. There has been a sharp increase in premiums for more run-of-the-mill cases, as the

---

[39] See the *statutory factors* in the Act, s. 8(2). This criterion does not apply in all cases, e.g. housing cases.

[40] In addition to providing guidance on the use of CFAs, the Law Society also produced a model CFA. Both have recently undergone review by the Law Society.

[41] Despite this link with damages, it should be stressed that CFAs are related only to the professional fees charged, *not* to damages. Any arrangements to recover costs by taking a percentage of damages recovered—contingency fees—are not lawful in England and Wales.

Box 10.1 Legal expenses insurance

By comparison with many other countries, notably Germany, the development of commercially provided LEI has been extremely slow in England. This is probably due to the fact that, by comparison with most other countries, legal aid in England has been relatively generously funded.

Legal expenses insurance comes in a variety of guises:

- Stand alone/'before the event';

- Add-on;

- After the event.

Stand alone or 'before the event' policies are those which are sold principally by specialist legal expenses insurance providers for those who wish to obtain general cover against the possibility that at some point they may have to incur legal expenses. Although this type of legal expenses insurance has been available in the UK for many years, take up has not been as widespread as its promoters would have wished.

Add-on policies are those where, as an additional benefit to other cover, e.g. household contents insurance, or travel insurance, or motor insurance, related legal expenses may be covered. It is thought that many people who have these forms of insurance cover do not actually realize this. It is part of the 'small print' of insurance contracts which they do not read.

After the event insurance is a newer form of policy devised to take advantage of the new rules relating to conditional fee arrangements. These are bought when the purchaser is contemplating taking legal proceedings but before the outcome of the case has been determined, and cover the solicitor's fees in cases where the case is lost. The rules relating to CFAs allow the costs of premiums to be recovered from the losing party by the winner: Access to Justice Act 1999, section 29.

insurers who provide this form of cover initially underestimated the cost of meeting claims under the policies and so lost money in the early years.

CFAs cannot be entered into in relation to criminal and most family proceedings. They must also comply with requirements prescribed by the Lord Chancellor in regulations.[42]

In addition to CFAs, section 28 of the Access to Justice Act 1999 introduced a new concept, the *litigation funding agreement*. This allows a party to be funded by a third party (rather than the solicitor) e.g. a trade union or other prescribed group. In these cases the funder pays the solicitor's normal fees. However, where the case is won, the funder is entitled to be paid the success fee by the losing side and is able to retain that element of the fee to cover losses on cases which are not won.

---

[42] See Conditional Fees Regulations 2000 (SI 2000 No 823).

Funding agreements which comply with the prescribed requirements shall not be unenforceable by reason of their being funding agreements, unless they relate to criminal proceedings, family proceedings or other proceedings which have not been specified as coming within the scope of a funding agreement. Where an agreement relates to such categories of proceedings, or otherwise does not comply with the requirements in the regulations, the Access to Justice Act explicitly provides that the agreement is unenforceable. The success fee is enforceable only where the agreement complies with the prescribed requirements; relates to specified proceedings; and the percentage increase does not exceed that set out in the order specifying the proceedings.

Comment

The principles relating to CFAs may be relatively easy to set down, but their operation in practice has been very complex. Although CFAs have arguably provided a means for increasing access to justice, they are open to a number of forms of abuse:[43]

(1) Lawyers may charge excessive costs knowing that their own client will not have to pay them.

(2) Lawyers may set the success fee at a level that is grossly disproportionate to any fair assessment of the risk involved in the case.

(3) Insurers may charge premiums grossly disproportionate to the risk being underwritten.

As a result of these factors, plus the general desire of insurers to minimize their insurance liability, a vast body of 'satellite litigation' relating to costs has been generated. This goes quite against the aims and objectives of the Woolf reforms, which were about keeping cases out of court as much as possible. There have been sharp arguments about what costs are reasonable, what costs are proportionate and what the appropriate percentage of uplift for success fees should be. This last issue, in particular, has been the subject of sharp debate both in the courts and the professional legal press. The difficulty has been to determine what are the appropriate cost benchmarks against which questions of reasonableness and proportionality could be tested.

Fixed fees

One category of cases where these problems are thrown into sharp relief are low-value cases, for example damages for modest personal injuries arising from road traffic accidents. It needs to be remembered that, in his report, Lord Woolf recommended that such cases should be subject to a fixed-fee regime. The Government did not follow that recommendation, but in the interim increasing complaint has been heard

---

[43] These were identified by Lord Bingham in his judgment in *Callery v. Gray* [2002] 1 WLR 2000 at 2003.

about the disproportionate burden of costs in this class of case. Lawyers acting for claimants insist that, in order to prepare cases properly, they must have the ability to get the material they need to prove that defendants are liable for the injury suffered by their clients. In response, defendants' lawyers (and more particularly their insurers) argued that unless costs are curbed they will become an increasingly disproportionate burden.

This has led practitioners, encouraged by the Civil Justice Council, to explore the possibility of creating an agreed fixed-fee regime, in the first instance for modest uncontested road traffic accident cases. In reality fixed fees have become a much more common feature of professional fee-charging practice; there is considerable pressure on the profession to reach agreement on this issue.

Conclusion

Access to justice is essential if the claim to have an efficient legal system is to be sustained. Debate on legal aid was, in the past, dominated to a large extent by the legal profession. The legal aid scheme was largely designed and developed by the Law Society. While there should be no doubt that those who undertook this work were determined to create a scheme that delivered a needed service to the public, it is also the case that the legal profession was the principal beneficiary of it. The injection of £1.7 billion into the legal profession—the total amount of current public expenditure on legal services—is not trivial. It was obvious that the rate of growth of public expenditure in this area—despite rhetorical claims that 'justice is without price'—could not be sustained.

Put another way, if policy-makers had started the legal aid scheme from scratch with a budget of £1.7 billion, would they have devised the legal aid scheme that eventually developed? Those who accept that the answer to this question must be 'no' must then think what the shape of any alternative might be. The Access to Justice Act 1999 provided the opportunity for a new scheme to emerge. It will inevitably build upon its historical legacy. It may not achieve all that those who have put it in place claim that it will achieve. There is every chance that the Community Legal Service will prove to be more fit for its purpose than the civil legal aid scheme it has replaced. The jury is still out on the Criminal Defence Service.

The potential relationship between public funding and the new incentives to encourage the private funding of litigation is less clear, though lawyers do have a considerable track record of turning new opportunities for earning a living to their advantage. In so doing, there is at least a reasonable prospect that the individual will have greater access to justice.

However, if the difficulties with conditional fees persist, voices are increasingly being heard suggesting that the next logical step would be to move from conditional fees to *contingency fees*. This is the principle used in the USA, but also every Canadian province save Ontario. The key feature of contingency fees is that lawyers get their fees by taking a percentage out of the damages recovered by their own clients. This issue is not currently on the policy agenda, but may well appear there in the medium term.

Questions for discussion

1. What should be the balance between the role of the state and the responsibility of the individual in funding litigation? Is the current balance correct?

2. Will a Public Defender Service weaken or enhance the criminal justice system?

3. Should the legal aid budget be 'cash-limited'?

4. Can access to civil justice be improved through new arrangements for the funding of litigation?

5. How can 'satellite litigation' on costs be avoided?

6. What are the arguments for and against contingency fees?

Further reading

DAVIS, G., DONKOR, K., and MORGAN, R., *Ethnic Minorities' Legal Needs and Perceptions of Legal Services: Report of a Pilot Investigation for the Law Society* (London, The Law Society, 1993)

GORIELY, T., and DAS GUPTA, P. (with Bowles, R.), *Breaking the Code: The Impact of Legal Aid Reforms on General Civil Litigation* (London, Institute of Advanced Legal Studies, 2001)

——, MOORHEAD, R., and ABRAMS, P., *More Civil Justice? The Impact of the Woolf Reforms on Pre-action Behaviour* (Research Study 43) (London, Law Society (and the Civil Justice Council), 2002)

KEMPSON, E., *Legal Advice and Assistance* (London, Policy Studies Institute, 1989)

Legal Action Group, *A Strategy for Justice: Publicly Funded Legal Services in the 1990s* (London, Legal Action Group, 1992)

LORD CHANCELLOR'S ADVISORY COMMITTEE ON LEGAL EDUCATION AND CONDUCT, *Setting Standards for Community Legal Services* (London, Lord Chancellor's Department, 1999)

LORD CHANCELLOR'S DEPARTMENT, *Striking the Balance: The Future of Legal Aid in England and Wales* (London, HMSO, 1996)

MIDDLETON, SIR PETER, *Review of Civil Justice and Legal Aid: A Report to the Lord Chancellor's Department* (London, HMSO, 1997)

REGAN, F., *et al.*, *The Transformation of Legal Aid: Comparative and Historical Studies* (Oxford, Clarendon Press, 1999)

ROBERTSHAW, P., *Rethinking Legal Need: The Case of Criminal Justice* (Aldershot, Dartmouth, 1991)

SMITH, R. (ed.), *Shaping the Future: New*

Directions for Legal Services (London, Legal Action Group, 1995)

STEELE, J., and SEARGEANT, J., *Access to Legal Services: The Contribution of Alternative Approaches* (London, Policy Studies Institute, 1999)

THOMAS, P.A. (ed.), *Law in the Balance: Legal Services in the 1980s* (Oxford, M. Robertson, 1982)

ZANDER, M., *Legal Services for the Community* (London, Temple Smith, 1978)

Websites

www.lapg.co.uk/ *(Legal Aid Practitioners' Group)*

www.lag.org.uk/ *(Legal Action Group)*

www.clsa.co.uk/ *(Criminal Law Solicitors' Association)*

www.legalservices.gov.uk/ *(Legal Services Commission)*

www.justask.org.uk/ *(The first port of call for legal information and help in England and Wales)*

www.civiljusticecouncil.gov.uk/

www.costsdebate.civiljusticecouncil.gov.uk/Home.go *(Links to pages devoted to discussion of the question of costs of litigation)*

www.lawsociety.org.uk/home.asp

www.das.co.uk/explorer.htm *(Legal expense insurance company)*

www.national-accident.co.uk/index1.html *(Site advertising services relating to personal injury litigation)*

www.foil.org.uk/ *(Forum of Insurance Lawyers)*

www.apil.com/ *(Association of Personal Injury Lawyers)*

www.nacab.org.uk/ *(Citizens' Advice Bureaux)*

www.lasa.org.uk/ *(London Advice Services Alliance)*

CONCLUSION

11

Is the English legal system
fit for purpose?

Introduction

At the start of this book, the question was posed whether the English legal system is currently fit to meet the demands placed upon it. In subsequent pages, a wide range of issues has been considered: what are law's functions? how is law made? what are the contexts in which it is practised? who are the different actors in the legal system? how are legal services funded? A number of specific issues about the fitness of the legal system to achieve its apparent purposes have been raised in context above.[1]

In this final chapter I return to that initial question. This chapter does not provide definitive answers but raises matters not specifically considered earlier, and seeks to encourage the reader to think critically about issues that have been raised.

Law plays a variety of key roles, not necessarily consistent with each other, in the organization of modern society. Countries where the rule of law seems to be less well established than in the United Kingdom may be seen to be at something of a disadvantage. However, the world is going through a period of rapid and considerable change. Is the English legal system able adequately to respond to this changing world?

Images of law

Chapter 1 suggested that those without direct experience of law or lawyers might come to the study of law with pre-conceptions about the legal system that were at best limited, at worst seriously distorted. Subsequent chapters have demonstrated that there is much more to law than criminal justice; that those providing legal services are far more varied in character than the 'fat-cat' lawyers sometimes portrayed in the press; that both the institutions of the legal system and those who deliver legal services are undergoing profound change; that problems of inefficiency and delay, particularly

---

[1] Just by way of example note the comments on the Child Support system, above, at Chapter 7, p. 179.

in the litigation process, are increasingly acknowledged and are beginning to be addressed.

Institutional innovation is driven in part by the present Government's modernization agenda, but also by the needs of an increasingly global economy which contribute substantially to the pressure for institutional change. The leaders of the legal profession may, on occasion, appear resistant to change as they seek to defend the interests of practitioners who may fear an uncertain future and are unwilling to embrace change. But many individual practitioners and firms of lawyers have shown considerable dynamism and imagination in shaping their practices to respond to clients' needs and wider pressures.

Many other indicators suggest that negative images of law and the legal system are unfair. There is still a great desire on the part both of professionally qualified lawyers and other lay legal advisers to deliver legal services to all sections of the public, not just the well-heeled and powerful. Standards of education and training of lawyers and other advisers have increased greatly in recent years. The judiciary are essentially free of corruption.

But to stop at this point would risk the complacent conclusion that the English legal system *is* the best in the world, requiring at most only modest further adjustment. The fact is that there are many other issues on which one can be more critical. It is important that those coming to the legal system for the first time think about those features which can be criticized. The future development of robust legal institutions lies at least in part in the hands of those now entering the legal system.

One key problem is the treatment of legal issues in the mass media. Apart from the drama of the big criminal trial or a scandal involving a miscarriage of justice, discussion about law in the mass media is not well-rounded. With notable exceptions such as the BBC Radio programme, *Law In Action*, or the weekly law pages in the broadsheet newspapers, together with a number of consumer programmes which touch on aspects of the law, there is little public discussion about law-making, the practice of law or the impact of law on the citizen. Unlike other aspects of our intellectual life, such as history or science or medicine, law is not regularly the subject of mainstream media programming.

Yet the centrality of law to different social orders suggests that the media neglect of law and legal issues is unsatisfactory. Programme makers may feel that law is too complex a subject to make it attractive for mass programming. But this simply contributes to the mystique of law and enhances the power of the lawyer in society, at a time when arguably opportunities for greater general understanding of and access to law should be growing.

Part of the reason public discussion of legal issues is so limited may be that those who operate within the legal system themselves have shown only limited interest in presenting their work to a wider audience. Much professional legal activity is conducted on the basis of secrecy and confidentiality, which may result in a lack of individual enthusiasm to enter the public eye. Furthermore, there are those in the legal profession who think that it goes against the professional grain to seek publicity for their work. However, a consequence of such attitudes is that the law and its practitioners tend to hit the headlines only when things have gone wrong.

Considerable effort is these days expended on placing stories in the media which form part of the public relations activity of promoting the work of individual legal firms or practices. Lawyers and other practitioners should also be willing to shape a more educational public information agenda, and to work with the media to develop opportunities for a fuller understanding of law and the legal system in all our lives. The difficulties of making a wider range of programmes about law may be substantial; nevertheless the challenge for the years ahead remains to provide a new, more informed, treatment of legal issues in the mass media, which would play an important part in the shaping of public perceptions about the legal system and those who work in it, which could in turn contribute to making the legal system function more effectively.

One particular idea is whether trials should be televised. This happens a great deal in the USA; there was a notable recent experience in the UK when a number of trials in Scotland were shown in edited form on television. While such a step might give the appearance of greater openness of the legal system to the public, it should be remembered that televising trials may merely serve to exacerbate current images of law—that the typical legal process is a criminal one, in which there is a lengthy trial of the case for and against the accused. There is little discussion about televising cases in the administrative justice, family justice or civil justice arenas; or programmes dealing with the vast majority of cases that are resolved without a full-scale trial.

In addition to the treatment of law in the media, other issues also need consideration. First, there are important questions to be resolved about the patterns of recruitment to the legal profession. Although there are now greater opportunities for women to become lawyers than was the case some years ago, they do not yet appear to be achieving their full potential to rise to the most senior positions in the legal world. In addition, the improvement in the opportunities for women to enter law does not appear to have been matched by comparable increases in the opportunities for those coming from working-class backgrounds or ethnic minority backgrounds. Given the importance of equality of treatment and even-handedness in the delivery of legal services, it is important that those running the profession and the institutions of the law take issues of recruitment and advancement seriously.

Secondly, are current modes of dress really appropriate in the twenty-first century? As noted in Chapter 9, a large number of actors in the legal system do not put on any kind of formal clothing before they undertake the services required of them by the public. The question still arises whether the use of wigs and gowns in the higher courts is necessary. Some find the use of such costumes as intimidating and creating a distant relationship between the lawyer or judge and those who appear in court. For this very reason others argue that such a sense of distance is necessary. It may be particularly desirable for some categories of judge, especially those in the criminal courts, to wear distinguishing garb to provide an added sense of authority to those who appear before them. But the question remains: is the present system of wigs and robes still essential? If not, how should it be altered?

Law's functions

A wide range of issues about the social functions of law were considered in Chapter 2. In relation to many of these, readers will have their own views, not all of which can be canvassed in an introductory work. The tension between the use of law to control and regulate behaviour and the use of law to protect people by giving them rights and entitlements was particularly emphasized.

The issue that arises out of that discussion which perhaps bears most fundamentally on the question whether the English legal system is fit for its purpose is whether there is now too ready a recourse to the use of law to try to deal with the issues facing modern society. There are occasions on which politicians and others pay lip-service to the proposition that law should not be used to regulate human activity more than absolutely necessary. But there are few incentives not to make law. Politicians' and civil servants' reputations are based on the laws they create, not those that they prevent. And the reputation of practitioners is enhanced by their pushing at the boundaries of law, as they try to establish new areas of legal liability, not by their seeking to limit the scope of law. The Human Rights Act 1998 has added to these pressures. Certainly the amount and complexity of the law that emerges from government and the courts are constantly increasing.

In this context, the proposition that ordinary citizens can in any real sense be assumed to know the law that governs their lives is just not sustainable. While it may not be realistic to complain that there is too much law, the implications for law-makers and others involved in the working of the legal system in providing better information about law are clear. The current lack of investment in the provision of useful information about the law and its procedures must be seen as a weakness in the current institutional arrangements of the legal system. As with the challenge of providing better general information about law through the mass media, there is also a considerable challenge to be faced, particularly within government, about the use of new information and communication technologies to make information about citizens' rights available to a much wider public than is presently the case. This is an area of activity in which there has already been much change[2] and where it may be anticipated that there will be rapid progress in the years ahead.

---

[2] In preparing this second edition, I have been very struck by the huge amount of legal information now available, free, on the web.

Law-making—legitimacy and authority

The primary law-making bodies today are the legislative institutions of the European Union and the United Kingdom. Both claim to derive legitimacy for the exercise of legislative powers from political theories of democracy. However, the extent to which ordinary people understand the nature of such assertions of legitimacy must be open to doubt. The processes of Parliament are poorly understood; those of the institutions of the European Union are shrouded in even greater mystery. There is great ignorance about the links between institutional assertions of legitimacy and the democratic will of the people. Even less clear is the relationship between majority opinion and the protection of minorities—a key issue in modern pluralist societies.

There is evidence that this is an issue that is beginning to be taken seriously. Many of the institutional and constitutional reforms, both in the UK and in Europe, are influenced by an increasing acknowledgement that voter apathy is not a satisfactory basis on which to claim legitimacy for the exercise of law-making power. At some point, unless more is done to encourage people to understand that, for example, elections are important, there will be a danger that those theoretically governed on the basis of consent may come to deny the legitimacy of their governors to govern. The decision, by the present Government, to introduce instruction on 'citizenship' into the school curriculum is a recognition of the importance of this issue.

A likely trend in the next decade is much greater effort by government institutions to explain what they are doing and to encourage input into the law-making process.[3] Many of the recent procedural innovations to the law-making machinery in the UK— considered in Chapter 3—reflect this need. Questions remain, though: do these changes go far enough? Should recent procedural changes in both the UK and European Parliaments be taken further? Should there be further changes to the electoral system? To what extent is there a 'democratic deficit'? If there is such a deficit, what measures are needed to reduce it? Should there be greater opportunities for lobbyists and other groups to influence the shape and content of legislation?

The law-making functions of the judges are also under intense scrutiny, particularly with the coming into force of the Human Rights Act 1998. Initial indications are that English judges have been very restrained and have not sought to use the Human Rights Act to usurp the essentially political functions of Parliament and the Executive to deliver its legislative agenda. But voices are being heard that the judges have been too timid. It is impossible to predict how the judges will respond to such pressure, though it may be guessed that they will continue to take a cautious line for some time yet.

In any event, most governments would claim that they already operate within both

---

[3] In fact, a vast amount of consultation already goes on between government and groups in society; indeed, some complain of 'consultation fatigue' as yet another consultation exercise arrives in the post or e-mail. But it is important that, whatever the problems, governments continue this trend.

the spirit and the letter of the European Convention on Human Rights. But a moment's reflection indicates that, in difficult cases, there is potential for considerable tension to develop between the legislative and executive branches of government and the judicial branch. If a significant political/legislative objective is declared incompatible with the European Convention on Human Rights by the courts, whether in the UK or in Strasbourg, this may at best result in embarrassment for the Government, at worst in considerable frustration. There is a powerful argument that adherence to human rights standards by government should be in general a political responsibility, not a judicial one.

Experience in the USA, where the Supreme Court has long asserted a power to review legislation in the context of the US Constitution and the Bill of Rights, may suggest that the impact of the courts on the legislative process has been limited. Experience in other countries—for example, Canada—suggests that such a view may be too sanguine. Whichever way the British judiciary goes, it seems inevitable that the constitutional role of the judiciary will become the focus of sharp debate in the years ahead.

This leads to a broader question: has the time come for the creation of a written constitution, which seeks to provide specific legitimacy for the different branches of government, and the systems of checks and balances that they should operate to preserve the rule of law and prevent abuse of power. At present, this seems to be an unlikely development, but is an issue which, following the present round of significant constitutional change, will not wholly disappear.

Notwithstanding all the procedural changes, there remain many practical questions about the law-making process which still need addressing. For example, where there is agreement that a particular rule of law needs changing, the problem of Parliamentary time means that this cannot easily be achieved. A significant number of Law Commission reports remain unimplemented.[4] Where the common law lacks clarity or certainty, the ability of the judiciary to develop legal principle is dependent on the right case being brought before it. Should special procedures, either in Parliament or before the courts, be made more readily available where the state of the law is clearly unsatisfactory?

A different issue relates to styles of legislative drafting. One of the reasons legislation, in particular, is so hard to understand is that legislative draftsmen seek to define everything in legislation—whether primary, secondary or tertiary—with a very high degree of linguistic precision. This leads to very considerable complexity. In turn this raises the question whether a more 'plain English' approach to the drafting of statutes might be appropriate. Certainly, the new Civil Procedure Rules were drafted on the basis that they should be easier to read and understand. And there are lawyers who have signed up to the Plain English Campaign's[5] initiative for clearer drafting of legal

---

[4] Recent proposals for changes to Parliamentary procedures may result in more efficient use of Parliamentary time. See Select Committee on the Modernization of the House of Commons, 2nd Report, 2002, at www.publications.parliament.uk/pa/cm200102/cmselect/cmmodern/1168/116802.htm.

[5] See www.plainenglish.co.uk/index.html.

documents. The question of the extent to which such initiatives should spread more widely into legislative drafting practice are being considered.

In fact, legislative drafting styles change. An Act or a Bill drafted today, is very different from one drafted twenty-five, fifty or 100 years ago. Currently the focus is on getting the architecture of an Act right so that the reader can acquire more easily a sense of what the legislation is seeking to achieve. This is supported by the new practice of publishing explanatory notes. A particular difficulty is to know whether new drafting practices would lead to more or less legislative uncertainty. It is likely that, to be fully effective, radically new legislative drafting practices would have to be supported by the senior judiciary.

Justice and efficiency

The chapters in Part 2 of the book reveal a number of common themes. Most prominent is the pressure in all justice systems to deal with cases as expeditiously and as economically as possible. These are perfectly proper aims, but nevertheless raise the question of the extent to which the shaping of the legal system should be driven by demands for efficiency and value for money, as opposed to other demands, such as the need for the justice system to be just. While unnecessary delay and expense must be deplored, it should still be asked whether current trends to dispose of cases rapidly or even to divert them completely from courts and other dispute-resolution fora will always operate in the interests of justice.

These issues cannot be addressed by vague assertions that 'justice has no price'. Justice quite clearly does have a price, which has to be paid for either by the citizen or by the state (whose resources come from the taxpayer). At the same time important principles relating to the need for fairness of the trial process must be borne in mind. There must be some doubt, especially in the context of criminal justice, whether the apparently increasing focus on the 'crime control' model of criminal justice is compatible with a 'due process' model. If taken too far, the question will arise whether the system will be compliant with the human rights standards set down in the European Convention on Human Rights.

Another set of issues relates to avenues of appeal. In the context of the criminal justice system, for example, some of the recent serious cases of miscarriage of justice seem to have been exacerbated, at least in part, by the rather restrictive bases on which the Court of Criminal Appeal may determine criminal appeals. The creation of the Criminal Cases Review Commission was designed in part to assist. Will this be enough to prevent further serious miscarriages of justice? What other mechanisms are needed to ensure both that the innocent are not convicted and sentenced, and that those who have committed offences are brought to trial?

In relation to administrative justice and civil justice, the question was raised whether there were too many avenues of appeal and complaint for the individual to pursue. Changes to appeal routes in the civil justice system have reduced the numbers of appeals that can be brought in that context. The outcome of Sir Andrew Leggatt's review of the tribunal system may be the first step in a similar process in the administrative justice system.

A fundamental issue that affects the whole of the institutional framework of the English legal system is whether all citizens, and particularly members of ethnic minorities, feel that they are dealt with fairly. Following the Stephen Lawrence case, the Lord Chancellor's Department announced a major programme of research on the experience of those from the minority groups in all parts of the legal system. Clearly, if the legal system is revealed as being unable to deliver equal treatment to all those who come into contact with it, as is now often asserted, this will be a concern of the utmost importance which will have to be dealt with as a matter of considerable urgency.

One pressure for change not considered in the main text is a set of ideas currently being developed within the policy-making bodies in Europe which might lead towards the development of a more European-wide court system. There could be some merit in these ideas. If the EU is able to encourage greater movement of its citizens around the different countries of Europe, should it not also enable those citizens to enforce their rights in the country of their choice? However, for many the very idea of such integration would be anathema. This is not an idea that is currently well-developed and has certainly not been widely discussed, and will not be pursued further here. But it is an issue to which attention needs to be drawn. Were such moves to be seriously contemplated, the major distinctions between the British common law approach to law and the Continental European civil law approach would be likely to prove a major hurdle to the integration of judicial systems. It is in this context that the suggestion of the need for closer legal integration between the common law countries of Europe, principally the United Kingdom and Ireland, might gain more significance.

Professional organization

Chapter 9 considered a number of questions relating to professional organization. It considered the increasing part played by government in seeking to regulate standards of professional activity. It was suggested that this could prove a worrying trend, for although there is no current suggestion that government will seek to limit the proper independence of the professionally qualified lawyer to take up controversial or unpopular cases, this does not mean that this could not happen at some future time if the trend towards greater government intervention accelerated.

There are a number of issues relating to professional regulation that are not currently well handled by the lawyers' professional bodies. In particular, there is an unsatisfactory muddling of the regulatory functions of the professional bodies—designed to ensure its members deliver services to proper professional standards—with the professions' 'trade union' functions—designed to ensure that the interests of professional lawyers are as fully protected as possible. Unlike in the medical profession, where the former function is performed by bodies such as the General Medical Council and the latter by the British Medical Association, the Law Society and Bar Council perform both functions. Perhaps the time has come for a similar division of responsibility in the context of the practising legal profession?

Related to this is another more subtle question about the effectiveness of the professional bodies, and in particular the Law Society, to perform their 'trade union' functions. Many argue that the interests of those who practise in the large global law firms in the City of London are so far removed from the interests of the sole practitioner in a rural area that it is absurd to suggest that they should be represented by the same professional body. Certainly one of the issues that will continue to need discussion in the years ahead is what the basic notion of 'the professional lawyer' should be, and how the identity of that professional person can best be sustained without fragmentation into a vast array of sub-specialisms.

The funding of legal services

The final issue addressed in the book is whether the new arrangements for the funding of legal services will—in some general sense—'work'. Here there is considerable uncertainty. The new arrangements for the state-funded Community Legal Service and Criminal Defence Service and the related arrangements for alternative ways of funding other forms of litigation are too recent for any conclusion to be reached.

Those who predicted a complete breakdown in the provision of quality legal services to the public will be confounded. However, the changes will have a big impact on the legal profession, particularly small firms or sole practitioners in small towns or rural areas, where it is hard to see their being able to generate the levels of business needed to stay afloat financially. It is likely that there will have to be the same sorts of mergers and consolidations to increase business efficiency that have already taken place at the more commercial end of the legal professional market.

More generally, whether all the promises offered by government for the effectiveness and impact of the new structure will be delivered must also be open to doubt. What will be needed is agreement on a reasonable level of government expenditure on the delivery of legal services, accompanied by an acceptance by legal practitioners that they must justify the £1.7 billion of public money that is paid to them. At the same time, it does seem inevitable that the line between legal services and lawyers' services will become even more blurred, with more legal services being delivered by those without formal professional legal qualifications.

Conclusion

Much of the English legal system is pretty fit for purpose, but it is not perfect. There is always room for change and improvement. Those coming new to law should seek to support what is good, but not seek to defend the indefensible. The discussion in these pages is designed to encourage the thought, reflection and action needed to bring about necessary change, while preventing undesirable change.

Table of references

Index